PRIEST AND FREEMASON

The Life of George Oliver

1782–1867

Geo. Oliver D.D.

PRIEST AND FREEMASON

The Life of George Oliver

by

R.S.E. SANDBACH

© 1988 Richard Sandbach

First published in England in 1988
This edition revised 1993
Published by LEWIS MASONIC, Ian Allan Regalia
Coombelands House, Coombelands Lane
Addlestone, Surrey, KT15 1HY, England

ISBN 085318 194 2

Printed in Great Britain by Ian Allan Printing Ltd,
Coombelands House, Addlestone, Surrey KT15 1HY

By the same author:
UNDERSTANDING THE ROYAL ARCH

FOREWORD

It is a special pleasure for a more modern priest and freemason to write a word of commendation about this excellent biography, which is of interest to the general reader as well as members of the Craft. It was high time that the copious writings of this Lincolnshire pastor received the due recognition that they deserved once more and anyone who takes the time and trouble to read this ordered narrative will discover both the wisdom and the relevance of so much that George Oliver produced. In a way which could hardly have been imagined, the themes of this prolific masonic scholar's work fit the contemporary scene in regard not only to the stance of the Church which he and I both served but also to the approach of the Craft to which we are also committed. In these pages the reader will find pointers to a rich vein of masonic study that is worth prospecting again whilst the author's colleagues in Quatuor Coronati Lodge will once again pay ready tribute to his ability as a biographer, linking the facts of an individual's life to the events of social history through which he passed. The result is a most valuable addition to the stock of modern masonic literature as well as a balanced reappraisal of one whose fame had become unnecessarily tarnished and whose researches were being under-valued. No one who reads this work can fail to be the better for it.

The Revd N. Barker Cryer,
Late Secretary, British and Foreign Bible Society,
Past Grand Chaplain, United Grand Lodge of England,
Secretary, Quatuor Coronati Lodge.

ACKNOWLEDGEMENTS

I thank the council of QCCC Ltd and the Lincolnshire County Libraries for permission to quote from *Ars Quatuor Coronatorum* and *Scopwickiana* respectively, and gratefully acknowledge the help received from many people, but especially from Edward H. Trevitt in Great Grimsby; Norman W. Tildesley and the late Ronald A. Stevens in Wolverhampton; Richard Hellier, John Sandall and the late J. M. Sneath in Peterborough; John M. Hamill (Librarian of the United Grand Lodge of England), Terence Haunch (his predecessor), the UGL library staff, Sir James Stubbs, KCVO, and the late Colin Dyer in London; the Revd Canon Frank Pickard; and most of all my wife but for whose patience and forebearance the book would not have been completed.

CONTENTS

ABBREVIATIONS
AND DEFINITIONS

A & AR	The Ancient and Accepted Rite (in this country, a Christian masonic Order).
Antiquities	*The Antiquities of Freemasonry*, G. Oliver, 1823.
Apology	*An Apology for the Free and Accepted Masons*, G. Oliver, 1846.
AQC	Ars Quatuor Coronatorum: the Transactions of Quatuor Coronati Lodge, no. 2076.
Constitutions	The Book of Constitutions of the United Grand Lodge of England.
Craft	*See* Preface.
DPGM	Deputy Provincial Grand Master (the second senior masonic officer in a Province).
Discrepancies	*The Discrepancies of Freemasonry*, G. Oliver, 1875 (posthumous; probably written c. 1840).
Dixon	*The History of Freemasonry in Lincolnshire*, William Dixon, 1894 (Macmillan).
FQR	The Freemasons' Quarterly Review.
Freemasonry	*See* Preface.
Golden Remains	*The Golden Remains of Early Masonic Authors*, collected and annotated by G. Oliver; 5 volumes, 1847–50.
Knights Templar	(Except where context shows reference to the historical Order is meant) the Christian masonic Order 'The Masonic and Military Order of Knights of St John of Jerusalem, Palestine, Rhodes and Malta'.
Ladder	*Jacob's Ladder, The Ascent to Heaven plainly pointed out'*, G. Oliver, 1845.
Landmarks	*The Historical Landmarks of Freemasonry*, G. Oliver; 2 volumes, 1845–6.
Masonry	*See* Preface.
Mirror	*A Mirror for the Johannite Mason*, G. Oliver, 1848.
NMJ	Supreme Council, 33rd Degree, A & AR for the Northern Masonic Jurisdiction of North America.
Offering	Pamphlet, based on FQR report of the masonic offering to Dr Oliver, 9 May 1844.

Papal Teachings	*Papal Teachings in Freemasonry*, G. Oliver, 1866.
PGM	Provincial Grand Master—the senior officer in a masonic Province.
Pr. or Prov.	Provincial (e.g. Pr. Grand Lodge).
Rose Croix	The 18th degree in the A & AR. Sometimes used (wrongly) to refer to the Order itself.
Star	*The Star in the East*, G. Oliver, 1825.
Symbol	*The Symbol of Glory*, G. Oliver, 1850.
Treasury	*The Freemason's Treasury*, G. Oliver, 1863.
UGL	The United Grand Lodge of England.
Valedictory	A so-called *Valedictory Address* which prefaced *The Symbol of Glory*, G. Oliver, 1850.

Note: reference to a specific edition of any of Oliver's works is only made where needed to identify a material alteration.

PREFACE

Priest and Freemason: George Oliver was only one among many clergy of all Christian denominations who have found in the masonic Craft happiness and companionship, as well as a moral code wholly compatible with their religious beliefs. In that Craft he was distinguished for his passionate interest in its traditions and history and his imperative urge to examine and justify its teachings in the light of his fervently-held Christian belief. He published many articles, sermons and books about it and achieved a world-wide reputation as 'the sage of masonry'; but his fascination as the subject of a biography lies in the nature of the man—in his complex simplicity, his unsought and unwilling involvement with the masonic and industrial problems of his time, the extraordinary vicissitudes of his career, the austerity of his character, and his mellow companionship. To search out and portray a nature at once so enigmatic and charismatic is the challenge that faces his biographer.

As a necessary preliminary, it must be made clear that in this book the terms 'freemasonry' and 'masonry' on their own are used only to describe the Craft as it is practised under the United Grand Lodge of England (UGL). There are movements which call themselves masonic but which the UGL does not accept as such since they do not measure up to its strict criteria for recognition; this is usually because either they do not insist that candidates for admission must profess a belief in a Supreme Being, or because the Bible does not lie open in the lodge room at all times when the lodge is open. There is no masonic God, in spite of what such authors as Stephen Knight allege; a freemason is expected to practise his religion, whatever it may be, and though he may not proselytize in Lodge, each person there knows that all present have publicly professed in Open Lodge to a belief and trust in a Creator God (that is, in some Supreme Being). A freemason or a candidate for admission to the Craft is required to take his solemn obligations with his hand on whatever book he regards as divinely binding him to observe any promise made on it. In masonic terms such a book is termed 'Volume of the Sacred Law'; and consequently this may mean a different book to members of different faiths; for a Christian freemason it will be the Bible.

After starting his adult career as a schoolmaster in Caistor and Great Grimsby, Oliver was ordained a priest in the Church of England and as curate of Great Grimsby determinedly set to work to restore the parish church and to carry out the duties which the absentee incumbent should have been performing; he was so effective that when he had to leave Grimsby the church building was in prime shape and a sizable congregation worshipped there. His later ecclesiastical appointments, to a Lincolnshire village where he was happy and to Wolverhampton where he was not, moved in eery parallel with his masonic career in which he attained high office and a world-wide reputation, but was nevertheless summarily and arbitrarily dismissed from that office to the consternation of freemasons all over the world.

Throughout his long adult life he was constantly writing for publication; we know of more than 60 books and pamphlets from his pen, on religious, archaeological, social, historical, and above all masonic subjects. By modern standards his style of writing was sometimes heavy, nor would he be deterred by a charge of prolixity from fully propounding a thesis, saying 'if brevity be the soul of wit, it is also a bar to the exercise of judgment, or the play of imagination'.[1] His works varied from advice to the Pope on the errors of a Papal Allocution condemning freemasonry to a delightful description of his country parish, as yet unaffected by the Industrial Revolution; they include a letter to the Archbishop of Canterbury which probably earned him a doctorate but of which no copy seems to have survived, and 'hints' to the rulers of Wolverhampton on how they should reform their treatment of their workers, which possibly was a major cause of his unpopularity with the Anglican community there. A peace-loving man of retiring nature who could nevertheless fight hard when roused, he became involved in some spectacular disputes, at Grimsby with the Corporation, in London with the Duke of Sussex, at Wolverhampton with clergy and laity, and in Lincolnshire with his Provincial Grand Master.

How all this happened is of course one of the main subjects of this book; but behind the actions and the excitements is the man himself. The best known portrait of him seems at first glance to indicate a character of stern angularity, but the lasting impression is of benevolence and sympathy. Some 30 years after his death, William Dixon, the historian of freemasonry in Lincolnshire wrote, 'Doctor Oliver is yet well remembered in Lincoln. All agree in their testimony to his good qualities . . . In business matters straightforward, charitable according to the limited means at his disposal, of a genial disposition, at the refreshment board would sing a good song, enjoy a good joke, and was excellent company'.[2] He might well have added that he also rescued a village from degradation and a masonic province from inertia, restored two churches and became, in spite of official disapproval, the adviser on masonic matters whose authority was universally acknowledged. But it was for himself that the Lincolnshire masons loved him, and to show why they did so is really why I have written this book.

Chapter One

BACKGROUND

(Nottingham, Lutterworth, Leicester)

The world into which George Oliver was born on 5 November 1782 was one which previous generations of his family would have recognized without difficulty; that in which he died on 3 March 1867 had changed greatly and was still changing. He himself changed, fully appreciating the advance of science and technology; but as priest and as freemason he adhered firmly to the fundamentals he had learnt from his father. Thus he believed implicitly in the truth of the Bible, from Genesis to Revelations; and he found the dechristianizing of the masonic ritual under the auspices of the Duke of Sussex, a son of King George III, distasteful. Yet he could say of the biblical legend of the seven days of Creation that we could not know how long each day was for 'from what data can we solve it? . . . A thousand years, in the sight of God, are but as one day. And what are thousands of thousands? The inquiry is too vast and too mysterious for comprehension. We must believe and adore'.[1]

When Oliver was born in 1782, freemasonry was well established over a great part of the civilized world. Its origins have been the subject of much dispute, but at that period it was unhesitatingly accepted as derived from very ancient times indeed, at least from the date of the building of the first Temple at Jerusalem by King Solomon (c.1000 BC). Its development as a coherent and cohesive discipline concerned with the ethics of life can fairly be considered as beginning when four London lodges formed the first (or Premier) Grand Lodge in 1717, an example soon followed in Ireland (c.1725) and Scotland (1736). This coming together of groups of lodges under a Grand Lodge, usually on a territorial basis, came to be the generally accepted form of its organization in all the many countries where it was established. Its ceremonials, though developing differently in different parts of the world, had on the whole become formalized during the 18th century and its reputation for secrecy, 'clubability' and philosophical dispute had proved attractive to men of all ranks in many countries, and is expressed in the phrase 'brother to a beggar, companion to a prince, if a mason and found worthy'. However the details of ritual or ceremonial might vary, there was a feeling of unity between freemasons.

The basic structure was the Craft, today regarded in England as comprising three degrees and the 'Chapter' (or 'Holy Royal Arch') which is considered officially as the completion of the third; but success breeds imitation, and it was not long before new 'degrees' and even whole rites were invented which claimed to be masonic; over a thousand have been counted. Many appear to have originated on the Continent, particularly in France, the West Indies, and North America, and the question of the acceptability of such new growths as truly masonic began to trouble 'regular' masons. There was perhaps less concern in England and Wales than elsewhere, because the attention of English freemasons throughout the second half of the 18th century was focused on an internal quarrel. In 1751 a rival Grand Lodge had been established in opposition to the Premier Grand Lodge whom their new rivals, claiming to represent 'true antient freemasonry', skilfully dubbed 'Moderns' while calling themselves by the masonically flattering title of the 'Antients'. This was the first of a series of propaganda victories they achieved in the early days of the quarrel, which lasted until 1813 when it was resolved by the union of the two warring Grand Lodges as 'The United Grand Lodge of England', which still rules all lodges under the English masonic constitution today. The union was effected with the help of the Duke of Sussex, as Grand Master of the Premier Grand Lodge and his brother the Duke of Kent as Grand Master of their rivals, and the former became the first Grand Master of the UGL. He was re-elected to that office every year until his death in 1843, during which period, in spite of occasional protests, he effectively dominated English freemasonry. A Christian, he was an ardent Hebrew scholar with a great sympathy for, and many friends among, the Jewish population in England and held firmly that freemasonry should be open to all who believed in a God Who had Himself created the world, whether or not they were Christians.

English masonic ritual prior to the union had evinced a strong Christian bias; lodges were opened and closed 'in the name of God and holy Saint John',[2] and the festivals of St John the Baptist and St John the Evangelist were observed by the Craft as high feast days. The union made it necessary to review the ritual to achieve a degree of uniformity, and the Duke used his power to see that in the review Christian references were deleted from it. The review did not in fact succeed in removing them entirely and the English rituals used today still retain some.

Of the large number of new masonic or quasi-masonic degrees invented in the 18th century some, notably the Christian degrees which became part of 'The Ancient and Accepted Rite' of which the Order of the Rose Croix of Heredom is the best known, became widely accepted on the Continent and in the New World. These had little effect in England and Wales, the Craft being too occupied with the quarrel between the two Grand Lodges to absorb them. Even the old-established Christian masonic order of Knights Templar decayed, largely as a result of the deliberate policy of the Duke to focus all attention on the Union and play down the Christian element in freemasonry. He also effectively managed to make it impossible for these orders to increase their importance in England during his long life. Oliver was later to be concerned in reorganizing them when, immediately after the death of the Duke, he was involved in the establishment in England of a Supreme Council for the Ancient and Accepted Rite.

It should be made clear at this point that the Rose Croix degree, in spite of the similarity of name, has nothing to do with Rosicrucianism, whose tenets it does not profess to share.

Some of the foreign Grand Lodges and quasi-masonic bodies later strayed into alien paths unacceptable to the UGL and to other 'regular' Grand Lodges, failing to insist on belief in a Supreme Being as a precondition for membership or that the

Bible should lie open in Lodge. Much of the blame for this must be laid on Napoleon Bonaparte. English freemasonry remained singularly unaffected by such matters and much of the credit for this must go to the Duke of Sussex; even if his rule tended to the autocratic on occasion, on the wider view it was unquestionably beneficial to the Craft and made the most of the reaction to the quarrels of the previous half-century by first stabilizing and then establishing English freemasonry in a mould which it has retained to the present day. Whether his determination to remove Christian references from the ritual was or was not justified may be disputed, but his sincerity was undoubted. Oliver was not alone in disapproving of the alterations but, unlike most others, made his views clear, while at the same time maintaining strongly that the revisions had not changed the essentially Christian character of the Craft.

When he was growing to manhood, all this was still in the future. The England which he knew as a boy was still essentially an agricultural community. The quarrels started by the Reformation had in general been laid to rest and from the point of view of the Established Church the kingdom seemed settled at last. The Wesleys had proceeded on their tempestuous course (John Wesley was still alive when Oliver was born) but had barely ruffled the torpor of the Church of England. Stuart hopes had been shattered at Culloden in 1746, though there would be those in Nottingham, which he knew well in his early years, who could remember the time when Prince Charles Edward's troops had reached nearby Derby before retreating to Scotland. The country was firmly established under the House of Hanover as Protestant, and though there might be quarrels between sects Christians were on the whole united in their unquestioning acceptance of the literal truth of the Bible. People might dispute about the adornment of the gates to the Garden of Eden or about whether Adam and Eve wore fig leaves or breeches, but not the fact of their existence or the Genesis legend of the Creation, which event was confidently believed to have occurred in 4004 BC as calculated by Archbishop Ussher. Satan and Hell were as real as the Pope and Roman Catholics, and for many Englishmen there was marked similarity between all four.

Politically, wars—or at least strained relations with the Continent—were a recurring factor. The American war of Independence was in its last stages but a new British Empire was rather casually coming into existence as trade and the flag advanced together. There was unrest and pressure for reform, but on the whole life seemed settled. London was a focus for intellectual ferment and political debate. Kant had just published his *Critique of Pure Reason*, and Watt had patented his steam engine; but the French Revolution was still in the future, and the industrialization of England had barely started. Dr Johnson's world was about to give way to that of Miss Austen—Oliver would live on into that of Trollope. But it was in rural England that the heart of the land was still to be found.

In 1838 Oliver wrote a pamphlet about life in the Lincolnshire village of Scopwick, where he was then vicar. *Scopwickiana* shows that in spite of the increasing industrialization of large parts of the Midlands and North and notwithstanding the redistribution of village lands under the Inclosure Acts—mostly it must be admitted in favour of the large landowners—rural England had changed little since the Civil

War. The picture he draws is as charming in its simplicity as it is perceptive in its observation; such comments as 'Our village population is not absolutely virtuous or vicious: the people are neither so high-minded or so slavishly abject as has been represented; and the most popular theories are rather speculative than true' contrast with lengthy descriptions of the perils of spring-cleaning in the vicarage or of the May-Day hiring fairs ('the Saturnalia of servants'), 'Goodying' (an organized perambulation for alms on Shrove Tuesday and 21 December, the feast day of St Thomas), harvest, and the annual patronal festival on 14 September.

When Charles Darwin astounded the world and shook the foundations of established Christianity in 1859 by publishing his epic *On the Origin of Species*, Oliver was 76 years old and had been living in semi-retirement from parochial duties for three of them; his clerical troubles at Wolverhampton and his summary dismissal as Deputy Provincial Grand Master (DPGM) of Lincolnshire were behind him, as was his brief career as head of a Christian masonic order. He was revered as 'the sage of masonry' everywhere except in the hierarchy of the UGL, and was still to write and edit several works on freemasonry, including his lively and forthright retaliation to a papal attack on freemasons ('If there were any valid reasons for this bitter phillipic, it might be pardonable; but it has not the shadow of a foundation to rest upon').[3] It seems that he nowhere expressed a view about Darwin's theories.

The Oliver family claimed descent from Andrew Oliver of 'Castle Oliver' in Scotland; there is a village of Oliver in Tweeddale, between Moffat and Peebles. This Andrew was alive when James VI went south to London to claim the English throne in 1603, and having a large family, he despatched three of his younger sons in the King's wake, scenting the possibility of prosperous pickings. They became established near Nottingham and from one, Augustine, six generations later, George Oliver was descended. His father was Samuel Oliver (1756–1847); any family property in the Nottingham area had long since vanished, and Samuel, until the last years of his life, had to struggle against poverty; he became a schoolmaster and married Elizabeth Whitehead ('Betsy') on 12 February 1782. George, their eldest child, was born on 5 November that year and baptized at Papplewick, just outside Nottingham, four days later; they had eight other children, at least one of whom died in infancy. Samuel had received a thorough grounding in mathematics, and became keenly interested in astronomy and astronomical calculations, interests which he passed on to his eldest son. In his earlier years he was much addicted to astrology, calculating nativities and horoscopes. But when his fourth child, for whom he had by these means predicted a long and prosperous life, died in infancy, he abandoned such pursuits. He is described as 'a perfectly original character'[4] whose actions sprang from impulse rather than experience and whose judgements could consequently be sometimes hasty. He had early acquired a dislike of dissenters as the result of an encounter with one described as 'a worthless follower of John Wesley' at whose hands 'he had been extremely ill-used and injured in his property',[5] which was in any event not great. In consequence he tended to speak out bluntly about 'the sin of schism' and when he became a priest of the Church of England he felt it to be his duty in that capacity to do so. But he was a charming and accomplished man in spite of his relatively lowly position in Church and Craft and his influence on his eldest son seems to have been considerable. Dixon, quoting 'one who well remembers him later in life', describes him as 'a host in himself, full of anecdotes and reminiscences of a long career, thoroughly appreciating his glass and long pipe and the good things of this life, extremely fond of a joke, yet withal a God-fearing man'.[6]

Six years after his marriage, Samuel was appointed headmaster of a school at Lutterworth by the Earl of Denbigh; by 1791 he was advertising his own school there, 'The English Academy'. It is reported of him that he was invariably at his desk by seven o'clock each morning and he appears to have been blessed with good health. For some of the time, George was a pupil at his father's school, but may also have attended one in Nottingham. Later he was to write of 1793, the year in which the revolutionaries executed the king and queen of France, 'the whole country was in a moral fervour; and I am old enough to remember that in the town where I went to school . . . the boys met in the market-place every night, and never parted till they had sung the national anthem, and concluded with three hearty cheers',[7] a description that would seem more applicable to a large town such as Nottingham than a village like Lutterworth.

In 1797 the course of life began to change for the family; Samuel was in that year ordained a deacon in the Church of England. In the same year he became a freemason in a 'Moderns' lodge, being 'made' in St John's Lodge, Leicester, founded in 1790 and still extant as No. 279 on the UGL register. (It is arguable that he may have already have been an 'Antient' freemason since George later 'had reason to believe' his father was initiated in 1781, the year before George was born and the year before Samuel's marriage. Neither of the two Grand Lodges recognized brethren initiated in the other as regularly-made masons, and a second initiation to regularize the matter would not have been unusual). At Leicester, Samuel was a regular attender, walking the dozen or so miles between the two towns. Having a minor talent for versifying, he wrote a song for each meeting in the year; some still exist.[8] Four years later he was ordained priest and an appointment to a curacy at Gotham brought him back to the Nottingham area. He closed his school in Lutterworth and opened one in Gotham; but almost immediately (1802) accepted a curacy for an absentee incumbent at Whaplode, a Lincolnshire village about 20 miles north of Peterborough. This was the family's first connection with the county to which George was to become so attached.

It is worth stressing that Samuel took Orders and became a member of the 'Moderns' lodge of St John in the same year. Clearly he, like many of his contemporaries in the ordained ministry from archbishops to curates and deacons, saw no conflict between the two, and throughout his life he retained his interest and enthusiasm for the Craft, visiting lodges in London, and joining (or at least attending) Union Lodge in Nottingham after leaving Lutterworth; he became Chaplain of a Peterborough lodge, and an honorary member of Scientific Lodge, Cambridge, now no. 88. From his sermon for the dedication of the Peterborough lodge in 1802 we know that he was a devotee of what was then the orthodox masonic school that believed in the pre-Solomon origin of freemasonry.

George was 19 years old when the family moved to Whaplode. Little is known of the earlier part of his life. As a boy he had become interested in freemasonry, probably after reading an article about it in 'Young Man's Companion' by W. Gordon. He was about 17 when Samuel was initiated in Leicester, old enough to note the attraction which the Craft clearly had for his father and the enjoyment which led him to walk to Leicester and back each lodge night after a long day's work.

There is indeed a mystery about George's youth. In a book published in 1850 he refers to a visit to Cairo;[9] this must almost certainly have taken place after 1794 (when, aged 11 or 12, he is recorded as at his father's school in Lutterworth) and before 1802 (which is almost certainly when, aged about 19, he became a freemason). However, between those years the Mediterranean was a theatre of war and hardly the place for a young tourist: Napoleon Bonaparte had sailed to Egypt in 1798, where Nelson had destroyed the French fleet, and in the subsequent years was making his way back overland to Europe. It is an interesting speculation that George Oliver as a youth may have joined the Navy, and this might account for his early acquaintance with Lord Kensington whose private chaplain he became on his ordination in 1814. He does not appear to have referred to his Mediterranean experiences anywhere else, which suggests that he was not proud of them; but it would not be in keeping with his general character that he should be romancing. The intriguing mystery remains.

Chapter Two

EARLY DAYS (1802–1809)

(Whaplode, Peterborough, Caistor)

Whaplode is a Lincolnshire village some six miles east of Spalding in the fens. To the south is Whaplode Fen, to the north Holbeach Marsh with the Wash beyond it. The landscape is flat and drainage channels of all sizes from ditches to broad canals are everywhere. It is a country of broad horizons stretching to infinity, and it breeds its own types of people. Communities tend to be scattered and small even today and there are few centres, the most notable being Spalding to the west and Wisbech to the east; further afield, and for practical purposes infinitely more remote, are Peterborough, lying between fen and 'upland', and King's Lynn, opening the way to the prosperous hinterland of Norfolk. There could hardly be a greater contrast to the rural east midland countryside around Nottingham which had for so long been home to Samuel Oliver and his family.

The church living at Whaplode was at that time held by an incumbent who was also Master of the Charterhouse, a canon of Salisbury and rector of a parish in Huntingdon and who had no intention of working for his reward in the depth of the Lincolnshire fens. He employed a curate to do that, and it was to this curacy that Samuel was appointed in 1802, being allowed according to Dixon 'less than £100 a year to keep up the dignity of the Vicarage and raise nine children'[1] at least seven of whom survived to adulthood.

It is not easy today to appreciate how far such evils as pluralism—the holding by one priest of more than one living—affected the organization and well-being of the Church of England in the early 19th century, though reform was imminent and George Oliver would encounter its force in Wolverhampton. The payment to a priest of a stipend from central funds is a relatively modern development, and in early days, in theory, each parish had its own priest who occupied the parsonage house unless excused from residence by the ecclesiastical authorities, and obtained his income from whatever historical resources such as capital bequests, land or tithes had become attached to the living, and from such gifts of his parishioners as they might be disposed to make, particularly at Eastertide. Once he had been confirmed in possession he could not be removed except by due process and for grave ecclesiastical offence. Any curate was paid by the incumbent as a personal arrangement which could be ended just like any other contract of employment.

In many cases the erosion of money over the centuries had severely reduced the value of the historical income while in others substantial rewards were attached to livings in country areas remote from the comforts and company afforded by the towns. Further, the right to present the next incumbent to a living was a saleable asset often vested in individuals and which obviously varied in value according to the worth of the living and the age of the incumbent; it could be sold without regard to the wishes of the ecclesiastical authorities or the parishioners. Not all those possessing the right to present to a living so abused their privilege, but abuses there were in plenty.

The result of all these factors was that Anglican priests without private means or a patron could find it difficult to obtain presentation to a living that would provide a livelihood. On the other hand, one able to afford to buy the right to be presented, or who succeeded in attracting the goodwill of a patron, might desire the status and the income, but be irked by the duties, of a parish priest; or might prefer the comforts of the town to the austerities of the rural parsonage in which he was required to dwell. Others again, by a mixture of purchase and patronage, might secure presentation to several livings to obtain the income, but with no intention of performing the duties of any or all, other than by appointing curates who, for a fraction of that income, would do the work for which their employers were paid.

Hence two evils arose, pluralism and the appointment of underpaid curates. A man so appointed was, in the eyes of the parishioners, the incumbent, with all the duties and responsibilities entailed in that important office; yet on the death or resignation, or even at the mere will of the absentee, the curate lost his status, house and income with no financial reward for his work and no provision for his future. It was such a curacy that Samuel Oliver undertook at Whaplode.

His masonic lodges in Leicester and Nottingham were clearly out of reach for the curate of Whaplode, as was Scientific Lodge in Cambridge; but he soon established contact with a number of masons who were setting up a lodge in Peterborough. The majority of the founders had been only recently initiated in an 'Antients' lodge in Norwich and the new lodge, to be named for St Peter, was to be of that Order and to be constituted on 26 July 1802; it had possibly been meeting for some months before that date. In spite of the 20 miles or so which separated his vicarage from the cathedral city of Peterborough, Samuel accepted an invitation to become chaplain of the new lodge, a fact which tends to support the suggestion of his dual membership.[2] He was however a 'Modern' at heart and by conviction and, whether or not by his persuasion, before the constitution date arrived the founders had apparently determined to apply for a 'Modern' warrant. The original date was nevertheless celebrated in style with a service in the parish church of St John, Peterborough, at which he preached a sermon, copies of which are still extant; he sent 12 to Scientific Lodge. It shows considerable oratorical skill, and as was customary is lengthy; in fact at one point the urges his audience 'Bear with me, Brethren, I am enraptured by my subject'. That subject was the compatibility of Christianity and freemasonry and at one point he said 'I can, and do, aver in this *sacred* place and before the GRAND ARCHITECT *of the world*, that I never could discover any property of *Masonry*, which is not only justifiable, but commendable according to the strictest rules of Religion and Society; being founded upon principles perfectly consistent with the holy Gospel; that is *doing* the will of God, believing in Jesus Christ, *subduing the passions*; and highly conducing to every sacred and social virtue'.

George desired to be admitted in the new lodge. He was not yet 21, the normal minimum age for candidates, but his application was accepted. It is not clear when his initiation actually took place as the lodge minute book has been lost, but the most likely date seems to be late in 1802.[3] The present St Peter's Lodge no. 442 constituted in 1836 seems to have acquired the furniture of its predecessor; and although most of that is reported as having been destroyed later in a fire, the original lodge pedestal seems to have survived and to be that which now stands before the Master's chair in the Peterborough lodge room. It is almost certainly that at which George Oliver knelt when he was received into masonry and, being under age, his father as his sponsor was required to kneel there by his son's side as guarantor of good faith, a practice not followed today and not prevalent even in those times. The pedestal is described in the books of Daniel Ruddle, a Peterborough builder, later a member of the lodge, who provided its furniture; the entry, dated 17 July 1802, refers to 'Pedestal with Drawr painted £3.13.6'. Female figures representing Faith, Hope and Charity are painted on the three sides with a representation of the arms of the 'Antients' on the fourth.

The 'Moderns' warrant for the lodge was granted on 23 December 1802 and it is said to have been constituted by the Earl of Pomfret, Provincial Grand Master, on the same day. After 1806, when the Lodge of Harmony (which also figures in the saga) was moved from Northampton to Boston, St Peter's Lodge may well have been the only lodge permanently situated in the Province until the Pomfret Lodge, now no. 360, was constituted in Northampton in 1819; at one point in the intervening period it actually claimed to have been established as the Provincial Grand Lodge of the Province of Northamptonshire; and in spite of a terse and chilling response to this from the Grand Secretary it continued to meet as such on occasion. But the days of its glory were short-lived and it was erased from the register of the Grand Lodge in 1830 for non-payment of annual dues. As it will be referred to again, it should be made clear that unless otherwise stated later references are to the lodge constituted in 1836 when the ceremony was performed on the orders of the Grand Master by an Officer of the Grand Lodge who was later to play a prominent part in the Oliver story, Dr Robert Thomas Crucefix. The story of the founding of the new lodge also introduces another character who appears in a supporting role in that story, an expatriate Scottish mason, Brother Thomas Ewart; he found the papers of the former lodge and not knowing it had been erased attempted to revive it. When the error was discovered a petition for a new lodge was granted; the petitioners wished it to be called the Crucefix Lodge but it was contrary to policy to allow a lodge to be named after a living brother and the Grand Master granted the petition 'with the exception of the name'. Crucefix was then sent to constitute it with the name left blank in the warrant and, after further discussion with the founders, wrote in the name 'Saint Peter's Lodge' in his own hand. This warrant perished in the fire already mentioned and the warrant in the lodge room at Peterborough is therefore unfortunately a replacement. Ewart later became Deputy Provincial Grand Master of Northamptonshire and was to be one of George Oliver's supporters.

Neither George nor his father seems to have attended regularly in Peterborough, though George does tell us he received his second and third degrees there.[4] But in 1803 he was appointed usher (assistant master) of a school at Caistor, a small Lincolnshire town 11 miles south-west of Great Grimsby, and over 80 miles from Peterborough.[5] According to an appreciation in memoriam on his death written by his publisher, he joined the Order of Mark Masons in that year.

In the following year he married Mary Ann Beverley, of a well-known local family and six years his senior. At this time he seems to have had little money apart from his salary; he had not yet started to supplement his income by writing. It is possible that Miss Beverley brought a dowry with her, but the family still seems to have had little to live on.

In 1806 their first son, George was born. There were to be four more children, Caroline Burnett (1808), Beverley Samuel (1811), Charles Wellington (1815) and Mary Ann Pierpont (1819). The eldest was of course named for his father; the second for his mother's family and his grandfather whose second son, also Samuel, became a beneficed priest in Nottinghamshire; and the third, born in the year of Waterloo, for the great national hero of that victory. Mary Ann was named for her mother, and the name Pierpont has family connections since it appears also among the children of Samuel and Betsy.

George and his wife remained at Caistor for six years until on 30 May 1808, aged 26, he was elected headmaster of a school at the flourishing Humber port of Great Grimsby. This was the moment at which his career really began.

Chapter Three

THE START OF A CAREER
(1809–1831)

(Great Grimsby)

Great Grimsby has been a fishing port throughout its history, but by the latter part of the 18th century the silting up of its harbour had caused trade to decline. This was remedied by diverting the river Freshney into the harbour, and in 1800 a new haven 14 acres in extent was opened. By the time George Oliver moved there in 1809 with his wife, son aged 3, and baby daughter, it was prospering again.

King Edward's school to which he had been appointed was controlled by the Freemen of the town, an hereditary body who as in many other towns before the Reform Acts formed the corporation which governed it. From the little we know about Oliver's relationship with his employers it would seem that it was not difficult to quarrel with them, and in one letter he wrote that his income was dependent 'on the caprice of Individuals . . . who are not wholly to be depended upon'.[1] Certainly he seems to have felt the need to supplement that income, because E.H.E. Wilson in a lecture about Oliver's time in Grimsby delivered in 1967[2] quotes a prospectus dated 10 July 1809 in which Oliver offered to instruct 'young gentlemen' in English, Latin, writing, arithmetic, geometry, algebra 'and all the higher branches of mathematics' for an entrance fee of one guinea and schooling fee of £2. Boarders were to be charged £20 per annum, plus 2 guineas for their washing, and had to provide their own sheets. Sea bathing was offered as an additional attraction.

At Grimsby he became familiar with the influential and ambitious Tennyson family. Dr George Clayton Tennyson, father of Alfred who was to become Poet Laureate, was from 1815 to 1831 the (absentee) incumbent of the Grimsby parish church of St James, a living which he held with other ecclesiastical preferments where the parochial work and the parishioners were left in the care of curates. Oliver became friendly with Dr Tennyson's brother Charles, who helped him in the masonic research he later undertook and to whom in the dedication of one of his early books[3] he referred as 'the friend and companion of all my labours'—though their friendship was later to be violently disrupted.

Soon after Oliver arrived in Grimsby, he received and dined the Duke of Brunswick who, with his corps of Black Hussars, had seized some ships and fled to England to avoid captivity in the Franco-Austrian war. It would be a practical reminder to him of his new status as a leader in the town.

Being now settled, he lost no time in resuming his masonry. There was an 'Antients' lodge in Grimsby, the Spurn and Humber Lodge, about which almost the only thing we know is that Oliver refused to buy its Bible from its Tyler (the officer responsible for guarding the outside of the lodge room). The Bible had most unmasonically been pawned to pay the rent; the 'Antients' did not in general prosper in Lincolnshire. Oliver determined to establish his own lodge for which purpose he acquired the furniture and, with questionable legality, the warrant of a lodge at Louth which had ceased to work; this warrant, no. 510, had originally been granted to another lodge on 17 October, 1792. He apparently paid 30 shillings for it, and whether or not he was entitled to do so, used it to set up a lodge which he called 'Apollo' and of which he became Master for the first time in 1813, the year in which the two Grand Lodges were united. It is unlikely that either Grand Lodge would have approved of the cavalier way in which he established it; but neither of them had exhaustive records, and Grimsby was a long way from London. One of the earliest members of the new lodge, Samuel Newby, bricklayer, is shown as joining from Spurn and Humber Lodge. In due course Apollo Lodge was renumbered 544 on the roll of the United Grand Lodge and its regularity was thereby acknowledged.

The episode was typical of the energy with which Oliver set about achieving any purpose on which he had determined; and the powerful nature of the persuasion which he was often able to bring to bear is shown by the fact that he arranged for a Brother Kitching to build a masonic hall in Burgess Street in 1812 to house the lodge. The inscription on the foundation stone recorded the event and probably explains the reason for the name Apollo: 'This building, erected for a Lodge, dedicated to masonry on the Festival of St John the Evangelist AD 1812. Bro. Geo. Oliver R.W.M.; Geo. Parker S.W.; T. Travis J.W.; W. Piercy P.M. This stone, a part of the temple of Apollo at Delos, was brought and presented to the Lodge by Bro. Potter'. The stone later passed into the possession of Pelham Pillar Lodge, now no. 792 and, after being found later in its lodge room doing duty as a hearthstone, was restored to a more suitable site. A report in the *Lincoln Mercury* for 20 August 1813 describes the dedication of the new hall, which seems to have taken place in conjunction with the holding of Provincial Grand Lodge there after one of the great public masonic processions of which the Craft was very fond in those days; the Chair was occupied by the Deputy Provincial Grand Master (DPGM), the Reverend Matthew Barnett. The building is described as being aligned east and west with a plain exterior; the west gable, being that nearest to the street, had the word 'Apollo' cut on its stonework. The entrance, an arched doorway, was reached by a flagged path lined with poplars—Oliver had a fondness for trees—and 'a pretty garden'. Within there was a lodge-room measuring 36 feet by 20 and 12 feet high, with ante room and robing or preparation room. According to a description by Anderson Bates,[4] there was a long table covered with green baize extending from East to West in the centre on which the celestial and terrestrial globes and various masonic emblems were placed. There was a dais with a chequered covering at the eastern end on which stood a pedestal and the Master's chair. The Bible, square, and compasses lay on the pedestal. The chairs for the Master and Wardens were 'suitably carved', presumably with the emblems of their respective offices. A kitchen was situated in the basement where there were also living quarters occupied by Kitching. A print showing the exterior exists at the Grimsby Masonic Hall. Oliver was Master of Apollo Lodge for over 10 years notwithstanding a Grand Lodge ruling that limited tenure to two successive years, another reminder that London was a long way off. He revelled in the new hall, and later (1848) wrote:

'It was a noble lodge room, appropriated to the sole purpose of Masonry. I had a private key, and many an hour have I spent in solitary enjoyment, when no-one knew that the building contained an inmate. Here my first aspirations to contribute to the benefit of the order were imbibed. Here vast projects were formed, with none present but my Almighty Father and myself, which have not yet been fully developed. Here, surrounded by the implements of Masonry, I became impressed with the sublime ideas of its superlative blessedness, and universal application to science and morals; and determined to work out principles which were then so feebly scattered as to give rise, amongst the uninitiated, to fantastic notions and absurd opinions respecting the design and end of the institution, that derogated from the virtue and holiness of this sacred handmaiden of religion'.[5]

How these projects developed into a 'Grand Design' is one of the themes of this book.

From this extract it would seem that it was at Grimsby he first began seriously to consider the nature of freemasonry and its relationship to the Christian faith. He soon concluded that it was the development of a moral code laid down at the Creation, a concept to be examined in due course but which, while it appears extraordinary to post-Darwinian generations, was not illogical in the context of the orthodoxy of the time when the literal truth of the version of the Creation as related in the Book of Genesis was accepted without question and to doubt it would be accounted blasphemous.

The Union of the two Grand Lodges took place almost at the same time as that at which as we shall see George Oliver was ordained a deacon and a year before he became a priest. Apollo Lodge was flourishing under his guidance and Bates gives its membership about this time as 7 clergy, 3 esquires, 10 gentlemen, 3 lawyers, 2 doctors, 18 mariners, 43 comedians, 2 customs officers, 3 lieutenants, 27 tradesmen and 1 farmer, a cross-section which well indicates the Craft's wide appeal. However, official records indicate that from 1815, when dues were paid to UGL for 13 members, to 1828, when payments ceased, the maximum number at any one time was 28 (1818).

The views he had inherited from his father, as expressed for instance in the Peterborough sermon, would be of the absolute compatibility of freemasonry with the Christian religion and there are grounds for thinking he may at about this time have been challenged on this point.[6] He was by now reading widely, probably with the help of Charles Tennyson's library and would certainly be aware that from time to time attacks were made on the Craft in the name of Christianity. It would be natural for him, as a newly-ordained man with his interest in freemasonry recently re-kindled, to consider whether the two were after all irreconcilable. To many of its members freemasonry was concerned with all aspects of morality, and morality was a code which had been established for mankind by the Creator just as religion had been. This was not a theory introduced by George Oliver, but one which had been accepted widely for many years, and was not out of keeping with the fundamentalist tenets of the time. To a more cynical age which prides itself on its worldly wisdom and self-sufficiency and appears to doubt the existence of any divine purpose, such reasoning is not easily understandable; but many men of intelligence and ability in the early 19th century accepted it without demur.

In fact, three things seem to have happened to direct his thinking at this time. First, he had been challenged by a skilful opponent to justify freemasonry as a reputable and worthwhile institution; second, he was appalled by the state of the Craft in Lincolnshire which had for many years been without effective control and guidance, and felt that his aim should be to become the Deputy Provincial Grand Master of the Province; and third, he felt that there was no ordered explanation of the nature of freemasonry to which brethren could turn for guidance when challenged about its objects. From this time forward he was intent both on his Grand Design of writing a series of books to expound the nature and aims of the Craft and its relationship with the Christian religion, and on the reform of freemasonry in the Province of Lincolnshire.

He had already made the acquaintance of the DPGM who, as was often the custom in those days, actually ran the Province. In 1813 the Revd Prebendary William Peters was the Provincial Grand Master; he rarely appeared in the Province for which he was responsible, living in the vicarage on his Prebend on the borders of Gloucestershire. Barnett obviously was impressed by Oliver's energy since he asked Peters to offer a Provincial Grand rank to the new Apollo Lodge. Peters' reply, dated from Sevenoaks on 1 July 1813 shows a strange ignorance about what was happening in his Province: '. . . Taking for granted that the Apollo Lodge (which name I have no recollection of having heard of before) will nominate two respectable men to be their Stewards at the ensuing festival, I should be glad to add to their consequence by giving them the rank of grand Steward on the morning of the Feast that they may then be invested by you with that honour in my name'. The fact that the Provincial Grand Master had not heard of Apollo Lodge is not only a comment on his own absenteeism but also on the cavalier way in which Oliver seems to have established it. The offer (of two stewardships) was made and accepted, Oliver writing to Barnett 'The honor [sic] you are about to confer on two of our Brethren by investing us with the red apron, merits a return of thanks greater than it is in my power to express'. (By way of note, Grand Stewards and Provincial Grand Stewards wore, and still do wear, a distinctive red-bordered apron in contrast to the normal blues of the Craft and, although the rank itself is low, the prestige of the red apron is often high.) Oliver promptly ensured that he should himself be the recipient of one apron and so gained his first Provincial rank.

In 1813 also he became a Royal Arch mason in Kingston-upon-Hull at a ceremony in the Industrious Chapter, attached to the Rodney Lodge, on 8 May; the certificate issued to him is in the possession of the Dr Oliver Lodge, no. 3964, Peterborough. Unusually, and presumably as a tribute to the esteem in which he was held in local masonic circles, he appears to have been promoted to the senior office in a Chapter almost at once. The Royal Arch (Chapter) is now regarded in English freemasonry as the completion of the Craft degrees. Before the union it was known to both the Grand Lodges and was conferred by the 'Antients' in their Craft lodges.

The 'Moderns' showed a somewhat equivocal attitude to it which resulted in the formation of a separate Grand Chapter to govern the Order, a position accepted if not formally recognized by the Premier Grand Lodge. At the Union it was eventually recognized as part of 'pure antient freemasonry' and is now governed separately but in close co-operation with the Craft.

Having been exalted into the Royal Arch, it is typical of Oliver that he immediately set about founding a Royal Arch Chapter in Grimsby, and he seems to have relied on his purchased Craft warrant for authority. That he could so easily do all this without (apparently) sanction by any higher authority is presumably indicative of his own forceful nature as much as of the state of the masonic Province of Lincolnshire at the time. Aletheia Chapter began its meetings in 1813; later that year the local head of the Royal Arch, the Grand Superintendent in and over Lincolnshire, proposed to visit it but Oliver wrote to him declining the honour on grounds of the low state of the Chapter's finances 'for, in fact, we are possessed of no funds at all and the expenses already incurred have been so serious, that the brethren have been under the necessity of contributing liberally to discharge the Debts. . .' What the Grand Superintendent thought of this rebuff is not recorded.

The Lodge and Chapter prospered for some years. But the ill-advised election of a disputatious candidate led, as we shall see, to dissension and ultimately it would seem that rather than have the lodge he considered peculiarly his own creation torn apart by strife, Oliver declared it at an end, burnt the minute books and returned the warrant to the Grand Secretary.

Oliver himself was later (30 July 1819) seeking action against his mother lodge of St Peter who, he complained, had pocketed the fees he had paid for his initiation and the conferring of subsequent degrees, but had not had his name enrolled in the records of the Grand Lodge as required by the laws! But that lodge was by then meeting only spasmodically and it was not until 1823 that he received the Grand Lodge certificate of membership which now hangs in the Lodge Room at Peterborough.

But the real importance of 1813 in his life is that it marked his entry into Holy Orders. He was ordained deacon in the Church of England by the Bishop of Lincoln on 19 December, and priest on 11 December 1814. He may have been becoming weary of his struggles with the Freemen and have looked to an alternative; but he remained headmaster for the time being. He was a man of strong religious faith and his revered father was a priest. Inclination and upbringing alike would urge him to seek ordination and he may well have felt that he had by now the connections that were so necessary for an Anglican priest in those days if he was to secure a benefice. He may possibly have known that Dr George Clayton Tennyson might shortly have a curacy to offer him. Dr Tennyson was in fact instituted Vicar of Grimsby St Mary with St James on 22 August 1815 and shortly afterwards George Oliver appears as his curate having also been appointed by the Bishop to the living of Clee, a small village near Grimsby, and where, as there was no vicarage, he was granted a licence excusing him from residence.

By 1814 George Oliver was becoming a person of importance in Great Grimsby.

As a priest he was in charge of the parish church and was vicar of Clee; he was also headmaster of the Grimsby school, while as a mason he had founded a lodge and a chapter, been awarded a Provincial rank, and had arranged for the building of a new lodge room and its formal dedication by the Provincial authorities as well as the holding there of the Provincial Grand Lodge. He was also becoming known and liked in important quarters. At the same time, though by now he must have learned to live with his employers at the school, he would no doubt still feel his position there to be precarious; and he was conscious too of the insecure situation of an underpaid curate, as a letter in the Grimsby library to Charles Tennyson shows;[7] he had heard of the illness and likely death of a parish priest and wished to ensure that when the time for a new presentation should arrive his name would be considered; but the priest survived. He was also becoming known as a writer, having contributed articles to various magazines, mainly about antiquities. And, presumably to enhance his importance, he got himself enrolled on the books of Trinity College, Cambridge, as a 'ten year man', a step towards acquiring a Cambridge degree without the necessity for going into residence in one of the colleges; this seems to have got no further and would have become unnecessary after he received a Lambeth doctorate in 1836.

His energy was immense; while still leading an active masonic life and discharging the work of headmaster he set about his parochial duties with vigour and was an interested observer of social habits, as is shown in his description of sailors' weddings in the Parish Church:

> 'At this altar about 30 marriages are annually solemnized; and the sailors' weddings are often conducted with much parade and show. A spirited tar will frequently be attended to the altar by eight or ten couples of young people, gaily attired in their best *bibs and tuckers*; and in the afternoon of the wedding day the bridal train will parade through the town in pairs with processional pomp, the Bride and Groom taking precedence, all decorated with Bride favours, consisting of White Ribbons curiously disposed in the form of a *True lover's knot*; a mystical favour that perhaps derives its original from the Rodus Herculaneus, the Knot of Hercules, resembling the snaky complication in the Caduceus or Rod of Mercury . . . The ship to which the happy bridegroom belongs is decorated with numerous flags of different colours and bearings, surmounted by A GARLAND of ribbons suspended from the topmast. This garland is mystical, having been composed by the bride-maids with many significant ceremonies. And let not the fastidious despise this humble emblem of connubial happiness; for it was used equally by Jews and heathens throughout the world long before the birth of Christ, as a symbol of joy and gladness; and the early Christians hallowed it with a solemn benediction.'[8]

He remained the Grimsby headmaster until 1826 (when, according to a petition later presented by his supporters to the Bishop urging that he be the next vicar, he gave it up because being 'advanced in years' it had become too laborious an office: he was 43 when he resigned!). We learn something of what he achieved as curate of Grimsby from the farewell sermon[9] he preached there in 1831 when, Dr Tennyson having died and Oliver in spite of petitions in his favour having failed to secure nomination to the vacancy, the new incumbent, the Revd Francis Attwood, terminated his appointment as curate, seemingly not without acrimony. Oliver was never one to retire gracefully, presumably a reflection of the hard school in which he had been brought up where everyone had to fight for survival or succumb. In the sermon he first summarized his religious teaching 'that man is *placed* in a state of justification by Faith alone . . . Good works . . . cannot justify,' and continued 'Such is a brief recapitulation of the fundamental doctrines by which I have anxiously endeavoured to instil into your minds the necessity of faith and a holy life, that I might enjoy the heart-felt satisfaction of leading you by gradual steps from earth to heaven, and receiving, at the consummation of my Stewardship, the appellation of a good Shepherd of the Flock; and that, at the last day, we might equally be welcomed with the salutation—well done, good and faithful servants, enter into the joy of your Lord'. He also defined what he saw as the main duty of a pastor: he 'must be *useful* and possess *influence* by attending without respect of persons with assiduity and unfeigned affection to the wants and wishes of parishioners'; and sadly commented on the difficulties of discharging those duties in a parish 'divided into parties, political as well as religious; the former conducted with the most vindictive feelings of rancour and revenge'. It was to be good grounding for what would confront him later in Wolverhampton.

He then turned to the 'temporal benefits which the parish has derived from my superintendence . . . When I entered in the church, I found the fabric damp, dirty and forlorn, without casements in the windows for a free ventilation; the windows themselves in the last stages of decay; the walls green from the effect of moisture, and the floor wet from its low situation compared with the level of the churchyard. You had no Church Sunday School to bring up the rising generation of the lower class of society . . . no public charity supported by voluntary contribution for the relief of indigence and the sick bed of cheerless poverty; no Organ in the church; no tunable bells; and only a single duty on the Sabbath day. Opposed to this melancholy picture, look at the state of the place now in any one of these particulars. You have a beautiful church, clean, dry and perfectly ventilated, with two full services every Sunday; a sweet-toned organ, of which my daughter has been the gratuitous organist from the period of its erection in 1822; eight musical Bells, a Dorcas charity well-supported, a Sunday School, and a District Committee of the Society for Promoting Christian Knowledge. The Churchyard I planted at my own expence; and there is another great improvement in this enclosure, of which, more than all the rest, I have reason to feel proud.

'For many years I saw and lamented the desolate stage of your burial ground from the effects of a defective drainage'. He goes on graphically to describe the macabre effect of coffins 'floating in a grave half-full of water', never being one to back away from the realities of life or death, and then recounts how, although 'a few individuals opposed . . . the expence' and the scheme was 'frequently foiled . . . this desirable object has been effectually accomplished'. (He was to have trouble with churchyards at Wolverhampton too.) Later in the sermon he criticizes the opposition to the repair of the church by those 'not possessed of sufficient discernment to foresee the inevitable consequences of suffering it to remain in the state of decay in which I found it; but I prevailed, though at the expense of some degree of unpopularity, which I endured cheerfully, conscious posterity will do justice to my motives, and thank me for my work'. Though normally a modest and retiring man, he was sometimes roused sufficiently to sound his own trumpet, and when he did so the music was usually rendered with a self-righteous bravado.

The determination shown by these passages was the same as that which would cause him so much trouble in Wolverhampton, and it is worth noting from the reference to his daughter's services as organist that she would only have been 14 at the time when she first undertook the duty. It is also noteworthy that during his time as curate he published a description of the parish church which achieves the often unattained object of being both scholarly and readable.

During the 22 years he spent in Grimsby (1809–1831) he persevered in his activities as an author and wrote two treatises supporting the fundamental teachings of the Anglican Church: *A Vindication of the Fundamental Doctrines of Christianity* (1821) and *The Apostolic Institution of the Church of England Examined* (1831), as well as *An Essay on Education* (pre 1826: no copy seems to be known). The *Vindication* was printed and published in Grimsby and although it was stated on the title page to be available in various Lincolnshire towns and even in London, this was modest, as we shall see, compared to that for the *Apostolic Institution*; Oliver was still flexing his muscles. The full title of the work was *A Vindication of the Fundamental Doctrines of Christianity Against the attacks of Deism and Infidelity in a series of Pastoral Addresses, from a clergyman to his parishioners*; and in the preface, Oliver wrote: 'If mankind would study the sacred truths of Holy Writ with the same avidity with which they read pernicious publications; if they would employ reason instead of prejudice; if they would attend to the admonitions of their authorized Minister, who wishes to give an account of them with joy, instead of hoarding up the sophisticated reasonings of designing men who lie in wait to deceive, they would renounce all idle disputes of faith and doctrine'. He could at the age of 38 write at times with the passionate idealism of the early 20s, and mingled with the worldly wisdom he had acquired it produced a heady mixture.

It was at Grimsby that his love of antiquarian study flowered. Later he wrote 'I dearly love these mysterious investigations. I love to wander through the obscure regions of dark antiquity; and a research into the hidden truths of history, science and topography is pleasing to my taste, and congenial to habits long indulged and deeply planted'.[10] Articles from his pen appeared in London journals, and in 1825 his first major work in this sphere was published. *The Monumental Antiquities of Great Grimsby* was a volume of considerable size, modestly sub-titled *An essay towards ascertaining its original and Ancient Population. Contains also a brief account of the two magnificent churches*. He describes himself on the title page as 'Vicar of Clee, domestic Chaplain to the right Honourable Lord Kensington'. The work was, as customary at that time, funded by subscription and among the subscribers were Charles Tennyson, the Bishop of Winchester and Charles Chaplin MP, the latter being a considerable landowner in the area of Scopwick, to the incumbency of which Oliver was later to be appointed. He seems to have had a knack of making friends, a fact which foreshadows the ability to inspire love and esteem that was so notable a trait of his character in later years. The origin of his association with Lord Kensington is not known.

Oliver has been criticized by historians—particularly masonic writers—for a too ready acceptance of unsubstantiated fact, in which connection it has to be remembered that he would have little access to primary texts, and some of those which he and many others then took at face value have been shown by the aid of our more sophisticated tools to be forgeries or otherwise unreliable; nor were communications as easy as now. In the preface to *The Monumental Antiquities of Great Grimsby* he clearly states the dilemma: 'Facts are a substantial groundwork for theory; and when theory is founded on facts, it possesses great claims to public credence. Nothing great or useful can be accomplished without investigation; nor can truth be elicited without an essay. I have freely offered my own opinion on the monuments which surround us, in the hope of inducing others, possessing more leisure for literary purposes . . . to prosecute the enquiry still further'. This was a position he would restate later in relation to his investigations into masonic history saying 'I conceive that I have merely opened the mine'.[11] He is certainly not above criticism but his critics do him less than justice when they fail to recognize the limitations of which he himself showed he was aware.

If his enthusiasm at times led him astray, the restrictions imposed by lack of easy transport facilities, absence of critical tools we now take for granted and, above all, the straightjacket of the religious orthodoxy of the time, should all be remembered in his defence.

Chapter Four

PRIEST, MASON, WRITER

(Great Grimsby)

The Monumental Antiquities of Great Grimsby was not the first major work George Oliver published. Apart from the magazine articles and pamphlets already mentioned and a number of masonic and other sermons (he had been appointed Provincial Chaplain in 1816, an honour which the brethren of Apollo Lodge commemorated by presenting him with a gold medal) he had begun his career as a serious masonic writer in 1823 with *The Antiquities of Freemasonry*, intended as the first step in the 'Grand Design'. Letters in the UGL Library suggest that he embarked on this work in 1820 when he was corresponding with the Revd George Adam Browne of Trinity College, Cambridge, one of those who had been concerned in the revision of the ritual, chaplain to the Duke of Sussex and from 1825 PGM for Cambridgeshire and Huntingdonshire. By July of that year he had sent some proof sheets for perusal by the Grand Master, and on the 20th Browne wrote acknowledging further sheets and expressing sympathy for the fact that the number of subscribers to the project (which was to be published by monthly parts) was less than the author had hoped. Browne had been trying to get subscribers, but had encountered opposition from freemasons who were appalled at the prospect of details about the Craft appearing in print, especially, Browne wrote, in the wake of a new exposé 'by Carlisle in *The Republican*'. He also advised toning down a passage in which Oliver had referred to certain forms of phallic worship practised by heathens in the past.

Oliver seems to have been mounting a two-pronged approach in this, for on 10 July he had written to the Grand Secretaries, the chief executive officers of the Grand Lodge, with a synopsis of chapter headings to 'obtain information respecting the proper method thro' which this undertaking may receive the sanction of the Grand Lodge'; and to ascertain whether it could be dedicated to the Duke of Sussex. The original letter is endorsed with a summary of the reply: 'HRH has made it a rule not to give his Sanction to a Pub. until an oppy. is afforded of first perusing the Work. If a copy were transmitted to us it would be laid before HRH & His pleasure made known'. Another letter indicates that the Secretaries had also told Oliver that it was not the practice of the Grand Lodge to give its sanction to works on freemasonry, though he would be aware that this had once been done (for *The Spirit of Masonry* by William Hutchinson in 1775, a fresh printing of which was published in 1843 with annotations by Oliver). He promptly asked for the matter to be placed before the Board of General Purposes for an executive ruling on whether he might quote the Secretaries' letter in the preface to his own proposed book. The reply, dated 1 October, reported that the Board had refused to give an opinion as the matter was not officially before them but went on to express some personal views 'which we feel are in accordance with the sentiments of the Members of the Board'; these were to the effect that 'such a quotation might induce a belief that applications had already been made to Grand lodge' which had refused its permission, and 'if such would be the inference drawn, it would certainly not accord with the fact'. He must have realized he was embroiled with experts.

Oliver described the inception of the Grand Design in a document of great importance to his biographer, the *Valedictory Address* published in 1850 as an introduction to the last work, or 'cope-stone' of the Design, *The Symbol of Glory* (1850), in these words:

> 'An event, too trifling to be recorded, originated my first publication . . . At that early period I had formed a plan in my own mind, which was intended to demonstrate the capabilities of Freemasonry as a literary institution . . . to convince the reading public that Freemasonry possessed within itself references of a more exalted character, and that it actually contained the rudiments of all worldly science and spiritual edification, I contemplated working out, in a definitive cycle, a detailed view of its comprehensive system of knowledge, human and divine. The plan was extensive, and the chances were, that it would . . . never be completed. But the mind of youth is elastic . . . Such an undertaking, to be perfect, must necessarily embrace History and Antiquities; Rites and Ceremonies; Science and Morals; Types and Symbols; Degrees and Landmarks; and, above all, it would require to be shown what connection the Order bears to our most holy religion; and how far it recommends and enforces the duties which every created being is bound to observe in his progress from this world to another and better . . . The first step was to show the Antiquity of the Order, and somewhat of its early history: for this was the only basis on which all subsequent reasoning could be safely founded . . . I therefore published a work on the Early History and Antiquities of Masonry from the Creation to the building of Solomon's temple.'

This passage, written when Oliver was 67, emphasizes that his view on the universality of freemasonry as a moral code had not altered. In one of his works he defined it as 'a science which includes all others, and teaches mankind their duty to God, their neighbour and themselves';[1] but at all times he was insistent on its subordinate status to religion, by which term he meant the Christian religion and it was in this sense that he on several occasions referred to it as 'the humble handmaiden of religion'.[2] The point has already been made that this conception of freemasonry was not unusual at the time, but to understand why this was so it is necessary to look back into the history of the Craft as it appeared to its members in the late 18th century.

The original freemasons were the workers in free-stone who were employed in the construction of great buildings, particularly cathedrals, abbeys and priories, throughout the Middle Ages. By the 18th century a distinction had developed between the 'operative' mason, who actually worked on buildings and the 'speculative' mason, who used the mason craft to provide the basis for the allegorical teaching of morality. There is argument about whether speculative masonry developed in or independently of any operative lodges, but whatever the answer the speculatives acquired an identity of their own and any link there may have been with the operatives was abandoned. Justifiably or not, the new freemasons looked to the operative craft as the foundation from which speculative freemasonry sprang, and no doubt wishing, like many other new movements before and since, to acquire a respectable aura of antiquity, set about determining the history of the mason craft and adopting it as their own. This history took them back to the days of Athelstan, King of the English in the 10th century, who was reputed to have granted a charter to the mason craft ratifying its organization in lodges. From these premises it could be assumed that the Craft had an even earlier origin; and in a society which believed in the literal truth of the Bible it would be natural to search the Scriptures for this. The building of King Solomon's temple about a thousand years before the Christian era had obviously been an occasion for the gathering together of a vast number of masons. The Biblical story of the Tower of Babel came from a still earlier era. It would be but a step to claiming that the operative craft of freemasonry had come into existence with the first building work after the Creation and that operative masons abided by a moral code promulgated even earlier, at the Creation itself (4004 BC): a conceit which neatly inverted the proposition that speculative freemasonry grew out of the operative craft. That Oliver accepted this reasoning is shown by *The Star in the East* (1825) shortly to be considered, in words which also demonstrate his conception of freemasonry as a fully comprehensive system of morality: 'Freemasonry was revealed by God himself to the first man'. It seems that this statement was challenged, as well it might be, for in later editions he added a footnote: 'This may appear a bold assertion, but I am persuaded that it is nevertheless true. Placed in the Garden of Eden Adam would certainly be made acquainted with the nature of his tenure, and taught, with the worship of his Maker, that simple science of morals which is now termed Freemasonry'.

The speculative masons could thus claim to have found in operative masonry an historical basis for their own Craft as well as for their belief that from the first there had been a philosophical side to masonry. Elsewhere I have suggested how Oliver and his predecessors might have come to believe this, bearing in mind the extensive view they took of freemasonry as an all-embracing system of morality, and I now quote from that paper:

'Like Preston before him, George Oliver believed Freemasonry to have existed from the beginning of the world and, accepting the Bible as literal truth, he believed that the Creation had occurred as stated in the Book of Genesis, though he did not accept that each day of the six in which the universe was said to have been created was necessarily of 24 hours, since a thousand years, even thousands of thousands of years could in the sight of God be but a day . . . Whether Oliver was right or wrong, he was sincere and the logical conclusion of his belief—using the word belief in its strictest sense—is in sharp contrast to all modern theories, which may of course themselves be wrong. The argument would run thus: God created the universe; men were created in God's image; it was to them that God revealed His purpose, and with one race of mankind that He later made His covenant; the early books of the Bible show that God's plan for mankind, or at least for that part of mankind He had chosen as His people, is all-embracing, covering every facet of their lives; therefore there is an all-embracing rule of conduct for man which has been in existence from before the Creation, and has been worked out for man in revelation and in history as he has come more and more to understand God's purpose, or as that purpose has been gradually revealed to him. That purpose reached fruition, in the Christian ethic, in the coming of Christ, Who was the Messiah, and in the giving of the New Covenant. A new system of morality and conduct thereby sprang from the old, and again embraces everything necessary for carrying out God's will for mankind; this system does not provide or purport to provide the rules for religious celebration, or to dictate dogma, but concentrates on what man must do in his daily life on earth, how he must behave—a handmaid in fact to religion. Freemasonry is exactly that, and is the embodiment of that system. Therefore Freemasonry is that system, and has existed from the Creation. Few today will accept this argument. But it seems to have been how Oliver reasoned, and how those earlier generations of freemasons, whose works were in his time accepted dogma, must have thought. It is therefore necessary to assess Oliver's works in the context of this belief.'[3]

In a book written in 1845 at the age of 62, Oliver stated his position once again: 'It is a mistake, however, to suppose that Freemasonry is a system of religion. It is no such thing. It is but the handmaiden to religion, although it largely and effectually illustrates one great branch of it, which is *practice*'.[4] Later in the same work he wrote '. . it is remarkable that there is not a single legend or tradition, which Freemasonry acknowledges, that can be construed into a type or emblem of any great truth, but is connected, directly or indirectly, with the covenant delivered by God, with the gracious design of redeeming his erring creatures from the consequences of that unhappy event which expelled the first created pair from their bower of bliss, and of producing their eternal salvation'.[5]

The Antiquities of Freemasonry was a success and he was encouraged to proceed in the Grand Design. For the next step he reasoned that 'it was necessary to show clearly to what religion, if any, the present system of masonry was analogous. On this question I came to the point at once . . . and unhesitatingly pronounced it to be Christianity'.[6]

His arguments were set out in *The Star in the East* to show 'the Analogy which exists between the Lectures of Freemasonry, the mechanics of Initiation into its mysteries, and the Christian Religion'. (The masonic 'lectures' are instructional catechisms which formed part of the ritual in Oliver's time but have now, as we shall see, fallen into disuse.) In the preface, he gave three reasons for writing it: the proscription of freemasonry as hostile to the interests of Christianity, the charge that it was 'established for purposes of sensual conviviality', and the reaction to the publication of his earlier book by freemasons protesting 'the intimate and necessary connexion which subsists between Masonry and Christianity'. He found a large body of opinion within the Craft to support him. Secure in his north Lincolnshire fastness and in the righteousness of his cause, Oliver probably did not realize that he might be setting himself on a collision course with the powerful forces that had worked to dechristianize the ritual, even though in one passage he wrote 'I presume not to say that masonry is exclusively Christian . . . I only contend . . . that being a system of ethics, and inculcating the morality of every religion under the sun, it is more particularly adapted to the Christian religion, because Christian ethics approach nearest to the standard of absolute perfection; and because the genius of masonry can assimilate with no other religion so completely as with Christianity';[7] but the feeling throughout the work was very much in keeping with a note included in a later edition: 'It is much to be lamented that the casuistry of the present day should be used to sever the connection between Freemasonry and Religion. It arises out of the mistaken notion that Freemasonry entertains the ambition of superseding religion altogether; which is as wide of the truth as the poles are asunder . . . It is a system of morality, inculcated on scientific principles, and morality is not the groundwork, but the result and fruit of religion'.[8] Though ostensibly a remark of general import, such a statement was not likely to be acceptable to the masonic hierarchy after all the agony of a reappraisal of the ritual, something to which freemasons do not take kindly even today. For the moment however all was well and as will appear the Duke of Sussex and the masonic establishment supported him.

The argument advanced in *The Star in the East* is not easy to follow, but in the light of his other works and particularly of the statement in the *Valedictory Address*, it may perhaps fairly be summarized thus: freemasonry is a cosmopolitan institution and so can only have an affinity to a religion which is applicable to all times and adaptable to all peoples; Christianity is at the appointed time to prevail universally and therefore is the religon to which a truly cosmopolite moral institution must relate. The 'permanent and unchangeable landmarks' in the masonic lectures are based on allegorical teaching founded on events in the Old Testament. That Book is the precursor and foundation of the Christian dispensation and so is in conformity with the teaching of that dispensation. Therefore freemasonry is compatible with Christianity and is in fact Christian.

Support for this summary can be found in the following passage from the posthumously published *The Pythagorean Triangle* which he probably wrote in his late 60s or early 70s: 'There is little benefit to be derived from Freemasonry in this Christian country, if it be divorced from all connection with the Christian religion; although admitting that it would be a violation of the true principles of the Order to close our Lodges against the sincere professors of any other faith which includes the belief of only one God, the creator and governor of the world . . . The great error of those who can find no Christianity in Freemasonry is, the very superficial view which they take of our most holy faith. They restrict its operation to the last eighteen and a half centuries; whereas, if they believed the Scriptures, they would extend it back to the beginning of time, as St Paul instructs them to do'.[9]

In the *Valedictory Address* he referred to an argument by some who felt that because freemasonry claimed an earlier origin than the Christian religion it could not be compatible with the doctrine of salvation. This he rejected because the lectures 'actually contain a pointed reference to all the principal types of Christ or the Christian dispensation which are to be found in the Hebrew Scriptures'.[10] The equivocal position of the lectures after the Union is considered later but for the moment it suffices to state that in spite of the attempted dechristianizing of the ritual, no such operation was carried out in respect of the lectures, nor has it been attempted since.

As *The Star in the East* and *The Monumental Antiquities of Great Grimsby* were published in the same year, it may fairly be stated that Oliver was now firmly embarked on his career as a writer; but whereas proposals for further grandiose schemes for books on antiquarian subjects languished and were abandoned, the Grand Design advanced one step further as (to quote again from the *Valedictory Address*) he 'commenced the superstructure with an explanation of the elementary tenets of the Order, as a preliminary step towards a general view of its claims to a favourable consideration which might spread throughout the length and breadth of the habitable globe';[11] he was nothing if not ambitious in the cause of freemasonry and by the time he wrote those words he was occupying a pinnacle of authority on which he was hailed as 'the sage and historian of masonry'.[12]

The book in which he undertook this explanation was *Signs and Symbols* which first appeared in 1826, the third in the Grand Design. In it he discussed the terms and technicalities of the Craft since 'no science can be mastered without a competent knowledge of the terms and technicalities'.[13] In the preface he wrote 'With pure intentions I have used my utmost endeavours to conceal from the prying eyes of insatiable curiosity, those essential points which have constituted masonry into an exclusive system' but noted that 'the very same symbols have been used for a similar purpose by every nation and people, and in all secret institutions which have existed from the creation to the present time',[14] a remark of wide import which he must have felt his intensive reading and research entitled him to make.

His growing reputation allowed him this time to secure permission to dedicate the work to the Duke of Sussex. How this was obtained is not known but a later letter signed by Grand Secretary Harper and sent in reply to a brother who had expressed indignation about the publication and dedication implies that permission was apparently given in Cambridge—presumably it was obtained through Browne instead of by the more regular channels of the Grand Secretaries; this would certainly account for the rather grudging tone of Harper's letter. The subscription list included the Duke of York, the Duke of Leinster (Grand Master of the Irish constitution) and many other notables and Oliver must have felt considerable pride in his achievement. Certainly he fared better on this occasion than when shortly after the death of the Duke he tried to obtain permission to dedicate another of his books to the Earl of Zetland, Pro Grand Master under the Duke and shortly to become Grand Master. The reply (dated 29 July 1843) read 'I have the honour to receive your letter of the 20th inst. I beg leave to say that as a general principle I am much averse to publications on Masonry and can therefore never give my sanction to any work on that subject without having ample opportunity of knowing and judging of its content. I regret therefore that I must decline to comply with your request'. After which his lordship had 'the honour to be, Sir, Your Obedt humble Servt'.[15]

On the present occasion however Oliver received ample co-operation from the masonic hierarchy and on 23 June 1826 we find him acknowledging a list of sub-scribers from Nantwich, forwarded to him by Harper, and commenting that he now has 750 names. On 20 October he sent (probably by water) nine copies of the book to Harper, seven being for 'the Grand Officers . . . as I am at a loss how to deliver the single copies'; the seven included those for the three subscribing dukes. Harper asked for a further six so Oliver, who was not averse to building on success, sent him a round dozen, writing 'I have recd from all quarters the most flattering testimonies of their utility to the Brethren . . . I think it would be advisable to send Bro. G.A. Browne's copy to Cambridge, as I do not know otherwise how it will reach him. I have a particular desire that the book should be seen in Cambridge, & he is the only subscriber there'. Whatever lay behind this particular desire, the object does not seem to have been achieved. The 'ten year term' which began in January 1814 never led to anything; but whether the motive was frustration, ambition or annoyance we cannot determine. Certainly the sale of over 750 copies must have been gratifying to him as an author and have been seen as a vindication of his thesis.

Another event now occurred which was to have far-reaching effects for his masonic career. The Provincial Grand Mastership for the Province of Lincolnshire was vacant, and in 1826 Charles Tennyson was appointed. He was a busy radical politician and had been equerry to the Duke of Sussex, himself a man of surprisingly radical views on some matters. Tennyson was in fact so preoccupied that he did not attend to be installed in his new office, and so was unable to act, until 1832, leaving the Province leaderless for six years, something which did nothing to improve its already somewhat unhappy state. The appointment would increase Oliver's hopes, already referred to and apparently having Barnett's support, of becoming DPGM and, as the principal executive officer of the Province, being able to restore its morale and practice to conform with his own high ideals.

The year 1827 seems to have seen the beginning of the demise of Apollo Lodge. It had from the first been conducted to Oliver's exacting standards with 'lectures' and discussions in lodge and controlled relaxation at refreshment. He enjoyed both and wrote of the latter:

> 'I am not ashamed to acknowledge that I like the good old custom of moderate refreshment during Lodge hours, because, under proper restrictions, I am per-suaded that it is consonant with ancient usage . . . At a certain hour of the evening, and by certain ceremonies, the Lodge was called from labour to re-freshment; when the "Brethren enjoyed themselves with decent merriment", and the song and toast prevailed for a brief period. The songs were usually on Masonic subjects . . . Each song had its appropriate toast . . . And I can say from experience, that the time of refreshment, as it was conducted up to the Union in 1813, was a period of unalloyed happiness and rational enjoyment . . . During these happy moments, the Brethren entered with much unction upon their refreshments . . . When I was Master of the Apollo Lodge at Grimsby . . . the refreshments were abstemious and moderate. The amount

for each Brother was strictly limited to three small glasses of punch, and this was seldom exceeded, except at the annual festival, when a pint of wine was allowed . . . It is not to be denied but there were some Brethren who displayed an anxiety to have the allowance increased; but the character of Masonry prevented them from persisting in their demands; and I should think an instance of a Lodge, in these days, addicted to intemperance was not to be found'.[16]

That there were nevertheless high spirits engendered may be gathered from the fact that one member, who lived in a nearby village to which he would return after lodge across country on foot, was accustomed to signal his imminent arrival home about midnight by blasts on a horn—not necessarily a popular action in the country at that time of night. Parenthetically, the custom of having refreshment during part of the time when the lodge was open was frowned on after the Union and the modern pattern of dining after the Lodge had been closed became established.

Oliver never forgot that Apollo Lodge was wrecked because of one wrong choice, and in his masonic writings there are frequent warnings of the need to be careful in electing men to membership of a lodge; the most famous is still printed on many lodge summonses and first appeared in *A Century of Aphorisms* (1849): 'Be very cautious whom you recommend as a candidate for initiation: one false step on this point may be fatal. If you introduce a disputatious person, confusion will be produced, which may end in the dissolution of the Lodge. If you have a good Lodge, keep it select. Great numbers are not always beneficial'.

Oliver's next works appeared in 1829. Historical and antiquarian notes on Clee, Ratcliffe, and Castor (or Caistor) were printed in the *Gentleman's Magazine*, and a *History of Beverley* was published; but he also resumed prosecution of the Grand Design with *The History of Initiation*, a review of the ancient, idolatrous mysteries intended to show that neither in origin or in subsequent history were they in any way linked with freemasonry which 'stands proudly on its own basis'.[17] The work was dedicated to Charles Tennyson, who had recently assumed the name of D'Eyncourt to comply with a 'name and arms' clause in a will; it expressed the author's pleasure at 'the gratifying intelligence that the friend and supporter of all my labours had been elevated, by His Royal Highness the Duke of Sussex, to the superintendence of Freemasonry in Lincolnshire, in the capacity of its Provincial Grand Master'. Oliver could not know how long it was to be before his friend entered upon his new duties or how that friendship was to be tried.

In a subsequent edition[18] and at the suggestion of his publisher he gave a list of the authorities consulted, but added 'It is now many years since the *History of Initiation* was written, and at that period I had access to many valuable works which were not in my own collection. I am now resident in a distant part of the country, and, to supply such a catalogue I must depend principally upon the strength of my memory, which is not particularly retentive; for even the greater part of my library is in Lincolnshire'—from which it would seem this was written shortly after his retirement in 1860/61 when he lived for a short time in Nottingham.

His position as an authority on freemasonry is emphasized from the fact that in 1829 he was entrusted with preparing a new edition of a book which was then the standard work on freemasonry and its history, *Illustrations of Freemasonry* by William

Preston. He did not presume to alter the original script, and his editing took the form of extra footnotes and an extension of the history of freemasonry which formed part of the work, to cover recent events; it was a signal honour which he must have appreciated. There is also evidence that he was active in a literary society in Grimsby at the time. He had already given up the headmastership of the school (probably in 1826 but possibly a little earlier) and received the public thanks of the town, even though he had on occasion felt compelled to maintain his ecclesiastical authority against civic intrusions, as when in 1821 the corporation draped their pew in the church with black cloth in token of mourning for Queen Caroline. As the estranged wife of George IV whom the King had tried to divorce for alleged misconduct in a trial before the House of Lords and had refused to admit to his coronation, she had been the object of considerable popular sympathy, and her death soon after his coronation made her a popular martyr. The Grimsby corporation evidently sympathized with her cause; but Oliver removed the drape. On 21 October the corporation demanded to know why this had been done. The reply was uncompromising: Mr Oliver was not aware that he was accountable to the Mayor and Magistrates of Grimsby or to any other Power except the bench of bishops for his conduct in the church. As a concession, however, he explained his reasons, that the corporation had ignored a previous (and less contentious) royal funeral, and 'been engaged in political controversy at the very moment when divine service was being performed in the church' on that occasion; though he indicated that had permission been properly sought it might well have been granted, and concluded 'but the mayor and magistrates may rest assured that Mr Oliver will respectfully but firmly resist any encroachments that may be attempted on the privileges of the Church'.[19]

A book he published in 1831, *The Apostolic Institution of the Church of England Examined*, shows how seriously he regarded doctrine. An acquaintance, Mr R.M. Beverley, had published an essay on the alleged corruption of the Church of England; whether the writer was related to Oliver's wife does not appear but that they knew each other only slightly was emphasized at the start of the work in terms which suggest that Oliver wished to distance himself at once from his opponent, presumably to scotch at the outset any suggestion of relationship: 'The slight personal knowledge of you, with which I have had the honour of being favoured by accident, will be amply sufficient to furnish an apology for the present address; and I anticipate your thanks, should I be fortunate enough to adduce sufficient evidence, to dissipate the train of misconceptions, which, like so many glimmering meteors, have beguiled you into the fathomless depths of error'. He excuses his attack by saying 'The clergy, Sir, are bound by the canons of their church, when the fortress is assailed, to gird up their loins in its defence'. Interestingly, he is for once on the defensive in regard to his own upbringing as having been 'excluded from the advantages of an academical education, by the limited income of a parent, who, for the last half century has been a humble curate in the establishment, and still remains in the same unostentatious capacity'. It is perhaps the only occasion on which resentment at his parents' hard life surfaces, and that it should do so shows how much at this stage of his life, aged 48, he still felt his own lack of a secure position.

In the book itself his argument is orthodox; Christ established an authorized priesthood which had full powers of delegation; the Christian priesthood is of perpetual obligation and authority; the Church of England is genuinely apostolic and the three orders of bishop, priest and deacon are 'invested with the high sanction of apostolic observance'. He does not claim that the Church is always in the right: 'I presume not to defend the evils of pluralism and non-residence, although they admit of justification under some peculiar circumstances. There are, in this kingdom, numerous livings which do not exceed the annual value of one hundred pounds, and many which do not reach fifty. On one of these it would be impossible for a resident incumbent to provide for the necessities of his family, and practise among his indigent parishioners those benevolent works, which constitute at once his duty and delight; . . . "feeding the hungry, clothing the naked, healing the sick" '. It will be recalled that £100 was the amount allowed to his father at Whaplode.

The work also contains a vivid declaration of his sense of purpose and shows how dominant were his senses of vocation and of the importance of his calling in spite of all his other interests, notably freemasonry and antiquarian study. 'I, more humbly, "amidst evil report and good report", will, with the divine blessing, use my ceaseless endeavours, *contra tantam vim sceleris*, to confirm the religious feelings of mankind; convinced, that if I succeed in turning but one soul, from the error of the disobedient to the wisdom of the just, I shall have performed an action, whose reward is superior to the transient burst of human applause; an action over which "the angels of heaven will rejoice with joy unspeakable" '.

An intriguing sidelight on his ministry at this period appears from a paper *On Popular Superstitions* which he delivered to the Lincolnshire Topographical Society on 15 March 1842;[20] expressing himself as 'old enough to recollect the time when an implicit faith was placed in Palmistry and Metallic Tractors for the cure of rheumatic gout', he confesses that he 'offered many a shilling' at the altar in Grimsby for a cure for ague 'not that I had the slightest belief in the efficacy of the charm; but I thought it probable that the patient might be relieved by the mere force of imagination'. If his language sometimes seems high-flown and his idealism too other-worldly, this is a passage to remember.

The Apostolic Institution of the Church was 'printed and sold' by a Grimsby firm, Goddard and Brown in Lowgate; but its author clearly felt it deserved a wider audience, and the title page recites that it was 'sold also by Rivington and Co. St Paul's Church-Yard; Hamilton, Adams & Co, Paternoster Row; Whittaker & Co., Ave Maria Lane; and by all the other booksellers in Town and Country'. Ignoring the last claim, the addresses were all in that warren of small streets in the City of London that used to lie adjacent to St Paul's Cathedral and their inclusion would be something of a triumph for the author. But in that same year of 1831 his life was turned upside down by the death of Dr Tennyson. On 19 August 1831 the Revd Francis Thomas Attwood was instituted to the living in spite of at least two petitions to the Bishop in Oliver's favour. It would seem there was a clash of personalities; his precarious tenure as curate ended, not without acrimony over the dismissal by Attwood of Oliver's daughter from her position as organist in September.[21] At the age of 48 he was without a job other than that of vicar of Clee (where there was no parsonage house); of his five children George (b.1806, now aged 25), Caroline

Burnett (1808, 23) and Beverley Samuel (1811, 20) were old enough to make their own way in the world, but Charles Wellington (1815) and Mary Ann Pierpont (1819) were only 16 and 12 respectively. He does not seem to have been altogether without funds, but now was the time when he had need of friends, and they did not fail him.

Chapter Five

'A SECLUDED VILLAGE'

(Scopwick)

On 12 October 1831 Oliver was collated to the vicarage of Scopwick by Bishop Kaye of Lincoln in whose gift the living was. He remained vicar of Clee. The change from town to village was probably not unwelcome; life in Grimsby seems to have been a continual struggle as witness the reference in his farewell sermon to 'a parish divided into parties, political as well as religious; the former conducted with the most vindictive feelings of rancour and revenge'.[1] In that address he also made rueful reference to enemies: 'alas! who is without them'. He had come to the town unknown, respectable and poor, and it was an age where advancement depended on birth, patronage or (particularly after the Napoleonic wars) wealth. Even the gentle novels of Miss Austen paint a picture of the rule of privilege, albeit invaded by the newly rich officers of the Navy; the reality of life for many was later portrayed with stark accuracy by Dickens, and the poverty of that world cannot ever have been far from young George Oliver's mind. His pleasant manner and sincerity of purpose in education, archaeology and freemasonry had brought him friends and supporters and this in turn had probably led him to seek ordination. His energy made him a difficult man to ignore and though a lover of peace he would fight hard, even against powerful opponents, when the cause warranted it, as his later life would amply show. But it was as curate of Grimsby that he found himself; he experienced a satisfaction in the daily task of a parish priest, the spiritual care of souls and the welfare of the poor and distressed which clearly shows in his pamphlet *Scopwickiana* published in 1838. However much he resented his dismissal from Grimsby, he was to find much happiness in his new living, though the income was only slightly over £100 per annum.

Scopwick is a village about 12 miles south of Lincoln to the east of the minor road from Lincoln to Sleaford, at a point where it crosses a stream. The main village street runs near the north side of the stream with houses, cottages, and a school building to the north and the church behind them. There is now open land between stream and street, and further building on the south side, reached by tracks which bridge the stream at intervals. Another street runs parallel a hundred yards or so to the north and the vicarage fronts onto that. Oliver called it 'a secluded village',[2] and that is the impression it still gives today; however Dixon says that at the time when Oliver arrived it was 'in such a state as to be a proverb and a by-word amongst the neighbouring villages. No schools or school-room; the church walls and floor covered with green moss from which drops of water trickled continuously; scarcely any congregation; the churchyard in a ruinous condition; and the vicarage house and premises uninhabitable'.[3] It would be a challenge to the energies of the new vicar and he set about meeting it with his customary energy.

We have two sources on which we can draw to see what Oliver achieved in a very short time. *Scopwickiana*, which gives a detailed description of the village and of some of its inhabitants in 1838, and a biographical article in *The Freemasons' Quarterly Review* (FQR) in 1840, which provides material about his pastoral work there. They are as intriguing for the general picture of a remote Lincolnshire village in the aftermath of the Inclosures and on the threshold of the Industrial Revolution as for the light they throw on Oliver and his work as a Christian pastor. *Scopwickiana* was written in response to a suggestion in *Blackwood's Magazine* that priests might write about their parishes for the enjoyment of readers and the benefit of posterity. It is probably fair to surmise that the description in this case became too lengthy for the magazine and that Oliver therefore had it published privately. The article in FQR was the result of the admiration for Oliver as a masonic writer by the founder and first editor, Dr Robert Thomas Crucefix, already referred to as the Grand Officer who constituted the new St Peter's Lodge at Peterborough in 1836; it dealt only incidentally with his parish work.

In the preface to *Scopwickiana* Oliver wrote 'The clergy may be fairly expected to give the best account of their own villages and people; because the familiar intercourse with all ranks which their profession induces, must enable them to describe manners and customs much more accurately than the casual visiter [sic]; and their education and experience entitle them to distinguish between motives and actions, and to pronounce a decisive opinion on the various scenes and actions which come under their notice', words which could only have been written by a man sure of his vocation and his mission. He goes on to stress the need for a parish priest to study the 'manner, habits, propensities and amusements of his flock' so that 'knowing their wants, their weaknesses, and infirmities, he may so shape his course as to lead them by easy steps to the systematic practice of piety and virtue in this world, which will contribute to their everlasting happiness in the world to come.'

The following passage from the preface reflects perhaps more of himself than the author would have realized:

'By making frequent visits to the cottages of his poorer neighbours, the minister of religion secures to himself, along with the approval of his conscience, a source of gratification by which the punctual discharge of his onerous duties will not only be ameliorated, but invested with a present reward. These humble dwellings may be small and inconvenient, and sometimes even slovenly and dirty; the mother and her children may be clothed in rags; but there is a joyousness of heart and countenance attending the resident minister's reception which it is delightful to witness. These poor people feel complimented by his call, and endeavour to render it agreeable that it may be repeated. And it is surely no inconsiderable satisfaction to a faithful pastor to reflect, that a gleam of happiness, however momentary, has been conferred on his humble parishioners and friends; on those to whom happiness appears to be a name almost destitute of meaning. And should he succeed in alleviating their sorrows, or rendering the privations necessarily attached to their station in life, less keenly felt, he may enjoy the pleasing reflection that he has advanced one step towards infusing into their minds a firm reliance on the goodness of Providence, whose dispensations are all intended for the general benefit of his creatures, and contribute to produce an equal distribution of happiness to the poor as well as to the rich. This impression cannot fail to induce an habitual sense of gratitude and devotion, which will soon manifest itself in their external conduct.'

As a man, he was able to accept the social order of the time with what today would seem an unquestioning smugness, but as a Christian priest he was no respecter of persons and had a deep sense of the miseries of poverty, something which was to get him into trouble later in Wolverhampton.

He knew his people and saw them 'warts and all', as the following passage, the opening sentence of which has already been quoted, will show:

'Our village population is not absolutely virtuous or vicious: the people are neither so high-minded or so slavishly abject as has been represented; and the most popular theories are rather speculative than true. Incessant praises have been lavished in modern novels on the fidelity of servants; as if the virtues of faithfulness and disinterested attachment were an excellence more to be desired than hoped for; whereas the instances of unfaithfulness in real life are very rare. But this virtue, in common with many which adorn a cottage, is mixed with other qualities, whose excellence, to say the least of them, is very questionable. In the professed Histories of towns and villages, we look in vain for illustrations of character; although it is from the authors of such manuals, who are generally located on the spot, and conversant with the inhabitants and their peculiar customs, that we expect to be enlightened on the subject. The massive tomes which contain the records of parochial and county History, frequently exhibit profound antiquarian learning and indefatigable research, which renders them invaluable as books of reference; but they are generally destitute of that display of mind and character in an unsophisticated state, which would make them interesting to readers who are unacquainted with the localities they profess to describe. It is this want of general interest which causes topographical works to be such a drug after the first demand has been exhausted; and is the true secret why these publications are found on no shelves but those of book collectors; by whom, it may also with truth be affirmed, they are seldom read. And if ever they appear on the drawing-room table, it is only for the display of their embellishments.'

Oliver had himself written several such books and it is no doubt the wearied voice of experience that speaks in those last words.

By the time *Scopwickiana* was written he had become responsible for a parish at Wolverhampton, and was clearly comparing the life of an industrial town with that of a 'remote village'; indeed he writes that 'The degrading vices of a manufacturing population certainly form no part of village practice; and drunkenness, gaming, and all the crimes incidental thereto are unknown at Scopwick; if we except one profanation which I hope will soon be abolished'. The 'profanation' related to the practice by a certain part of the population who were only temporarily resident in the village of playing a game analogous to 'pitch and toss' in the village street, particularly on Sundays.

Oliver being what he was, it was inevitable that several pages of the pamphlet should be taken up with an historical background; perhaps it was also to be expected that early mention should be made of the local gentry:

> 'The locality is pleasant, the country round being well planted, and the neighbourhood enlivened by several noblemen's and gentlemen's seats, which impart an air of great interest to it. Blankney Hall, the seat of Charles Chaplin, Esq., is distant a short mile; Nocton, the late residence of Earl Ripon, and still of the Dean of Windsor, 4 miles; Coleby Hall, where Lady Kaye resides, and Haverholme Priory, the seat of the Earl of Winchelsea, each 6 miles; and Bloxham Hall, the residence of—Christopher, Esq., and Walcot Hall, of Capt. Peacock, each 3 miles.'

The list is interesting to his biographer because of the subscription to *The Monumental Antiquities of Great Grimsby* in 1825 by Chaplin, who, as the local squire, may have been instrumental in obtaining the living of Scopwick for him; while the Dean of Windsor was also, by an historical quirk, Dean of Wolverhampton and certainly responsible for his appointment to that town. Curiously, the manor of Scopwick had been transferred after the Norman conquest to one Walteyr D'Eyncourt whose family held it until the time of Henry IV—Charles Tennyson, it will be recalled, changed his surname to D'Eyncourt. The original church had been built by Ralph D'Eyncourt in 1135, but of that only the tower seems to have survived. The Chaplin family had held the manor since its confiscation in the aftermath of the 1715 rising.

Oliver's ability to write readably about architecture has been referred to already. The description of the church at Scopwick affords an example:

> 'The building is plain; the tower has square bell windows, each divided by a mullion and transom to represent the Holy Cross; to which the church is dedicated; and to commemorate that solemnity, the feast of the Holy Cross is annually celebrated in the village. And what remains of the interior, viz., the columns and arches which support the roof, and separate the two aisles from the nave, are of an uniform style, except the eastern arch of the north aisle, which was evidently erected by a lady, whose bust, beautifully executed, occupies the point where the archivolts emerge from the capitals of the column. In this situation was probably a private chapel; but all vestiges are removed by which such a conjecture might be confirmed. In the south pier at the entrance into the chancel, is a niche with a canopy, ornamented with pinnacles, crockets and finials, which perhaps contained the holy rood in the absence of a loft for that purpose. The high altar was accessible by three tall steps which still remain. All else is new, and every ancient memorial has been carefully destroyed. The interior of the church has no monumental inscrip-

tions; but within the altar rails is laid an old stone, on which is carved in high relief, a knight on his back in tegulated armour, as I suppose, for it is very much defaced, with the cylindrical helmet, crossed legged, and hands on the breast, elevated in prayer . . . It is a simple but good specimen of a village house of prayer, placed beside the running stream which springs from beneath its foundations, and bubbles forth in all its brightness and purity; an emblem of the sacred fount of piety which the edifice was erected to promote.'

He is not so complimentary about other buildings in the village; of them 'little can be said, and that little anything but satisfactory. The old Rectory and Vicarage[4] were low, damp habitations, unfit for human residence; with rooms five or six feet in height, and altogether destitute of convenience. The former is inhabited by servants'(!). The vicarage had been replaced at his instigation by 'a new stone house of moderate dimensions . . . It consists simply of dining and drawing rooms, two kitchens, and five sleeping apartments, with the customary offices, an excellent garden, and a lawn, flower garden and shrubbery of half an acre in front of the house'. Such was the building which was to be the family's home until 1855 and to see the completion of many books as well as the arrival of many guests of eminence in the masonic world.

Of other buildings in particular he says:

'The labourers' cottages are inconvenient, both with respect to construction and locality. They have been placed on the borders of the stream (an arrangement which has has ever constituted a prolific source of ague and rheumatism) built of stone and thatch; through the chinks and crannies of which the wind visits the inmates somewhat roughly in cold unfavourable weather. Some of these habitations are so totally inadequate to the purpose for which they are intended that, in more than one instance, a man, his wife, and five children, are domiciled in a room open to the thatch, 12 ft. by 10, which serves them "for parlour, for kitchen, for bedroom, and all", as they have no other place whatever, even for their repose; and father, mother, and children of both sexes, some of them ten or twelve years of age, all "turn in" together, and sleep by each other's side. The existence of this state of things is to be regretted, because it is unfavourable to morality . . . Preparations, however, are in progress for rebuilding some of these huts and I would suggest the propriety of placing them in a more dry and healthy situation, on each side of the cross lane which forms a junction between the Lincoln and the Heath roads.'

There was a good turnpike road along the higher ground but he records that the road eastward to Kirby Green was 'not only low and narrow, but flanked on each side by tall hedges, which exclude equally both sun and wind; and, consequently, it is dirty and disagreeable all the year round'. There had also been problems with the village roads. They were repaired by the use of the soft limestone which abounded in the area; when wet and under pressure this turned into a substance resembling mortar. During the winter wheel carriages could only enter or leave the village by the stream bed 'as the street was axle deep, and passed by pedestrians through the medium of stepping stones'. However, he adds there had recently been very considerable improvement.

It is worthy of note that in several places he refers to recent improvement. Given his character, it seems reasonable to suppose that his forceful ability must have been behind much of this; it would certainly appear that he worked well with Chaplin and the result could only be beneficial to the village. Dixon, after his reference to the lamentable state of the village when Oliver arrived there, continues 'all these were remedied in a few years. A new vicarage built at the expense of the Vicar,[5] the church made fit for service; a new school room built, and a regular attendance of children both on Sunday and weekday'. In 1840 FQR could refer to 'a well-filled church of attentive hearers, who are partial to his ministry'.

The parish covered about 3,500 acres. There were 'four principal farms and a few cottages' as well as several freeholds which conferred votes for south Lincolnshire. Charles Chaplin was the main landowner, with about three-quarters (2,760 acres) to his credit; the bishop, who owned the rectory land and leased it to Chaplin, had 500 acres and the vicar 17. Only two of the remaining eight freeholders had more than 50 acres.

Oliver lists the population as: '321 souls; and is thus distributed:

'The Vicar. 1
Farmers 5
Cottagers 7
Tradesmen 15
Labourers 35
Children } Males 66
            Females 63
Servants hired } Males 32
   by the year } Females 20

The remainder being adult females'.

He also gives a summary of burials over a 20-year period; there had been 65 deaths which he analysed thus by ages:

Infants 22
Under 10 years of age 1
From 10 to 20 2
From 20 to 30 1
From 30 to 40 5
From 40 to 50 5
From 50 to 60 2
From 60 to 70 9
From 70 to 80 12
From 80 to 90 5
From 90 to 100 1

During the same period there had been 160 births. The high mortality rate for infants would not be unusual and the figures show that once that hurdle had been surmounted there was a good chance of survival beyond middle age.

Marriages were infrequent 'but when the unusual sound of a publication of banns does occur in the church, the congregation appear all on the *qui vive*, although the choir do not respond, as in some village churches in the county, "God speed 'em weel!" Sermon over, a peal on the bells is sure to follow; and everyone who was not present enquires, "Who has the parson been talking about?" '. The choir consisted of 'a few agricultural labourers and their wives; led by a clarionet and a violoncello. There are three tenors, four trebles, and as many bass singers, besides the two instrumental performers; and very decently do they sing the Psalms of David'. But, as will be seen, the peal on the bells was a questionable blessing.

Oliver describes the village people as 'very quiet, sober and provident; unvexed by politics, and performing their daily avocations honestly and conscientiously to the best interest of their employers' but adds 'It must not be supposed, however, that the village is exempt from the leaven of idle and thriftless persons. I speak of the generality, who are uniformly industrious; and the patience and good feeling which accompany the discharge of their most onerous duties are beyond all praise' and refers particularly to harvest-time, when a labourer's day would start at 3 a.m. as he walked with his whole family to the cornfield where they would work for 16 hours to get extra wages to buy a pig for the winter or some other necessity, returning in the evening 'tired it is true, but not out of temper'. Charles Chaplin allowed a garden of about a rood (about 0.1 hectare) for each of the labourers on his land, 'amply sufficient, by judicious management, to furnish them with as many vegetables as each family can consume during the year, and potatoes to feed a pig'.

Time was governed by the sun. 'This noble luminary' Oliver wrote 'is almost the sole guide at Scopwick; for there is something very singular amongst the inhabitants respecting the measuration of time. Small as is the population, time is so differently estimated, that no two clocks are alike throughout the village. Every family appears to entertain its own distinct ideas respecting this invaluable treasure; for it is not regulated either by a town clock or sun-dial. One has a fancy for keeping his clock too fast; another entertains some special reason for having his too slow; and hence the two extremities are scarcely within as many hours of each other. I am not aware that any serious inconvenience arises out of this combination of whims, because each family has a tolerable guess at the correct time . . . [It] only seems to show how fond men are, even in the lowest grades of life, of possessing and displaying some independent principle of action in their own private concerns, by which they succeed in satisfying themselves that they really enjoy the privilege of self-control'.

Rents were low because the land could not be cultivated without the expense of bones as well as manure, and also because of the prevalence of loose limestone near the surface which had to be removed by hand after ploughing. Turnips, barley, seeds, and wheat were grown in rotation; oats and beans were not considered profitable and only grown for domestic consumption. There was also a local cheese which Oliver considered 'superior to the Stilton kind' and would have liked to see promoted commercially; but this was a scheme he does not seem to have been able to persuade anyone to undertake. The usual poultry was fattened for sale—geese, ducks, turkeys, chickens, guinea fowl, and peacocks. Wages for a labourer were normally 12 shillings a week, two strikes of malt (a strike was a measure of capacity which varied from place to place) and the possibility of extra money at harvest time; a man could earn five shillings a day cutting seeds or grass, and wives and children earned extra by stonepicking. Gleaning could add 'seven to eight strikes of wheat, and as much barley as would buy a pig'. There was good money to be had too by wool-gathering, but 'this is a very laborious employment; for they must travel perhaps 20 miles a day in the pursuit, climbing gates, crossing ditches, and struggling through hedges in their course, oppressed with a heavy burden; and the operation of cleansing and preparing the article for sale, is so disgusting that few are engaged on it'. Boys found special employment 'tenting birds' from which they would graduate to weeding, picking stones, dragging turnips and similar jobs until at the age of 14 they were adjudged capable of following the plough. Parish rates averaged two shillings in the pound.

Not all the workforce came from the village; indeed there seems to have been considerable mobility of labour, largely because of the custom of annual hiring fairs. Oliver described them thus:

'The annual period when servitude terminates is old May-day, and a series of statute fairs are held in all the large towns and principal villages for renewing the contract. Servants of both sexes assemble early at the statute, and place themselves in groups, the girls decked out in their best bibs and tuckers; and their personal appearance displayed to the greatest advantage for the purpose of attracting attention; while the "young chaps" sport blue or white slop frocks according to their respective taste, and their avocation is designated by well-known symbols. The shepherd has a lock of wool stuck through his hat-band; the waggoner mounts a thrum of whipcord, and the groom a bunch of horse hair. They are usually engaged for a year at a stipulated rate of wages, and the agreement is sealed by giving and receiving a small sum of money in addition to the wages, which varies from *one* to *five* shillings, and is denominated a "Fessen [fastening] Penny". Should the servant change his mind before he takes possession of his place, he may cancel the bargain by returning the Fessen Penny; and on the other hand, if a master should hear anything prejudicial to the servant's character before the same period, he may get rid of him by announcing that he is at liberty to retain it. A servant can demand the privilege of attending two of these statute fairs, provided he has not been previously hired; but after the actual receipt of his Fessen Penny, without which the hiring is imperfect, the master can legally withold his consent.

'At these fairs mothers attend with their young daughters; and before leaving home make calls on the neighbours for the benefit of their good wishes; and nothing is witnessed on the statute morning but sunshiny faces; and the heart cheering words, "Good luck! Good luck!" follow the several parties as they pass by every cottage door.

'These fairs are the Saturnalia of servants; and every kind of licence is indulged with impunity. The young men appear, like sailors on shore after a long voyage, to have no idea of order or propriety; and the unpopular master is sure to hear of his faults, real or imaginary, at these places, if he be seen among the crowd. Drinking, dancing, fighting, and every other irregularity prevail; and practical jokes without regard to personal consequences, are played off to an unlimited extent. Removing the linch pins from carts full of female passengers that they may be overturned, is very common; and it is seldom that a statute fair passes over without some accident of this kind occurring. Old quarrels between Farmers' servants are generally potponed till the fair, when they terminate in a battle. In this respect the statute bears some resemblance to the Irish "pattern", and the civil power is frequently in requisition to check these ebulitions of private feeling. A lady attended at Sleaford last year to hire a housemaid. While in the act of talking to the girl, a fellow in a slop came up, and rudely seizing the lady by the sleeve of her dress, shouted,

' "Hoi say, maaty, wool yaw let me cooam and see that lass when shaw lives wee yaw?"

'Which was followed by a horse laugh, echoed amongst the by-standers of his own grade; for he knew nothing of the girl or the lady. This is accounted wit, and men receive the applause of their companions in proportion as they display a superior excellence in practical audacity and insult.

'When the business of the statute declines, and the "hiring" appears to be at an end, the girls parade, in pairs, and are soon picked up by individuals of the other sex, who are on the lookout for sweethearts; and attachments are here formed which frequently end in marriage. They then adjourn to some public house for a dance; and here jigs, hornpipes and reels, as well as country dances are performed with equal agility and toil; for it appears that they strive to please their lovers more by muscular exertion than by graceful movements. Here is such stamping, and twisting, and bending, and spinning round, as cause the perspiration to pour in streams down the performers' faces; for the more they labour, the more they are applauded. A buxom lass, who has some reputation for dancing now spreads herself out to astonish the natives by the sonorous clatter of toe and heel, which beat the floor like a drum. A circle is soon formed round her, and she becomes the sole object of attention.

> ' "Queen regent of the scullery, the pretty Mrs Kitty
> Holds her check'd apron up with simpering agility,
> And thinks she is glissading it as graceful as nobility."

'The lads are delighted, and the lasses envious; and while the former cheer her with, "Go it, lass! Toe and heel! Stamp away! Shaw shaks hersen capital! Dang her, but she's a reyght gud 'un!"—the latter sneeringly exclaim, "How fussy shaw is! Shaw thinks shaw does it!" Meantime the Taglioni of the party, regardless of these observations, with her elbows akimbo, sails away in all her glory. Fatigue at length warns her to desist, and she finishes her *pas seul* with a loud rap, tap, tap, and swims proudly to her seat upon the bench followed by her enraptured swain.

'The girls are now treated with sweet wine and cakes, and it often happens that fun ends in fighting. Two fellows perhaps institute a claim to the same damsel—then what a dispute and chattering succeed! It generally commences with a very simple provocation. For instance; at the moment when a "young chap" is putting the important question to his sweetheart—"Cooam, Bess, weeant ye shake a bit?" some half drunken fellow amuses himself with throwing a handful of nut shells at her, which induces the common reply;

'"Yaw'l thraw yer nut shells where yer luv lies, hoi reckon."

'"May be hoi dow."

This is succeeded by another handful of shells in her face. Then her "fancy man" takes umbrage and looks daggers, which, if looks could kill, would annihilate his antagonist; but the stare is returned with a cool and steady eye, till the former is provoked to give vent to his feelings.

'"Yaw needn't stare so—ya'll know me agean—it's me—it's nobody else."

'"Yaw'r a desp'rat sharp lad—hoi wish hoi knawd yer muther."

'"Yaw'l behave yer sen, hoi reckon, and let moy lass alooan."

'"Yawer lass—whaw, shaw's moine, mun—what's yaw to dow we' her? Haw! Haw! Haw!" (laughing.)

'At this the girl bridles up and gives herself a scornful toss with—"none o' yer imperence, fellow"; which puts her companion on his mettle, and he sharply retorts;

'"It mun be a better chap than yaw are, to ta' her frae me."

'"We'll sune try that."

'The fingers, which have been itching for action in both parties, are now put into requisition; the fellows seize each other by the collar, and the weakest soon measures his length on the floor. The friends and acquaintances of each party, both male and female, now take different sides, and a regular row ensues. Words are followed by blows; bonnets and shawls are demolished; black eyes are given and received, until one party resigns his claim to the disputed belle; and then dresses are adjusted, blood washed off; dancing is resumed as if nothing whatever had happened; and the time passes merrily until the setting sun warns them of the hour of departure to their respective homes.'

The statute fair was not the only holiday or occasion for fun. There was one day each year which was observed as a public holiday when the entire population decamped to Mr Chaplin's house for the village sports—foot races, jumping in sacks, jingling matches, blindfold barrow-wheeling, the greasy pole and diving in a meal tub are noted. Perhaps a cause of the survival of this when so much else was disappearing was the fact that prizes were given by Chaplin, even though Oliver tells us that one individual generally carried off most of them and 'because of a want of stability in the man, causes his triumph and its reward to lead him to the neighbouring beer-shop, where the produce is expended in dissipation'.

The great day however was Holy Cross Day (14 September), the dedication feast of the village church, when an influx of visitors took place. The previous week was spent in preparation; cottages were scrubbed and scoured, plaster floors washed white 'and decorated with a running pattern in black' made from soot and water and intended to imitate a carpet. Food was stored in pantries and on the eve of the feast the squire, Charles Chaplin 'who resides in old English state' provided each cottage with a hare. After greetings, 'the children are dismissed with a few half-pence to the gingerbread stalls'. The inevitable meal was followed by visits and promenades which gave the young men the chance to walk with a girl on each arm 'with flaunting caps and ribands and artificial flowers—for bonnets are carefully eschewed at these times', their escort looking round out of the corners of his eyes to see that he and his companions were properly admired. A dance in the evening ended the celebrations and if disputes broke out 'respecting the proprietorship of some favourite lady . . . these petty squabbles never disturb the general harmony of the party': rather a large claim when it has to be accompanied by the statement that a man is no less pleased with his friend 'should he, in such a case, chance to treat him with a cracked crown . . . a broken head breaks no squares between them'. All this leads Oliver (after quoting 'Stubbs, the puritan, who wrote in 1585' as condemning such proceedings) to write 'I confess that I feel much gratification at witnessing their unsophisticated festivity, which dissention, either private or political, does not embitter. And I think the true philosophy of life, grounded on religious principles, is to keep the people in good humour by cheerfulness and innocent enjoyment, and to promote peace and harmony between man and man. I may be wrong; but it is an opinion which I imbibed in my youth, and I have not hitherto met with any argument to change it'.

The traditional keeping of Christmas Eve as a festival was still observed. 'The *Yule clog* blazes on the fire; the *Yule candle* burns brightly on the board, which is amply replenished with an abundance of *Yule cake* cut in slices, toasted, and soaked in spicy ale, the ancient British fare; and mince pies, decorated with stripes of paste disposed crossways over the upper surface to represent the *rack* of the stable in which Christ was born; and the evening usually concludes with some innocent games.'

Oliver was an astute observer and had an analytical mind. Although an idealist in many matters, particularly where freemasonry was concerned, he was alive to realities and had no illusions about the idyllic nature of the life of the poor in country or in town. By the time this was written he had become involved in the problems of the Industrial Revolution and having experience of the realities of poverty in both country and town clearly felt it was more bearable in the country, writing that 'The inhabitants of Scopwick are not in the slightest degree affected with the apprehensions that prey on the manufacturing classes, occasioned by anticipations of distress and ruin at some remote period'; but it has to be remembered that Chaplin was by Oliver's account a conscientious squire who cared for his workers and tenants.

Oliver was also aware of the drawbacks that exist for the worker in the country. 'I am reluctantly constrained to think that the poet's dream of absolute contentment in a cottage amongst the lower ranks of the people is without foundation; and displays an ignorance of human nature in its rude and uncultivated state. Comparative happiness may be attained; such a thing is possible; but positive felicity is inconsistent with this imperfect state'; and after quoting somewhat ecstatic lines by a poetess who professed to find more contentment among agricultural workers than among the rich ('Why dost thou to the hut repair, And from the gilded palace fly?') remarks 'This must be received with some allowance for her Ladyship's want of experience in those humble scenes to which she so enthusiastically refers; for there really exists much of murmuring and discontent—much of ingratitude for favours received, amongst the uneducated working classes; which, it is hoped, with the blessing of God, will be removed from the next generation by mental culture'.

The mutual care which the villagers showed for each other was exemplified in the custom of 'goodying', which Oliver says consisted of 'calling periodically on the farmers and others for the donation for winter comforts to which, as the women conceived, custom entitled them. On Shrove Tuesday and the feast day of St Thomas (21 December) they made the round of the village, 'dressed in all the rags they could muster up . . . as if all the maukins in the parish had deserted their station in the corn fields, and stalked forth for the astonishment of the neighbourhood', followed by the children whistling, shouting and carrying out practical jokes on one another, until 'the women, having appropriated the welcome offerings, retire to their respective habitations to resume their accustomed labours, and the little village is once more in its quiet state of noiseless repose'.

Another pastime of the women was tobacco. It had been introduced to the village as an antidote to ague but by Oliver's time 'the women, after they arrive at a certain age' were much addicted to smoking it in the belief that it was necessary for their health and alleviated the pains of old age.

The church would by 1838, when *Scopwickiana* was written, have been restored by Oliver's efforts and the services were well attended. However not all was perfect; the bells, for example:

'In the tower at Scopwick are three bad bells; one of which was baptized before the reformation and received the name of Gabriel. It contains the following inscription in Lombardie capitals:

MISSUS DE CELIS;
HABEO NOMEN GABRIELIS;

with two shields curiously charged with the monogram and cross. At a wedding, or any other rejoicing, these bells are brought into requisition, but with a most untunable effect; for the ringers do not excel in the art. The question does not appear to be, who shall perform with the greatest degree of accuracy, but who can effect the greatest number of strokes on his bell in the least poss-

ible space of time. This competition produces a discordant jangling which cannot fail to disconcert all nerves that are not composed of *bell metal*. "Those
evening bells" are enough to frighten every old woman in the parish. The
science of ringing has not yet attained to any degree of perfection in these
parts, although the neighbouring churches of Blankney, Timberland and
Ashby, possess some tolerable peals. This may be attributed to the par-
simonious system which has recently been introduced into the parochial
funds. The rewards usually paid on public days having been discontinued, and
the ringers being unable to devote their time gratuitously to this purpose, the
merry peal has ceased, and the excellence of the operators in the art has rapidly
declined.'

Nor were all the villagers as regular in their attendance at the church on the Sundays
as their vicar would wish. Though most came with great regularity 'habited soberly
in their clean white or blue slops, which is the favourite uniform of the village; and
the females in print gowns and shawls and straw bonnets, all clean and neat, the very
picture of decency and order', there were exceptions. 'The agricultural serving men
. . . being personally strangers, and changed every year, do not consider themselves
under any subjection to the ecclesiastical discipline of the village; or entertain any of
that feeling of respect and affection for the resident minister, which is becoming
hereditary with the rising population. Thus on the sabbath-day, knots of these servants congregate at the corners mixed with the half-grown men and boys who are
natives; and while the latter touch their hats as I pass by, with a smile and a familiar
"How do you do, Sir", almost as they would accost their own parents; the former
will turn their backs with a stupid leer, as if equally ashamed to display or to
withhold the same degree of cheerful reverence and attachment to their pastor'.
This revealing remark, which can be related to his earlier reference to the welcome
he customarily received from the cottagers and is an unconscious tribute to his own
pastoral success, leads to a disquisition on religion and morality which shows at once
Oliver's strictness and his tolerance, something which bears on his views about the
relationship between religion and freemasonry. 'It is a pity that these persons cannot
be made to understand the distinction between right and wrong more perfectly.
They appear to be totally deficient in correct ideas of the true nature of Christian
morality; which consists in the performance of those duties which promote domestic
and public peace, and tend to the protection of property by a strict observance of the
laws. I would make the line of distinction between real and fictious morality as
broad and evident as possible . . . Morality does not consist merely in the use of formal expressions of religious protestations'.

On the issue of village morality he speaks with approval of the conduct of the
local public house, 'The Royal Oak'. Only ale was sold there and the widow who
kept it 'allowed no drunkenness or late carousing'. If need be, she would tell a man
he had sat long enough and send him off. Oliver attributed much of the 'proverbial'
sobriety of the village to her management. At 74, she had never been more than 20
miles from her home in her life, nor was she then happy until she could return, a fact
which calls from the incumbent of Wolverhampton the heartfelt comment 'A

village is the most delightful of all locations, and Scopwick is the most delightful of all villages'.

Times were changing; cock-fighting had gone though the pit was still visible behind the church; bonfires and dancing on the green had vanished; 'The hopper cake remains unbaked; and the frumenty alone keeps its place'. May day with its maypole and 'Lady of the Common' and a game known as 'duck under the water kit' played to the neighbouring village of Kirby Green returning with that village's young people playing too, were things of the past. 'Plough Monday' had formerly been celebrated with a procession at the conclusion of which the men 'used to congregate in the street, and endeavour to bind each other within the coils of the plough rope, for the purpose of being jerked into the stream. Considerable dexterity was evinced on this occasion, and it frequently happened that the sport was concluded by the immersion of the whole party'. Beating the bounds had been discontinued at the time of the Inclosure—something which must have been a relief to the boys, who were habitually made to stand on their heads in post holes on the boundary. The vicar's sense of history led him to regret the passing of these old customs, but times were changing even in Scopwick.

But as he says, 'it is useless to lament the discontinuance of customs which do not appear to be suited to the genius of the age'. Provided he could effect improvements when they were needed, he was content with Scopwick as it was, and he saw it clearly with all its faults and virtues. It was here that he always returned as long as the vicarage was his home, and here that he was happy. And here most of his writing was to be done. In the double dedication of a book of sermons published in 1845,[6] one, that to his parishioners at Wolverhampton, was addressed to 'My dear friends' and subscribed 'Your faithful brother in Christ'; but the other was 'to my beloved parishioners of Scopwick' and subscribed 'Your faithful pastor and friend'.

Chapter Six

SUCCESS (1831–1834)

(Scopwick)

Life at Scopwick was to Oliver's liking; the new vicar and his parishioners were happy together; and he must also have been on excellent terms with Chaplin for so much to be achieved in so short a time. Some of the money for refurbishing the Vicarage may have come from his writing, but though both restoration of the church and building of a school had largely resulted from his own efforts, both must have involved the support of a local patron, presumably Chaplin. There were other improvements too, which he only indicates in *Scopwickiana* had been recently effected, without claiming any part in them; but in view of Dixon's remarks about the state of the village before Oliver arrived there, and with the evidence from his Grimsby curacy of the energy he could show in such matters, we can assume that he was responsible and that they took place in the early years of his incumbency. These were the curbing of the excesses of the stream that flowed through the village, and the repair of the roads.

The stream was fed by springs that provided every cottage with an ample supply of fresh water. In wet weather there was widespread flooding, and then the water spread to the walls of many of the houses and completely covered much of the street. When the water level dropped 'the borders of the brook were left stagnant, and soon assumed the form of a quagmire of soft black mud and cresses . . . interspersed with patches of putrid water, covered with a white and silvery film, which had a most unwholesome operation on the atmosphere; and damp houses, and the prevalence of ague and rheumatism were an alarming scourge to the village within the last few years'. To remedy this, the line of the roads on each side of the stream was changed; and by way of further improvement the land between roads and stream was so far as possible made into gardens which 'added much to the beauty and salubrity of the village'. It also allowed the villagers, or at least the more provident of them, 'such as are blessed with managing wives' is Oliver's description, to store loppings of fir trees (called 'kids') for winter fuel in 'kid stacks' on the banks of the stream near their cottage doors. The kids were bought cheaply from Chaplin's plantations.

As a result of these improvements Oliver claimed that by 1838 there were almost no cases of ague and far fewer of rheumatism though admitting that the stream was not yet fully tamed, 'for, even now, after heavy falls of rain, the quick springs . . . burst forth with great violence and rapidity in every part of the valley; boiling and bubbling amongst the sand, and attracting attention equally by their force and purity' and breached the road in places so that boots and 'patterns' were still regularly required.

These projects, coupled with the need to get to know his parishioners and their ways, occupied much of his time in the first years at Scopwick; he was also still vicar of Clee in those early years, though from the lack of any mention of affairs there (the place was in any event small) it is likely that a curacy had been arranged; Oliver would no doubt get a certain satisfaction from being able to do as he had until now been done by. There was a lull in his writing for some years though one directory credits him with several minor publications in 1832–1835, mainly sermons. But on the whole he seems to have been far too busily occupied to write much even though in a letter dated 11 May 1833 he sketched a proposal for a history of Kesteven which he says he was being pressed to undertake; nothing came of the idea.

But the cares of Scopwick were not his only concern. The archaeological site of Temple Bruern, a former preceptory of the Knight's Templar, was not far away. By 1832 he was busily investigating 'manifest tokens of an extensive internment'[1] on this site and these explorations there continued into 1833. There are strong indications that he published a note of his findings. It would have a double attraction for him—as an antiquarian because it was an important historical site, and as a freemason because there was (and is) a Christian masonic order of Knights Templar in England and there are grounds for thinking that he had become a member of one of its Encampments during his time in Grimsby. The original Order of Knights Templar, which was suppressed in the Middle Ages, figured in the mythical history of freemasonry current in England at the end of the 18th century.

The two years 1833 and 1834 also brought him additional responsibilities in both religious and masonic spheres. It was about this time that he published the *Letter to the Archbishop of Canterbury*.

Apollo Lodge had been troubled for some time and one writer states that Oliver took the warrant with him when he moved to Scopwick;[2] as a lodge cannot meet without its warrant this was a drastic (and illegal) step to take, but we do know that internal dissension had greatly grieved him and that the lodge which had been his pride had become a source of trouble and pain; the available evidence suggests that prominent freemasons who were members, including the Provincial Grand Secretary, approved the action he took. In about 1833 he burnt the minute book and papers. It was a high-handed and, on the face of it, unjustifiable action; that anyone so conscious of the value of historical material should wantonly destroy such records is all but incredible, and Oliver must have been deeply moved or very angry to have done so. Later he returned the warrant to the Grand Secretary. Though the full story is not known, some light on the unhappy state of the lodge's affairs can be obtained from letters that have survived. On 9 April 1829 Oliver had written to the Grand Secretaries asking for an informal opinion about possible irregularities in the conduct of a lodge. The letter does not name the lodge but the terms of the correspondence make it clear that it was Apollo. After mentioning the provision of a lodge room in 1812 by 'a spirited brother (since dead) . . . for which we agreed to pay him an annual rent of £20; but it was subsequently reduced as low as £8.0.0. a year', he states that a dispute with the new owner, who was not a mason, led to meetings being moved to a public house because of 'the small number of members and the depressed state of their funds'. If Apollo in its heyday indeed had about 90 members, there must have been an extraordinary number of resignations in a short space of time and this is itself evidence of great internal dissension. The Master died and some of the members agreed that the lodge should move to a billiard room. Oliver says the rules governing the movement of lodges were ignored—as indeed they had been when he had 'transferred' the lodge to Grimsby, but times had changed and such matters were now more effectively controlled—and writes 'From the beginning of these irregularities I have seceded from the Meetings, as I was determined to be no party to any practice which I considered to be unmasonic'. He had now been asked to attend again, and wrote to ask what was the lawful meeting place for the lodge and who were legally the officers as no Master had been installed. The reply has not survived, but on 24 April he wrote again, thanking the Grand Secretaries for their considered opinion and enquiring whether official sanction for the billiard room as a place of meeting for the lodge would be forthcoming. He clearly thought it should not be.

No more correspondence on this has been traced, but a further letter in the Grand Lodge library gives the other side of the picture; it was apparently written from Grimsby in September 1833 as a date 'Sept 26 1833' has been pencilled on it. A Brother Robert Richmond asked that an inquiry should be set up into the conduct of Bro. George Oliver, Provincial Grand Chaplain, Bro. Wm Smith Prov Grand Secretary, and Bro. Jno. Richmond, Provincial Grand Steward as Masters of the Apollo Lodge, and also Bro. Robt Cropper, Provincial Grand Warden 'to see if any one of them is qualified to hold the above Offices or in future how far they can be trusted in an office in any Lodge'. Robert Richmond is shown in UGL records as a surgeon who became a member of the Apollo Lodge in 1819; he is still shown as a member in 1828 though he does not seem to have paid any dues after 1819. John Richmond, also a surgeon, is shown as becoming a member in 1819 and paid dues until 1828.

After complaining that a previous letter had been ignored, Robert Richmond now wrote at length about efforts made by the Provincial Grand Secretary (referred to above as a member of Apollo Lodge but here acting for the Province) to get the lodge to pay its dues and finally alleged that without his own knowledge a meeting of the Lodge had been called and 'the property sold and the Lodge broken'. He then stated that the minute book had been destroyed so that it could not be established how much was due to superior authority (the payments being calculated per capita) and challenged the right of the brethren against whom he was lodging his complaint to hold Provincial office because they were no longer members of a lodge in the Province. This seems to have been ignored, which is hardly surprising since if the Lodge was in default on its dues it would be erased from the roll of lodges. However high-handed Oliver's action had been it seems to have had the approval not only of the Provincial masonic authorities but also of those in London, though the historian cannot approve the destruction of the records. It would seem not unlikely that Robert Richmond was the disputatious member whom Oliver blamed for the collapse of the lodge.

In spite of all this, Oliver's interest in freemasonry continued unabated. He had preached his first sermon as Provincial Grand Chaplain at Barton-on-Humber in 1816. The following year the Provincial meeting was held at Spalding; Oliver later said that about that time Barnett began to take him into his counsels; the office of PGM being vacant, Barnett, as DPGM-in-charge, would have complete responsibility for freemasonry in the Province, nothing new to him for Oliver says Peters never held a P.G.Lodge 'in my time'.[3] From 1818 onwards Barnett consulted Oliver in everything, though he did not always follow his advice. Annual Provincial meetings were reinstituted but Barnett's infirmities sometimes made it impossible to hold them. When D'Eyncourt was appointed PGM in December 1826 and during the lengthy period that elapsed until his Installation on 19 November 1832, Barnett was a sick man and quite unequal to the work of administering the Province; but he had no power to appoint a successor and though Oliver might be the power behind the throne, he had no authority. He later wrote 'During this inauspicious period, Freemasonry declined so much that there was scarcely an efficient Lodge in the Province. The St Matthew's Lodge at Boston, the Doric at Grantham, the Apollo at Grimsby, and the Hope at Sleaford, had entirely discontinued their meetings; and even the Witham, at Lincoln, and the Lodge of Harmony, at Boston, were extremely feeble'.[4] Such was the Province that D'Eyncourt found awaiting him, and kept waiting for six years because of his involvement with politics and other pursuits. When he at last took over, he reappointed Barnett as his Deputy, but this was a stop-gap measure. Barnett was anxious to be rid of his responsibilities and hoped to see them transferred to Oliver whose energy and interest in the local masonic scene were well known and whose masonic writings had made him the outstanding figure in Lincolnshire freemasonry, particularly as he had been allowed to dedicate one of his books to the Duke of Sussex. He had proved his practical abilities in Grimsby and the new PGM was well aware of his zeal and capacity. Everything pointed to him as the right man to control the Province and to set about reviving it. He became Deputy Provincial Grand Master of Lincolnshire on 11 October 1833 at a ceremony in Horncastle at which D'Eyncourt said of him, 'His profound investigations into the science we profess . . . have earned him the thanks and gratitude of every Mason who values the true beauties of his science'.[5]

This all happened in the same year as the furniture of Apollo Lodge was sold by auction and Oliver's intimate association with Grimsby thereby ceased, though as later events would show, his connections with that town were not forgotten.

He started his work as DPGM with urgent application. Provincial Grand Lodge had not been held for some years apart from the Installation of the Provincial Grand Master, and he summoned it forthwith. New appointments were made, probably to the surprise of those who had held them so long as to consider they had a divine right to them. By-laws were prepared and proposed by the new Deputy who made his wishes and intentions clear. Freemasonry in the Province was revitalized; a new broom had arrived and the dust was being disturbed and the waste jettisoned.

Six months after his appointment the first number of a new masonic quarterly appeared in London. This was *The Freemasons' Quarterly Review* (FQR), founded and edited by Dr Crucefix. Its stated objective was to provide freemasons under the

English Constitution throughout the world with information about the Craft, both as to background and current affairs. On reading the first number Oliver at once wrote to the editor, whom he did not then know, expressing support and approval for a project whose aims accorded so closely with his own views.[6] He would not appreciate that in so doing he was stepping into the minefield of masonic politics as the publication was largely designed to act as a power base for a number of brethren, of whom Crucefix was by far the most important, who were about to come into collision with the Grand Master. There was also a considerable body of opinion that deprecated such openness about freemasonry as the *Review* was dedicated to providing. Oliver became a regular contributor and though it would be some years before he actually met Crucefix, his position as an authority on all things masonic would considerably enhance the reputation—and the circulation— of the *Review*. He also saw to it that the activities of the Province of Lincolnshire were regularly reported in it, something which was to ensure that when the Province was thrown into turmoil by his dismissal the principal actors in the drama would already be well known to its many readers. But for the present the publication of such favourable reports about his Province must have gratified the new PGM.

The association between the two men ripened into a warm friendship and was to have profound consequences for Oliver. When, later, Oliver needed advice and comfort, Crucefix was unstinting in his efforts to provide both—even though it is arguable that in doing so he turned a 'minor local disturbance' into one of the great masonic rows of the century, and may possibly have had an ulterior motive.

Chapter Seven

PROBLEMS (1834–1842)

(Wolverhampton)

No sooner had Oliver begun his new masonic task than further ecclesiastical preferment came to him. It has been noted that the Dean of Windsor lived near Scopwick;
the holder of that office at the time was the Hon. and Very Reverend Dr H.L.
Hobart, not so far as is known a freemason but clearly someone who was impressed
by George Oliver. By a quirk of history the Dean of Windsor was at that time also
Dean of Wolverhampton and responsible for the Collegiate Church of St Peter
there, a Royal Peculiar, a status which meant that the Ordinary, the authority responsible for ecclesiastical discipline there and who would normally be the diocesan
bishop, was, exceptionally, the monarch; this status was to prove an unexpected
stumbling-block to Oliver later. The Dean's dual role dated from the reign of King
Edward IV who in 1480 had entrusted the deanery of Wolverhampton to a Royal
favourite, the then Dean of Windsor, to provide him with additional income; as is
the way with such illogical arrangements, the union had lasted ever since. The Dean
was the titular occupant of the Wolverhampton living but from his point of view it
was a sinecure, the duties he was required to perform being limited to a little preaching, which he could and did do by deputy; and, in case he wished to stay in the town,
two days' and three nights' entertainment was specified, which could be a matter of
considerable expense for those who had to provide it, and probably of inconvenience as well.[1]

These arrangements had perhaps been reasonable when Wolverhampton was a
small town of no particular importance; but it was now growing fast in the first flush
of the Industrial Revolution and what was more it had considerable civic pride and
thought of itself as a prosperous, progressive and well-laid-out modern town. The
Dean was rarely seen there, though in August 1828 he had arrived in state to lay the
foundation stone of the new church of St George, performing the ceremony in the
full splendour of his robes as 'Register' of the Most Noble Order of the Garter and
perhaps trying to make up in pomp and importance for his consistent neglect of his
Wolverhampton deanery hitherto. This second church was necessary because of the
rapid growth of the place; the old parish church of St Peter continued to cater for the
bulk of the old town which, as time soon showed, was even so too large and populous a parish; marriages for instance were running at between 300 and 400 each year
with all else in proportion, far too great a load for even two clergymen.

The glory and splendour of the Dean's visit were soon forgotten in a storm over the appointment of the Reverend George Boodle Clare, B.A. of Worcester College, Oxford, as first incumbent of the new parish. A local diarist wrote 'as soon as it became known that . . . a person of irregular, idle habits was appointed, every person who had subscribed for seats withdrew their names, and one and all relinquished their subscription'.[2] To an outsider it seems almost as if there was a compulsive resentment against the ecclesiastical establishment at Wolverhampton at that time. First Clare, then Oliver, then Oliver's curates and finally his successor were all the subject of resentful attack—perhaps because each of them was foisted onto a town which was fiercely independent and proud and quite properly determined that its new status as an important industrial centre should be recognized.

The Sacrist, or Perpetual Curate, was the equivalent of incumbent at the Collegiate Church and in 1834 the Dean appointed Oliver to the post, effectively making him Vicar of Wolverhampton. Bearing in mind Hobart's own attitude (and that of his predecessors) to the Wolverhampton Deanery and the prevalence of pluralism in the Church of England at that time it is possible that the Dean envisaged that the new post would provide additional income for a clergyman he favoured, and that the parish work would be entrusted to a curate.[3] That Oliver did not regard it in that light is clear from his description of the careful consideration he gave to the offer before he accepted the appointment. We have seen that he took parochial responsibilities seriously and that he had already successfully managed at least two parishes and did not willingly accept interference with what he considered to be his pastoral responsibilities. But at St Peter's he had as churchwardens two formidable, powerful, determined men who were of importance in the town and who had seen to the renovation of the church. They had their own very firm ideas about the conduct of its affairs. Given Oliver's insistence on the rights of an incumbent, the stage was set for a collision.

The historians of Wolverhampton (Mander and Tildesley) admit that Oliver's intentions were proper, though their chapter on his time there clearly shows the resentment which he left behind him in ecclesiastical circles, however successful he may have been in others. Some of this resentment may have been caused by the rather patronizing tone of a Pastoral Address he circulated almost as soon as he took up his post; it is difficult to assess how it would read to people of that age. Entitled *An Introductory Address to the Inhabitants of Wolverhampton. By George Oliver, M.A. S.E., Perpetual curate of the Collegiate Church, Vicar of Scopwick and Clee, in the County of Lincoln, Domestic Chaplain to the Right Honourable Lord Kensington*, it was printed in the town by William Parke and priced at sixpence. The term 'perpetual curate' is used to distinguish curacies such as those held by Samuel Oliver at Whaplode and George at Grimsby from those where the individual had a 'freehold' and so was protected against arbitrary dismissal by the incumbent.

Some play is made by Mander and Tildesley about the letters 'M.A. S.E.', which they print as 'M.A.,S.E.', the extra comma suggesting two descriptions are involved and the point is made that Oliver was pretending to a degree to which he was not in fact entitled. It is not clear from the actual title page whether the larger gap between the letters A and S is intentional, nor what the four letters stand for; the construction claimed would be tenable if the extra comma were inserted; but it is not there. What the letters stand for must be the subject of conjecture (possibly the antiquarian society in Edinburgh of which he was a member?) and whether it was a silly attempt to gain prestige cannot be established. He did, however, so describe himself on the title pages in his *Farewell Address at Grimsby* (1831), a *Candid Statement* (1835) referred to later, and a *History of the Trinity Guild at Sleaford* (1837).

The tone of the *Introductory Address* does sound patronizing to modern ears; but it is sincere and demonstrates that at this time he intended to supervise his new care personally; it would be to emphasize this that he now resigned the living of Clee and took up residence in Wolverhampton.

The Address adopts a firmly pastoral stance and starts with a statement of his determination:

'Having become personally known to many of you (an acquaintance which I shall endeavour to extend to every family in the parish with all the expedition in my power), I deem it necessary to state publicly and explicitly the line of conduct I intend to adopt for the purpose of discharging my conscience of the important duties which I have voluntarily undertaken. I have been sent amongst you for the purpose of directing you into the road that leads to everlasting salvation; and, as I must give an account to God of the flock committed to my pastoral care, I shall feel it a duty incumbent upon me to exhort you, boldly but affectionately, to do what is right and to abstain from what is wrong, by reminding you of the promises attached to faith and piety, and the judgments which the Gospel denounces against the ungodly and profane. That we may mutually rejoice in the results of my ministry, it is necessary that the most implicit confidence should exist between us. This will require time . . . Above all things it is my duty to set you a good example. An example of piety, morality, and every domestic and social virtue—an example of quietness, peace, and civility, to Christians of every denomination; with an entire devotion of my time to the arduous duties before me. It is my anxious desire to be courteous and affable to all men, whatever be their rank or station in life, and to afford every accommodation to the poor as well as to the rich; fully impressed with the great truth that they are equally my parishioners, that their souls are alike the objects of the Redeemer's atonement, and that they have equal claims upon me as their legitimate parish Minister.'

He would hardly have written in these terms had he not intended to spend much of his time in Wolverhampton; but he still had his home in Scopwick and was responsible for the parish there, and he also had his masonic duties as Deputy Provincial Grand Master to an absentee head to carry out. His energy was unbounded but he was setting himself a hard task. Whether or not his new parishioners would feel him to be presumptuous, the language which could seem appropriate in a rural setting might strike the senior members of an industrial community as out of place; nor would the reference to the claims of the poor be universally welcome in an industrial town with the rigid social structure common in the early stages of such development. It would not be the only time that Oliver caused trouble for himself by a naïve and candid expression of his worthy but not necessarily politic views.

Another passage in this *Address* discloses an openness of mind on religious toleration that was well in advance of the normal thinking of his peers and clearly at variance with his father's views about dissenters, a matter of some interest as they rarely disagreed. It was apparently the first time Oliver had encountered nonconformists in any strength, though there must have been some in Grimsby, and it will be recalled that in *A Vindication of the Fundamental Doctrines of Christianity* he had written of 'idle disputes about incomprehensible points of faith and doctrine'. But in Wolverhampton it was not only a question of doctrine but of cash; the fabric and upkeep of the parish church largely depended, as elsewhere, on the proceeds of a Church Rate levied on the inhabitants at large, and in an industrially-oriented town there was likely to be a substantial body of dissenters who would be entitled to vote on determining the amount of the rate and indeed whether a rate should be levied at all. Even though it was the official policy of the Wesleyan Methodists at least that such rates should be supported, little in the way of resistance would be needed to fuel the resentment of those who actually had to do the paying. Oliver tried to defuse the situation in his *Address*, writing: 'I have said, and I repeat it, that I shall ever entertain the utmost respect for the private opinions of those who differ from me on points of discipline or doctrine, and carefully refrain from every species of religious controversy; but I must be allowed to express my own decided preference for the Church of England as by law established—a preference which is founded on a conviction of the excellence of its rites, ordinances, and doctrines, and their efficacy in contributing to save the souls of men'. In the biographical article on Oliver in the FQR for December, 1840, this attitude is confirmed by the following words: 'He is no politician; and in accordance with the spirit of the Church to which he belongs, he is tolerant towards those who differ from him in their religious or political opinions, because he wishes to be in charity with all mankind—the chief desire of his heart in this world is—PEACE AND UNITY'. Alas, 'peace and unity' is seldom the lot in this world of one who 'is no politician' but whose path crosses that of men of action and determination. To make matters worse, he became involved early in his ministry in an unseemly argument about fees with the incumbent of the new Church of St George. He was not at his best when seeking to defend what he considered as the rights of his office. He attempted to justify his actions in print with a 'Candid Statement', only to be blasted by a 'Reply' from Mr Clare and find that though his contentions were supported by the ecclesiastical authorities, they were opposed by both churchwardens as well as by such of the inhabitants as could understand the arguments of the parties. The honeymoon was over.

From the number of words he spent on this in the *Address* on his duty to instruct his parishioners, he may well have suspected that what he was saying might not be entirely palatable to those who would read it. Quoting the advice of St Paul to Timothy to 'take heed to thyself and thy doctrine; continue in them; and in doing so thou shalt save thyself and them that hear thee', he goes on 'With a deep sense of this solemn responsibility upon my mind, I undertook the extensive duties of your extensive parish with great diffidence, and not without mature deliberation and anxious prayer for the Divine assistance. And the inducement which ultimately induced me to accept the appointment was a confident anticipation of counsel and aid from the members of my congregation . . .; with civil or parochial matters unconnected with the Church, I shall never interfere'. In the state of church politics and of Wolverhampton's own affairs at that time this was not an option that was open to him.

In spite of his forbearance in other matters he was not prepared to tolerate those who thought they could 'profitably wander from church to church, and from preacher to preacher, and oscillate between different and conflicting views of Christianity, as inclination or caprice may prompt them'; an interesting comment on the habits of the populace and perhaps on his own popularity as a preacher. His sermons may have been too serious and couched in too simple terms for those of his hearers who looked for oratorical cadences and comforting doctrine.

The last part of the *Introductory Address* dealt with his immediate proposals about the church itself which he acknowleged to be 'magnificent and imposing in its general appearance'; but he criticized the interior as 'greatly deformed by an injudicious disposal of the pews' asking their owners to agree to a rearrangement to allow more people to be accommodated—a proposal he managed to carry through—and after airing his own suggestions for more seemly ordering of the 'New Burying Ground' casually offered a stick of political dynamite to his flock: 'I have been urgently pressed to afford the families who have ground in the old Church-yard for burying their dead, such access for the convenience of interment as they possessed before it was closed in the year 1819. The request is perfectly reasonable, should it be true that the causes which induced the inhabitants to discontinue the use of it have disappeared'. He asked for their opinions but he was determined to effect the reopening if he could. In the following year (1835) a *Second Pastoral Address* shows that the work had been done, and he claimed that it was universally approved, the soil being 'perfectly clear from all vestiges of mortality, and the churchyard space sufficient for the whole population of the district for half a century to come'. He may have been right but the event did not soothe ruffled feelings or quieten apprehensions which apparently had originally led to the closing of the graveyard; and when he went on to profess himself 'acquainted with no valid reason why interments should not take place within the walls of the church' he added fuel to the fire.

In the *Second Pastoral Address* he confessed that he had not appreciated the workload that his office would entail and referring to the argument about the church rate between the Established Church and the Dissenters optimistically expressed himself as 'convinced that the religious peace and civil welfare of the community depend, in a great measure on a mutual forebearance and good understanding among the inhabitants, whatever be their religious or political opinions'. The realities of the situation and the stresses attendant on the town's rapid transformation were making themselves felt to the peace-loving Sacrist and it is hard to avoid the feeling that he was already becoming despondent: 'In the former Address I made some professions which I may justly refer to as having been amply redeemed; although the process has been interrupted by cares and troubles that I had never contemplated. I have been called upon to interpose between the Church and its temporalities. The unhappy dispute in which I was involved respecting St George's

Church was a sore stumbling block in the way of my first efforts among you; and although that has been amicably settled to the mutual satisfaction of all the parties concerned, yet the aspect from other quarters is threatening'.

Nor was the devotional life of his church taking the form of which he could wholly approve; the parishioners, true to the spirit of the time, wanted sermons; Oliver thought that 'an overwheening fondness' for them generated a dislike for prayer, 'the most beautiful exercise in which a rational soul can be engaged' and declared in unequivocal terms his love of the language and ritual of the *Book of Common Prayer*. The congregation seem to have been taking a somewhat independent line in the services for he urges them to repeat what the ritual requires them to repeat and answer what they are required to answer, protesting particularly at the Absolution being repeated after the minister instead of 'being received with humility'. The size of congregations was also disappointing; perhaps other churches where the ministers were more given to oratorical display were proving more attractive? Oliver says particularly 'I do not wish to excite any unnecessary alarm, or inflame your passions by popular declamation'.

In fact, his normal method of preaching seems to have used more simple language and fewer rhetorical flourishes than some of his printed sermons might lead us to expect. The 1840 article in FQR reported: 'his style of public speaking and preaching is quiet, deliberate and persuasive, attended with inflexions or intonations of voice, and a little subdued action . . . His sermons are written in a plain and simple style but we have reason to believe that he does not much use them in the pulpit, having the subject generally well up'. He himself said in the first Wolverhampton *Address*, 'The style of preaching which I have adopted is intended, by its energy, to impress your minds with a true sense of the value and importance of religion, and to make the seed sown penetrate to the very bottom of your hearts, and bring forth fruit an hundredfold. If this effect be not produced, no solid results of practical holiness can be anticipated, and Christianity will be but a dead letter to you'. In the *Second Address* he expresses himself more directly: 'I may be deficient in flowery language—but I am not deficient in ardour when I urge on my hearers, in plain terms, the great truths of Christianity'. Later, in an Introductory Letter to *Jacob's Ladder* (published in 1845), he said of the sermons it contained, and which had been preached in the Collegiate Church: 'Their chief peculiarity is an extreme simplicity of language. I have been careful to exclude every word or phrase which I conceive might be misunderstood, or misinterpreted by the unlearned portion of the congregation. They will, therefore, be found plain and easy to be understood, although, it is hoped, without any coarseness or vulgarity which might be offensive to persons of superior education'. It was not likely that such an attitude to preaching would appeal to the more socially important part of his congregation.

Clearly he thought deeply about the presentation of his sermons and this self-consciousness was an important part of his character; if it saved him from becoming conceited it also stirred him sometimes to protest with vigour when he felt himself slighted or unappreciated.

The good intentions in the Addresses foundered on the twin hazards of the hostility of the churchwardens and the difficulty of finding the money to restore the fabric of the church. In the *Second Address* he drew attention to the 'ruinous state of the nave . . . the battlements are actually down, and the west wall is falling periodically by masses of a ton weight and upwards'. The parishioners had refused to agree a Church Rate and Oliver pointed out that the energies of the churchwardens had thereby been crippled. Plunging into the fray with a reckless disregard of consequences, or more probably without political awareness of how dangerous was the course he was taking, he said 'You will probably expect my opinion on that occurrence, and I will not disappoint you; for it is right that the line of conduct which I intend to pursue in the conscientious discharge of my duty, should be laid fairly and openly before you. I beg, therefore, thus publicly to declare, in the best faith and most kindly feeling towards the Dissenters, I shall consider myself in duty obliged to call annually on the inhabitants to contribute by a Public Rate towards the Repairs of the Church, and the Registration of Births, Marriages, and Burials, in which every individual, whether Churchman or Dissenter, equally participates', though adding that he would rejoice should the legislature devise some other way of paying for the repair of the fabric. He had expected the support of the Roman Catholics 'because they are friendly to the existence of an Established Religion', and of the Wesleyans because their conference had so resolved; but in the end the rate was lost by a majority of 40 votes. Typically he proclaimed his determination to defend the legal rights and privileges of the Church to the utmost, while still cherishing 'that uniform good feeling towards those who differ from me in their views of discipline or doctrine'. But saintly expressions did not secure the cash.

The Dissenters regarded the refusal of the Church Rate as matter of principle, 'the injustice of calling on persons to contribute to an establishment *from which they derive no benefit*'. Oliver, after taking his stand on the legal ground, turned his attention to this:

> 'I enter upon this subject with extreme reluctance, but in a review of the transactions relating to the Collegiate Church for the past year, it is unavoidable. To this Church are attached two Public Schools, in one of which the sons of parishioners receive gratuitous instruction in the higher branches of learning; and may be qualified for the Universities or the learned professions, at the option of their parents; and the other, being of a humbler character, though not less useful, clothes and educates 150 children of both sexes, and boards 12; all of whom are selected from among the class of persons, who principally recorded their votes against a Rate for the support of the very Church to which these institutions belong. Again we have National Schools connected with the Church in Wolverhampton, which impart instruction to more than 700 children in the same class of life. To the Church the poor are mainly indebted for many of those valuable institutions which confer countless blessings upon them. Are they sick? The Dispensary is open to them; the Charity for the relief of the Sick Poor supplies them with money and other necessaries for their comfort and convenience during that season of calamity; and the Ladies' Charity conveys its benefits to them in another shape of equal utility. It is true, to some of these institutions many well-disposed Dissenters contribute; but I believe it will be at once admitted, that they so far depend upon

the support of churchmen, that if they were to withdraw their aid from any one of them, it would not exist for a single season . . . My only desire is to show that the Church of England is not entirely an useless Establishment, even in secular matters.'

His appeal may have had some effect, for a church rate was granted in 1836 and 1837; but in 1838 it was refused by a large majority and after that it was never levied in the town again.

All this time he had been under increasing pressure in respect of his masonic duties. Controlling the Province from a distance as D'Eyncourt's Deputy was proving increasingly difficult. The granting of Dispensations is a case in point; these were needed if a deviation from normal masonic procedures was to be authorized, such as a public appearance in regalia. His signature would be necessary to validate the document and there is at least one instance recorded where this caused problems; the brethren of the Doric Lodge at Grantham wished to appear in regalia at the funeral of one of their members and Oliver was in Wolverhampton. In that case he wrote a letter giving the necessary permission and regularized the situation by later granting a Dispensation, but it was an example of the unsatisfactory complications that the absence of the executive head of the Province could cause. Under his guidance freemasonry in Lincolnshire had experienced a revival, though he was careful to give the credit to D'Eyncourt. At a meeting of the Provincial Grand Lodge at Louth in the autumn of 1834 he referred to the founding of three new lodges and in proposing the health of the PGM said 'When you first undertook the superintendence of our Order in Lincolnshire, Masonry was declining; but under your fostering care it has not merely revived, but has reassumed a triumphant influence of an increasing and we hope of a permanent character'.[4] On 11 June of the following year a Provincial meeting was held at Spilsby and yet another lodge, Shakespeare (now no. 426) was constituted, the first Master being Major Brackenbury who as Provincial Senior Grand Warden was, after Oliver, the senior officer of the Province. The Provincial meeting started at 11 a.m. and the constitution of the Lodge was followed by a church service; at 3 p.m. 'the Brethren sat down to an excellent Dinner, after which many toasts were drunk, and the Brethren separated, much gratified with the days proceedings'. Shakespeare Lodge claims still to conduct its ceremonies, which are distinctive, in accordance with the precepts enjoined by Oliver.

Provincial Grand Lodge was now being held twice a year after a period when it might not have taken place at all for two years or more. The Spring meeting for 1836 was held on Thursday 12 May; Oliver presided in the absence of the PGM. At the dinner which followed, he referred to his problems: 'As the distance at which I reside makes it inconvenient for you to communicate with me personally on subjects which may render the advice of the PGM or his Deputy essential to your welfare, a sense of propriety has pointed out the necessity of resigning the office which I now hold, into the hands of the PGM, who will place it, I have no doubt, before the [Provincial] Grand Lodge in the autumn'. As he left at the end of the proceedings, Major Brackenbury took the chair and proposed a parting toast, 'The DPGM once more and God bless him' which, says the FQR report, 'was received with cheering;

and thus terminated as pleasant a meeting as can be recollected in the annals of Freemasonry in this county'. The fortunes of freemasonry in the Province had indeed changed for the better.

The autumn meeting was held at Market Rasen, where D'Eyncourt's house, Bayons Manor, was being repaired by one Nicholson, a freemason who was later to play a prominent and equivocal part in the dismissal drama.[5] The matter of Oliver's proffered resignation was referred to when D'Eyncourt proposed his Deputy's health in glowing terms. He announced that Oliver had been induced to consent to remain in office by the unanimous request of the brethren but 'at much personal inconvenience' and said that 'they could not have spared such an example of Masonic worth, whose absence would have left him without a rudder to steer by' and praised him as 'an author whose writings illustrative of the principles of Masonry were esteemed as standard in every Lodge in Europe'. An arrangement had been agreed; Oliver would spend six months of each year in the Province; as most masonic activity would be in the autumn and winter, this would greatly alleviate the administrative problems; the other six months would be spent in Wolverhampton.

It will be noted that this confirms the seriousness with which Oliver took his pastoral responsibilities at Wolverhampton and argues against the suggestion that he was a mere pluralist who had taken on the Sacrist's work there as a sinecure. Less than justice has been done to him in this respect. On the other hand, it is clear that a serious conflict of personalities had arisen which made it impossible to carry on the work of the Collegiate Church in amity. Both sides may have been to blame, but it is unfair to put him forward as caring only for the financial reward and having no interest in the work. He had succeeded in his proposals about the pews; but his relations with the churchwardens continued to deteriorate. He could not spend more time in Wolverhampton without giving up his haven of peace at Scopwick and his masonic duties in Lincolnshire, neither of which he was willing to forgo. Nor was he prepared to give up the increase in income which his appointment as Sacrist brought him, and with the example of his father's lifelong struggle with poverty he can hardly be blamed for admitting defeat and surrendering to the prevailing custom of appointing a curate to do the duties of the parish. In August 1836 he left the Reverend John Boyle, B.C.L., in charge at St Peter's and retreated for the time being to Lincolnshire. A hardier man with a less sensitive temperament and a thicker skin might have reached some sort of accommodation with the churchwardens, but Oliver must have felt that his agreement to spend only half the year in Wolverhampton was justified by the hostility shown to him by those whose duty it should have been to counsel, advise and support. In the result it would seem that he did not return to Wolverhampton for over two years.

Boyle, not surprisingly, soon found himself in trouble. The parish was far too big for one priest to manage on his own and by 1840 the pamphlets were in full flow again. The churchwardens protested that marriages could not be celebrated, women could not be churched, babies could not be baptized and the sick were not visited because the curate was overworked and had no time. Bearing in mind the figure of 300 to 400 weddings a year already mentioned it is obvious that even two men would have found it difficult, probably impossible, to carry out effective pastoral care for the parish. The fact was that the ecclesiastical arrangements made by Edward IV for a small and unimportant town had been rendered unworkable by its rapid growth and were ripe for reform; but with the security of tenure and the vested interests involved little could be done until an opportunity offered; meanwhile there would be quarrels and troubles as those concerned tried to work an unworkable system. When to such a tinder pile was added an incumbent who in exasperation had ceased to reside in the area, a curate who seems to have given up trying and churchwardens between whom and the incumbent there had from the beginning been an unresolvable clash of personalities, combustion was guaranteed.

In about 1839 Oliver returned again to Wolverhampton. He was by that time anathema to the churchwardens, and they now tried other means to get rid of him. This was the point at which he found himself in difficulty over the special provisions affecting a Royal Peculiar. An incumbent in the Church of England was bound to reside in his parish. This was, admittedly, often more honoured in the breach than the observance and permission for non-residence was freely given; Oliver had twice been given such a licence in respect of Clee. He had obtained a similar licence in respect of St Peter's from the ecclesiastical legal authorities at Doctors' Commons in London. The legal officer of the Collegiate Church now held this to be ineffective 'as the Archbishop has no jurisdiction within a Royal Peculiar'; quite what was to be achieved by this is not clear as the usual rules as to residence would not apply either. But it was enough to start a campaign. William Parke, one of the Churchwardens, wrote to Mr Birkett, the Official, requesting his attendance personally at the next Visitation 'for his doing so is the only hope we have [of] seeing anything like peace restored to our distressed church. Dr Oliver is again here in lodgings with a new Curate and nothing but confusion reigns to the utter disgust of all the friends of the church'. Oliver issued a pamphlet 'in Reply to the misrepresentations in a Circular issued by Messrs Thorneycroft and Parke', but hardly improved matters by telling them 'the affairs of the church are under my management'. In the end it was the churchwardens who were replaced. Oliver however left his new curate, the Reverend G. Cotton, to run the parish and once again retreated. Cotton was succeeded in 1842 by the Reverend Henry Roger Slade, a freemason and a regular contributor to FQR. When, in 1841, the wooden cross on the tower of the church, 40 feet high and 15 inches in diameter, was destroyed by lightning in a storm, this was to those who wished to see it so, a portent of further trouble.

Nevertheless there was a substantial body of opinion that held Oliver to have been brutally victimized.

Chapter Eight

INDUSTRIAL REVOLUTION

(Wolverhampton)

In 1838 Oliver published a pamphlet containing six letters to his Wolverhampton curate, Boyle. It is dated from Scopwick and he writes that he is 'precluded by inadequate health from active co-operation'. However, his health did not prevent him from taking part in a number of other events in Lincoln in that year, as will appear; and though he did on occasion complain of not being well he seems to have enjoyed good health until about 1849. The truth is probably that he did not want to face the trouble and quarrelling which a return to Wolverhampton would inevitably have entailed; he would not be the first, or the last, to plead a mild incapacity to avoid unpleasantness.

He had taken an interest in education long before he went to Wolverhampton. Though no copy has been traced, he had published a pamphlet about it at some time before 1826, and at Scopwick counted it one of his main achievements to have established a Sunday school for the village children, though it took some effort to get it started as 'I found some difficulty in inducing the children to exchange the freedom to which they had been accustomed, for the confinement of the school-room . . . Preferring an unrestrained licence to the observance of discipline, it took two years to reduce the disorderly elements of which the school was composed, to regularity'.[1]

At Wolverhampton he had found much to catch his attention in this field and within two years of his arrival published a pamphlet *Hints for improving the societies and institutions connected with Education and Science, in the Town of Wolverhampton*. The title was perhaps less than flattering to a town which prided itself on its orderly growth, and the somewhat pompous foreword which was addressed to its inhabitants may have given offence: 'Placed by Divine Providence in this extensive parish, as the resident head of the protestant ecclesiastical establishment, I feel a high responsibility resting with me, not only that the religious duties be performed with regularity and zeal, but also that the morals of the people be carefully guarded and advanced, both by precept and example, to the highest degree of excellence of which they are capable'. He was indeed taking his new responsibilities seriously, probably too seriously, and might have done well to wait longer before preaching from so high a pulpit; it is strange that he, normally so sensitive to the susceptibilities of others, should have failed to appreciate those of a large body of his new parishioners; but diffidence in discharging his duty as a clergyman of the Established

Church was not one of his characteristics and in this case he was confronting those who had made their mark in the tough world of industry. He would never understand the reasons for his failure there any more than those he opposed would ever understand why he was so widely revered and admired elsewhere.

To appreciate the position it is necessary to explain the historical background. Primary education in England had been a matter of contention for some time. The Established Church had in effect claimed a monopoly in educating children in spite of the growth in numbers of Dissenters, and demanded that any money allocated for schooling by the State should be under its control; the Dissenters were not prepared to agree. With the onset of the Industrial Revolution the Dissenters grew in wealth and importance and could not be ignored, yet the Church of England would not accept any diminution of its privileged position. Cash was collected by both parties to build and fund day and Sunday schools; and as the various sects of Dissenters could not agree among themselves all was indeed confusion. Inevitably it was the poor who suffered. Two main institutions eventually emerged, the 'National Society for the Education of the Poor according to the Principles of the Church of England' (the National Schools) and 'The British and Foreign School Society' (the British Schools). Primary education in the villages of England was usually provided by the National Schools but the British schools, largely funded by the Whigs, were often found in towns and provided an undenominational schooling. Oliver not unnaturally criticized the British Schools, claiming that they offered too superficial a system of instruction because 'it implants no principles, it restrains no vicious habits . . . The mass will remain, if not in their primitive ignorance, at least without a sufficient portion of knowledge to direct them effectually, to avoid the snares and quicksands of the state of life into which they will enter, when they quit the school'. This partisan view would be typical of the average thinking Church of England minister of the time and was due to a genuine fear that the proper religious instruction necessary to salvation would not be given in the non-conformist schools; so that even Oliver whose attitude to dissenters was tolerant and understanding shared the fears of his fellows about the shortcomings of the education such schools provided. To some extent obstinacy and jealousy of privilege may have shaped the attitude of the Established Church but that cannot impugn fears genuinely held. In fact he had not always approved of infant schools, considering that 'air and exercise were absolutely required by nature to develop the physical faculties of children, which I conceived would be rather obstructed by being shut up so many hours a day in a confined school room'; practical experience and close inspection had changed his mind.

Having made his point about the superiority of the National Schools, Oliver left the sectarian ground. In the only definite reference we have to a visit to Wolverhampton before accepting the proferred preferment he expressed the dismay he had felt then at 'the dingy figure presented by the lower class of the working population' and bewailed the wretched state of their accommodation. He was never afraid to express his strongly-held views about the troubles of the poor or his championship of their cause; in a manufacturing town such as Wolverhampton where a source of cheap labour was necessary to the prosperity of the employers this must have started conjecture that the new Sacrist should be watched. But it was the parents that Oliver blamed as much as the employers, lamenting their indifference to the children's need for education.

To his mind a neglect of religion and 'profanation of the Sabbath' were symptoms of a collapse of moral standards. It is clear from the Pastoral Addresses, as well as his writings about Scopwick, that non-observance of the Sabbath caused him real apprehension for the souls of his parishioners, and in such a case he would not keep silent whatever the cost.

The 'hints' foreshadowed in the title now began to appear. He advocated 'Schools of Industry . . . which I am old-fashioned enough to believe are of more actual service to the poor than schools of learning'; but he was alive also to the dangers, for 'how often do men become the tools of system makers'; and he was not proposing a mere factory for providing untutored labour but instruction in science, 'not only geography and astronomy; but experimental philosophy, natural history, chemistry, optics, electricity etc, all inculcated in familiar language, and illustrated by entertaining experiments' and argued for a method of instruction by games of learning. Expounding the duties of a master, he advocated praise 'when boys act virtuously' and a constant watch 'that the disposition and propensities of his young charges should be ever before him.'

Having made his pleas for a more positive attitude to schooling for the young and for an improvement in accommodation, he turned his attention to adult education. 'Mechanics' Institutions' had first made an appearance in 1823 on the inspiration of a Scot, Dr Birkbeck, and under the powerful urging of Henry Brougham had spread widely in England's manufacturing towns since. They were by-products of the Industrial Revolution which had made it necessary for workmen who wished to cope with the rapid advance of knowledge to study to improve their skills. Oliver hoped to see a Society for Apprentices and an Adult Institute as well as a Mechanics Institute and referred with approval to a Literary and Philosophical Society founded in 1833 and struggling to establish itself; the membership was only 20.

He took part in the social life of the town so long as he remained in residence, and became president of the Literary Society. He also helped to revive freemasonry. The situation was not unlike that at Peterborough; a Lodge of St Peter had languished and effectively been inoperative for many years. In 1834, the year of Oliver's arrival in the town, it was reconstituted, and St Peter's Lodge, Wolverhampton, is now no. 419 on the register. Oliver is reputed to have joined it on 2 March, 1835 but there is no mention of this in the minutes.[2] The effects of his energy and drive are shown by a report in FQR for June 1836: 'WOLVERHAMPTON. Masonry progresses in this town with considerable success. The Brethren are about to build a Masonic Hall, for which nearly 1000 l. is already subscribed! The exertion of Dr Oliver is the theme of universal admiration, and some fond hopes are entertained that he may be prevailed on to accept the Mastership of the Lodge recently established here'. He did not become Master but his third curate, the Reverend H.R. Slade, joined the lodge.

In 1842 his was the first signature on the Petition for a new Chapter to be attached to the St Peter's Lodge and named after it; the Petition was dated 15 February and he signed it as 'Exalted in the Industrious Chapter, No. 39, at Kingstone upon Hull.

Certificate dated 8th March 1813'; the Charter for the Chapter was granted on 4 May, 1842. Slade was its first candidate.

It would seem that by this time he had accepted that he had no mission in Wolverhampton; in 1842 he finally left a curate in charge and returned to Scopwick.

Oliver himself does not seem to have taken any active part in St Peter's Chapter after it had been established; Wolverhampton had been damaging to his pride in himself and in his calling and he wanted no further part in it. But when in 1850 he published *The Symbol of Glory*, 'cope stone' of the Grand Design, the sixth of the thirteen lectures into which the text was divided, was dedicated to the Master and brethren of St Peter's Lodge, Wolverhampton, and in the 'Epistle Dedicatory' which began it he wrote of 'the hostile denunciations of a clique of interested individuals who were leagued in an unnatural coalition to ruin my peace of mind at the least, if they should fail to establish more destructive purpose'; the wounds had penetrated very deeply.

Outside church circles he seems to have been popular; but when he eventually departed the division of feeling he inspired is clear from two differing newspaper reports. In 1841 a Wolverhampton correspondent wrote 'The retirement of Dr Oliver from this town has cast a gloom over us'; and in 1847 the *Wolverhampton Chronicle* reported 'We understand that the long-talked of retirement of Dr Oliver . . . is about to be effected'.

It is however clear that the appointment of new churchwardens had resulted in a more harmonious atmosphere in the Collegiate Church. In September 1840, the new appointees inserted an advertisement[3] in the *Staffordshire Examiner* that 'having been asked by numerous parishioners to receive SUBSCRIPTIONS towards the PURCHASE OF SOME MEMORIAL to be presented to the REVD DR OLIVER, in testimony of the high regard in which his merits were held by the great bulk of the Inhabitants of Wolverhampton, and of the spirit of sincerity in which they sympathize with him at this juncture . . . they . . . are ready to receive contributions. The churchwardens cannot allow this opportunity to pass, without congratulating the proposers of this design upon their zeal to do honour to the excellent Incumbent of their Parish; and without also congratulating their fellow-townsmen generally that such an opportunity occurs for presenting one solid testimony to the esteem and attachment of an unbiased public, in successful opposition to the machinations of those who factiously seek to prejudice the character of a meritorious Christian Minister'. All of which proves two facts; that there was more than one view taken of Oliver's efforts in Wolverhampton, and that advertising space in newspapers must have been much cheaper then than now. The editor of the paper added his own comments that 'nothing could more triumphantly testify the fact, that the disgraceful misrepresentations find no response but indignation in the voice of a liberal public'; and urged 'the humbler classes' to support the proposal 'in order to show that Dr Oliver is indeed looked upon as the minister of "the poor man's church" should be—as the poor man's friend . . . The honour of Dr Oliver must consist less in the amount contributed than in the number of contributors'.

It was in 1840 that Oliver finally settled the matter of the Church Rate at Wolverhampton. There was little likelihood that a rate would ever be granted freely again and he must have decided to make victory of defeat. On 27 April, at a Vestry Meeting he made his announcement:

'As to the legality of Church rates . . . I continue to hold the sentiments I have heretofore professed; but when I consider that the granting of such rates is optional, and that the discussion of the subject only tends to create feud, divide the town against itself—to set father against son and son against father—to sever long-standing friendships, and to dissolve mutual ties; when I reflect also that the agitation of that question is little less than a scourge on the public peace of the town, I cannot consent to aim a blow so heavy and a discouragement so great on what I consider to be the interests of the Church. I shall not give my consent, therefore, to the agitation of the question of the Church Rates. My motto is 'Peace', and the banner I unfurl this day is the banner of Unity—a banner which cannot, as it shall not, be raised to lead you into contests in which all is to be lost and nothing is to be gained.

I know I shall be asked how I purpose, without a rate, to provide for the congregational expenses of the Church? My answer is simple. I have no doubt whatever of the success of the voluntary system if it is properly tested. I shall with the assistance of my warden and the colleague you may appoint to act with him, give this plan a fair and free trial; and so long as I continue to be the resident incumbent of this parish, I pledge myself never to go for a rate if you will support me, which I repeat, I have no doubt you will, in defraying the congregational expenses of the Church by your voluntary contributions'.[4]

It is interesting that, although effectively compelled to retreat, he should have chosen to do so in a way so very much in keeping with the modern reaction of the Church of England to its own financial problems, and one which of course has long been familiar to non-conformist denominations.

Though the task of running the parish of Wolverhampton with the collegiate structure was probably impossible, and though he was deliberately made unwelcome, his withdrawal could only fuel the fire which the continued absence of the Dean had already lit. Oliver was not the right man for Wolverhampton at that time. It is doubtful whether any man of spirit would have succeeded in so large and demanding a parish, with such disparate social needs and such determined partisans. There could be no 'peace and unity' for one who was not prepared to walk in the wake of his determined churchwardens but insisted that the management of the church was in his hands alone; his outspoken and patronizing advice would hardly be welcome to a town whose chief inhabitants felt proud of what had been achieved; and in his resolute determination over such matters as the burial ground (and other things which he considered improvements to the church but which to others were anathema) he seemed to go out of his way to court disaster. He saw himself as a leader; the leaders of his congregation wanted him to be a puppet. In appointing a curate and absenting himself instead of resigning, he followed the custom of the time but did not enhance his reputation.

Chapter Nine

FAMILY LIFE

(Scopwick)

George Oliver was nearly 49 when he and Mary came to Scopwick; she would be about 55. Their eldest son, George, was probably already established in a medical career; a letter he wrote to his father on 21 July 1842, addressed from Newton, shows that he was married and had children as well as demonstrating the closeness of family ties. It reads in part 'Sarah and I had intended to be at Scopwick tomorrow but I expect to be at Nottm, I will thank you to send the boys to meet the Sliding Scale at Metheringham on Saturday morning it leaves Boston at 7 o'clock so I shd suppose it will be there about ½ past eight. The coachman will set them down at our house & we will pay him the fare. We have sent them coat and cloak'. He had been initiated as a freemason on 5 November 1838, his father's birthday, in Witham Lodge, No. 374, at Lincoln by his father who had joined the Lodge in the same year, and to whom the Lodge gave a silver salver to mark the occasion. In making the presentation the Master, Nicholson, already noted as in charge of the repair work at Bayons Manor, paid tribute to 'industry that has never wearied, ardour that has never cooled or abated', and continued: 'However much we might venerate his learning, however highly we might esteem his talent, our feelings would be cold indeed compared to what they really are, had he not, in every relation of life, and under every circumstance, shown himself to be not only influenced, but controlled by the purest principles of masonry. This is the highest gem in his character; this it is that has gained our affectionate esteem, and that has given additional lustre to that most dignified of all human characters—a Christian Pastor'. The son unfortunately died young, being drowned in the Foss Dyke.

The second child, Caroline Burnet Oliver, was the organist at Grimsby over whose dismissal by Attwood there had been such a furore. On 21 June 1849 she married a widower, the Scopwick miller, William Pears, who owned an eight-acre smallholding; the marriage would seem to have been childless, and lasted less than nine years, for the Scopwick registers record the burial of William Pears on 14 January 1856.[1] Caroline became her father's assistant in preparing his works for the printers.

Beverley Samuel Oliver was born in 1811. He became a freemason, probably also in Lincoln and was present at the laying of the foundation stone of the Witham lodge room on 15 April 1841 when D'Eyncourt performed the ceremony with the eloquent help of his Deputy. Later he was a printer (and probably also a bookseller) in Nottingham and a number of his father's books and pamphlets bear a reference to this on the title pages. In 1842, when his father decided to publish an account of his dismissal as D'Eyncourt's Deputy, Beverley wrote to him (30 June) offering to print it and divide equally the profit or loss at the end of six months 'but if it sells to a greater extent [than locally] then I anticipate I will take as much as pays me for the printing and you shall take the remainder'. He is also recorded as present in 1846 at a dinner given in Nottingham to his grandfather, Samuel Oliver, then Vicar at Lambley and aged 90, and seems to have been a member of a Nottingham lodge.

The third son, Charles Wellington, was born in 1815, the year of Waterloo, and so would be 16 at the date of the move to Scopwick. He later appears as a printer in Uppingham and his name too appears on some of the title pages. Later still he went to Bath and was the lessee of the famous Assembly Rooms and an alderman of the city; he became well known there for his keen interest in freemasonry. The second edition of his father's *Book of the Lodge* was dedicated to him in 1855 on his father's birthday in these affectionate terms:

My dear Son,

The accounts which have reached my ears respecting your zeal in behalf of Masonry, accompanied by a strict attention to constitutional authority in working the details, and a ready obedience to the edicts of the Grand Lodge, have been exceedingly gratifying.

To express my entire concurrence with the judicious course you have pursued, I dedicate to you this new edition of a well-known Work, where you will find many maxims and precepts which may confirm your adherence to the laws and usages of the Craft, and elevate the tone of your masonic life.

Believe me to be
Your affectionate Father
GEO. OLIVER, D.D.

Bank Street
Lincoln.
Nov 5, 1855

In his will, George Oliver referred to a security he and Charles had jointly given for £300, from which it would appear their dealings remained close throughout the doctor's life.

The youngest child, Mary Ann Pierpont Oliver, was born in 1819 and so only 12 at the time of the move. She was more fortunate than her sister, for after her marrige to Edward Gilby Rainforth, miller and baker of Sleaford and later of Kirton, which took place at Scopwick on 20 October 1842, the Scopwick registers record the baptism of two daughters, on 15 April 1850 and 10 September 1851, and it would seem likely there were other children born to them. In her father's will she is given £10 for mourning, 'she being already provided for'. She died at Boston in 1891.

As will appear later, in 1844 a silver cup formed part of a gift to Oliver funded by public subscription; there was a public banquet in Lincoln, but different arrangements were made for the actual presentation of the cup which allow us a brief glimpse of the family at Scopwick Vicarage where a 'symposium' was held to handsel the cup, a ceremony it was the Doctor's wish should have been performed in public, but the Committee ruled that the offering should pass 'in its purity' to the care of Mrs Oliver and family.

The proceedings at the Vicarage were described in FQR:[2]

'The previous meeting had certainly been a joyous one. Of the Symposium, we may truly term it a happy one. The doctor, no longer nervous, but more than cheerful, he was himself, his excellent wife and charming daughters elevated the scene; his two eldest sons (the youngest was absent), joined the merry throng, and shared the proud moment of their sire's happiness, in entertaining his friends on such an occasion . . . Bro. Crucefix was by the hostess invested with the dignity of the master of the revels—by whom all homage was exacted, and to whom it was most readily paid. There are secrets in Masonry, but of Scopwick secrets we are unaware . . . Mirth and good humour presided, and the joyful occasion introduced an old-fashioned visitor yclept "forgetfulness of time"—but we will not profain the mysteries of Scopwick.

'Sunday came! and then, reader, the historian of Freemasonry—the learned classic, assumed the sacred character of his ministry—the Vicar of Scopwick, a parish containing scarcely 200 souls—entered the little rustic church, where his flock were assembled to hear the word of God delivered to them in language easy and comprehensive, with an earnestness that convinced them of their pastor's sincerity, to which they paid an attention that betokened their increased desire to observe his directions. The village choir, assisted only by a clarionet, altogether so simple in its melody, was not lost on their hearts, and the children, male and female, who ever and anon peered at the strangers, betokened that if curiosity for a time prevailed, the "mind" was cared for among the lowly and the young.'

On 15 February, 1842 the Reverend Samuel Oliver and his wife Betsy celebrated the sixtieth anniversary of their wedding and the fortieth of his arrival at Whaplode as its curate. A dinner at the Vicarage there was attended by children, grandchildren and great-grandchildren. George, as their eldest son, presided and proposed the health of 'the patriarchs of the family'; in his speech he referred to his venerable father as 'a good man struggling with adversity, and conquering, by the aid of Christian fortitude, the impediments which adverse fortune has arrayed against him . . . braving the storms of the world, and triumphing over them'. The church bells were rung in honour of the curate and his wife, and 'the Whaplode brass band played favourite airs in the evening, on the lawn in front of the Vicarage' when a great number of friends 'joined this united family' in their celebrations.[3] In spite of the fact that 1842 was not to be a happy year for the patriarchal pair, even though all turned out well in the end, this occasion would mean much to them—and obviously the weather was kind, for there would be February evenings in that windswept area when even the local band would be hard put to it to perform with any credit at all.

Another and more light-hearted glimpse of life at Scopwick is given in a description in *Scopwickiana* of spring-cleaning at the Vicarage there:

'In this part of the country, as I have before observed, it is customary for servants of both sexes to engage themselves for a year at the May-day Statute Fair. That every annual succession of maids may have an inducement to cleanliness, it is usual for the mistress of a family to have her house, and everything it contains, well scarified before the old servants quit their places; or, in other words, before Old May-day. For it is presumed that, if the new-comer find a house clean, she has no excuse for not keeping it so. A few weeks previous to this period, therefore, is a season of hurry and bustle, which is any-thing but comfortable for the male part of the family. As for the lady of the house, she is quite in her element. Fairly set to work in this important concern, nothing seems so delightful to her as "confusion worse confounded". The process commences with the purchase of brushes for scouring and white-washing, and an enquiry after char-women. Then comes the tug of war. The chamber windows are dismantled of their curtains, and the beds of their hang-ings. Boxes, trunks, and drawers, chairs and dressing tables, are displaced to make room for the lustration of the upper stories; and nothing is heard but the slopping of mops and brooms and buckets of water; so that a stranger would fear a recurrence of the universal deluge, and make a precipitate retreat to avoid the consequences. A noise as if

> ". . . eldest Night
> And Chaos, ancestors of nature, held
> Eternal anarchy, amidst the noise
> Of endless wars, and by confusion stand.
> For hot, cold, moist, and dry, four champions fierce,
> Strive here for mastery, and to battle bring
> Their embryon atoms."

MILTON.

'This being effected, crockery ware, china and glass, are distributed over every room in the house, while the closets and pantries are purified, shelves scoured, and walls daubed with lime and water. Then what a hammering, and clashing, and opening and shutting of doors, do we hear. Every nook and corner is ferretted out; not a mousehole is left untouched in this general purgation; and happy it may be considered, if, in the scramble, your most valuable pieces of ornamental glass or china escape destruction. Then follows the rubbing and scrubbing of tables and furniture; cleaning of windows, kill-ing of spiders, and whitening of ceilings. Crash! "What's that?" screams the lady president of the uproar. "Jane's broke the window, Ma'am." "Careless jade; but I'll make her pay for it; I'll stop it out of her wages."

'"It aint me, Ma'am, it's Jem, a pushing so hard on the other side."

'"It was you," says Jem.

'"It wornt, now then!"

'What is the afflicted husband doing all this time? Confined to his own penetralia, he expects every moment that the storm will burst upon him and overwhelm him with its violence; for, between mistress and maid, his chance of peace is at a discount. Even the dogs and cats keep at a respectful distance; knowing instinctively that "monkey's allowance" will be their portion if they intrude themselves familiarly in the way on this weighty occasion.

'But every thing has an end, and so has the ceremony of "cleaning for May-day;" and the calm that succeeds this domestic storm is pleasant enough; as both mistress and servants appear filled with complacency at the contemplation of the wonderful effects which their united exertions have produced.

' "Ar'nt we nice and clean?" says the lady to her husband; and he, glad to purchase peace at any price, gives his ready assent.'

In the *Freemasons' Quarterly Review* for December 1840 an appreciation of Oliver appears, some parts of which have already been quoted. Crucefix, though no longer the editor, had written it; though he and Oliver had been in touch by correspondence for several years, they had only met in 1839, at Grantham where Crucefix had attended Provincial Grand Lodge, a meeting which had confirmed their friendship. The article was, as would be expected in view of Oliver's constant support of the periodical, rather fulsome in its tone but allowing for that it still gives a picture of the man at the age of 58, troubled by his problems at Wolverhampton but happily successful in his village parish and in the respect of freemasons not only in Lincolnshire, but increasingly in all the many countries where the English Craft flourished. The introduction set the tone:

> The Revd George Oliver, D.D.,
> the minister, whose piety is the best
> illustration of his function;
> the friend, whose friendship dignifies its object;
> the freemason whose intelligence is the
> handmaid to his philanthropy & philosophy;
> to the son, the husband, and father,
> who in each separate relation of life
> vindicates the worth and beauty of
> the domestic virtues, This The Seventh
> and Master Masons' Volume
> is respectfully and gratefully
> Dedicated

The article described him in his capacity of Vicar of Scopwick as having won by labours of love a title to the respect and esteem of his flock. Of his relations with the members of Apollo Lodge in Grimsby it reported that they were left with 'great veneration for his zeal, and a remembrance of his great liberality in maintaining the hospitality of the Lodge, and of those social qualities which chastened and enlivened the banquet, whilst his moral qualities illustrated the discipline of the Lodge', though it would be interesting to know what was behind the statement that he was 'in earlier life rather convivial in his habits, but always temperate', a remark quickly followed by the assertion that he enjoys good health, with a constitution unimpaired. Of his masonic intentions at that time the writer said his aspirations were not those of vaulting ambition, but that he had 'the common impulses of humanity . . . and indulged the hope that he might obtain higher masonic honours, and to that end he untiringly and ardently devoted himself to the cause'. There was no mention of the malcontents with whom he had come into conflict in the last years of the Lodge.

There is also an interesting glimpse which will stir a cord in the minds of many freemasons who have had to work hard at mastering ritual: 'In many a ramble he has been known to be practising the ceremonials of the order; indeed, his desire being known, his walks were often so far respected as not to be intruded upon for a given time—and more than once he was guilty of the extravagance of entering the Lodge Room in the day time, and delivering a lecture to the empty benches'. He is stated to be as strict a disciplinarian in lodge as 'his early mode of practice permits', a statement which clearly shows his preference for the 18th century masonic procedures to which his later works *The Book of the Lodge* and *The Revelations of a Square* were to bear witness and which was further referred to in the article: 'Masonry, since his initiation, has undergone vast changes for the better . . . Some alterations . . . we believe Dr Oliver does not regard as improvements'—an interesting exercise in applauding the efforts of the Duke of Sussex while pointing out that they were not entirely approved by at least one of the most prominent freemasons of the day. But once the lodge had turned from business to refreshment, and the disciplinarian took charge of the social part of proceedings 'as the chairman . . . his manners are graceful and unassuming—he wins by courtesy the esteem of his company'.

Of Oliver as an author it was stated that he had written for the periodical press for many years 'on Detached subjects', something which surviving letters in the keeping of the UGL and of the Great Grimsby public library support; and the extent of his masonic research is stressed as involving 'the most extensive reading . . . in various subjects, and in various languages, many of them unconnected with his previous studies as a Christian divine; and . . . all this time . . . attending to the important duties of the headmastership of the Grammar School, and had under his pastoral charge two parishes, one of them very populous'. Nor did his Wolverhampton problems go unnoticed, where he was 'called and destined to the most difficult but most eventful duties'—surely a classic example of understatement.

The simplicity of language of which he was capable in spite of the Pauline obscurity of some of his work, is again noticed here: as DPGM he 'brings into (Provincial) Grand Lodge the exercise of those attainments which make his addresses as conspicuous for their Masonic principles, as for the beautiful simplicity in which they are conveyed'.

The article sums up his character in words already quoted in part: 'a man of retired and unassuming habits, and much annoyed at the idea of having been brought forward as a leader in any public or polemical dispute . . . He is no politician; and in accordance with the spirit of the church to which he belongs, he is tolerant towards those who differ with him in their religious or political opinions, because he wishes to live in charity with all mankind—the chief desire of his heart in this world is—PEACE AND UNITY. Brother he is to all Masons, and friend he is to the world'.

But indeed he was 'no politician'; events would shortly most amply prove the truth of that remark.

Chapter Ten

DISASTERS (1842)

(Scopwick, Whaplode, London)

When Oliver was first appointed to Wolverhampton, he took a house in North Street and made that town his priority. But the masonic Province of Lincolnshire still needed a strong guiding hand to foster its growth and the memory of the neglect of the interregnum would die hard. It is difficult to understand how he could think it could be governed effectively from a main base in Wolverhampton. The agreement whereby he would spend half the year there and half in Lincolnshire was more a tribute to D'Eyncourt's need of him than to his own sense, and had he not abandoned Wolverhampton the arrangement would almost certainly have broken down. Even so, squalls lay ahead which presaged a storm that would rage not only in Lincolnshire, indeed not only in England, but in every country where the English form of freemasonry was practised. The other protagonists in this, HRH the Duke of Sussex, Charles Tennyson D'Eyncourt, and Dr Robert Thomas Crucefix, have already been introduced, but only the Duke has so far made any substantial appearance and to understand the story it is necessary to consider the other two.

D'Eyncourt[1] was a Lincolnshire man whose home was Bayons Manor, Market Rasen; he had a town house in London at Albemarle Street and in 1805 had graduated as Bachelor of Arts from Trinity College, Cambridge, the college on whose books Oliver was registered as a 'ten year man' in January 1814. He was called to the Bar in 1806 but it is doubtful whether he ever practised as a barrister. His main interest was politics and he was Member of Parliament for Great Grimsby from 1818–1826. It seems to have been there that he met Oliver; both were deeply interested in freemasonry and Oliver's dedication of the *History of Initiation* to him as 'friend and supporter of all my labours' suggests a close association in masonic research. When Oliver later referred to having access in those early days to the resources of a large library it is almost certain that he was referring to D'Eyncourt's collection.

In spite—or perhaps because—of his upbringing, D'Eyncourt was a radical politician and it may have been this that brought him to the notice of the Duke of Sussex. He became Sussex's equerry and a lasting friendship was formed between them. From 1832 they stood also in the relationship of Grand Master of the Craft in England and Provincial Grand Master for Lincolnshire.

In Parliament D'Eyncourt supported the case for constitutional reform. He was energetic and forceful and was listened to, achieving considerable success. A bill he sponsored to disenfranchise the 'rotten' borough of East Retford may well have paved the way for Lord John Russell's Reform Bill. However, he did become member in 1826 for a pocket borough (Bletchingley); but by 1830 he was again on the reform trail, contesting an election in Stamford to demonstrate opposition to the influence of the Marquis of Exeter; he was not successful, but there was another election in the following year and after a bitter contest, in the course of which he fought a duel with Lord Exeter's brother, Lord Robert Cecil, he won the seat by a handsome margin. At the next election he became member for Lambeth which he continued to represent for the next 20 years. He was made a member of the Privy Council in 1832 but retired from active politics in 1852 after being defeated by 193 votes at Lambeth. For the latter part of his political career he was known as 'the Radical Member for Lambeth' and must have been popular there because after his defeat he was in 1853 presented with 'a magnificent vase of the value of 400 guineas'.

He had a good reputation as a speaker, and Dixon says that 'on the rare occasions when he presided at Provincial Grand Lodge' his addresses were 'eloquent and interesting'.[2]

When King George IV fell out with Queen Caroline he supported the Queen's Cause in a pamphlet, and in the Commons urged the restoration of her name in the Liturgy. (Oliver of course had quarrelled with the Grimsby corporation about the Queen's Cause, apparently on the other side).

After a brief honeymoon period D'Eyncourt took little interest in his Province; on several occasions he cancelled the annual meeting of Provincial Grand Lodge and there are letters which show that he left his wishes about holding it in doubt, causing Oliver some difficulty in deciding whether or not a meeting was in fact to take place. On the other hand, he was well content to have at his right hand an energetic and efficient Deputy with a great reputation in the masonic world and whose actions would bring him credit without any need for exertion on his part.

Dr Crucefix was essentially a Londoner, a doctor of medicine who seems to have had a reasonable practice and financial resources; above all he was a political animal. He became a freemason in 1829 and had been Master of Burlington Lodge, now No. 96, and Bank of England Lodge, now No. 263, among others. In 1832 he was a Grand Steward and about two years later put forward a proposal for a third masonic charity, those already existing being the forerunners of the Royal Masonic Institutions for Girls and for Boys. This new charity would be devoted to caring for aged and sick freemasons in a home which was referred to as the Asylum. At about the same time he launched *The Freemasons' Quarterly Review*, which undoubtedly filled a need, in spite of the opposition which has already been noted; but its main purpose was to keep the 'Asylum' project before the masonic public. The paper itself provided its enemies with ammunition to use against it being in general critical and lacking in tact in spite of its somewhat laboured protestations of loyalty to the Grand Master; as a result, although it was popular with the Craft in general it was frowned upon by the hierarchy, including the Duke who showed an increasing aversion to it. At the quarterly meeting ('Communication') of UGL on 3 March 1841, it was even referred to as guilty of a 'traitorous violation of secrecy'.

Crucefix, as editor, was able to ensure that FQR supported the Asylum project in the face of the Grand Master's disapproval—something to which the Duke was not accustomed and which he was effectively powerless to stop in view of the popularity of the periodical, in the Provinces in particular. Relations were strained and only a spark was needed to create an explosion. The contrast in views between London and the Provinces is highlighted by the fact that in 1836 Crucefix was blackballed in his application to join the dinner Mess of the Grand Chapter Officers, but was elected an honorary member of the Royal Cumberland Lodge at Bath, now no. 41.

In 1837 the Grand Lodge voted that the formation of the new charity was expedient. However, the Duke let it be known that he did not approve of it; the reasons for this are not entirely clear and have been attributed to an opinion that the Craft could only effectively support the two existing charities; later he accepted the view that something should be done for the aged and sick, but that a system of annuities would be preferable to the construction of a building. It is probable that he had to bow to the approval of support for the aged and sick which the masonic Provinces were showing.

Crucefix had masterminded the formation of a committee to forward the Asylum project and following the vote of the Grand Lodge in favour of the scheme the committee proceeded on the basis that they now had the approval of the Craft and in spite of the opposition of the Grand Master they called a special General Meeting to consider the matter on 13 Novembr 1839. A scurrilous pamphlet was circulated at the meeting which impugned the motives and honesty of the promoters of the project and such violent emotion was generated that the meeting was in danger of getting out of control. Dr Crucefix presided. Two of the speakers, Alderman Wood and John Lee Stevens, later referred to by Crucefix as 'my lance-corporal' and a prominent man in the City, were incautiously outspoken in their comments. They were not checked by the Chair, and shortly afterwards a complaint about their remarks was lodged with the Board of General Purposes, the executive arm of UGL. The Board had judicial as well as administrative powers, and suspended Crucefix and Wood for six months and Stevens for three. A sentence of suspension prevented the brother concerned from attending any masonic Craft lodge for the period of the sentence.

The three then appealed to the Grand Lodge. Crucefix was advised by three prominent barristers that the suspension would not start until it was confirmed by the Grand Lodge and continued to exercise his masonic privileges, something which led to a violent confrontation with the Duke in the Grand Secretary's office. At a meeting in June 1840 Grand Lodge confirmed the sentences on Crucefix and Stevens but discharged that on Wood. Crucefix, whose appeal had been dismissed on a technicality, was extremely angry and wrote a strongly worded letter to the Grand Master, who took no action about it at first, waiting, as he later announced, to see whether Crucefix would publish it. When it was printed in FQR along with editorial comment that was far from acceptable, he at once had it laid before the Board of General Purposes. The Board summoned Crucefix to appear before it, a summons which he ignored; his reasons for doing so were not convincing and the

Board, with almost indecent haste, produced a tediously long report in which it recommended the Grand Lodge to expel him from the Craft, that body being the only masonic authority having the power to impose such a sentence. Crucefix was summoned to appear before a special Grand Lodge on 30 October to show cause why this should not be done. He parried this by writing to the Grand Master and the Grand Secretary on 11 June resigning as a Grand Officer, stating that he was no longer a member of any English lodge; later he used this excuse to claim he was no longer subject to the jurisdiction of the Board. He must however have realized that expulsion would deprive him of any credibility within the Craft and in all probability mean that the Asylum project would be shelved. Accordingly he decided to take his medicine while trying to render the dose relatively harmless. He attended the Grand Lodge meeting on 30 October, to make his apology, though not without gestures (such as appearing in Scottish regalia as considering himself no longer an English Grand Officer) which to say the least enlivened the proceedings.

The Deputy Grand Master, the Marquis of Salisbury, was in the Chair, having only that morning been invested in that rank by the Duke at Kensington Palace, and handled the matter with a courtesy and calm that did much to restore the dignity of the proceedings. Crucefix's speech in his own defence was masterly and having made it he retired, leaving his friends to arrange the terms of the apology he would sign. D'Eyncourt spoke, apparently at more length than suited the meeting, in favour of the expulsion. However an amendment was moved that the apology be accepted and this being eventually carried on a division, the motion for expulsion was lost. Neither party had won or come out of the affair with much credit, but it had been a public humiliation for the Establishment. Crucefix's public resignation as editor of FQR in 1841 defeated the attempt of the Establishment to condemn that journal by punishing him, but the appearance of the Board's report to Grand Lodge in its next number, side by side with detailed, and uncomplimentary, comment, showed clearly that the leopard was not going to change its spots. He remained a marked man, though his long record of support for charity and his popularity in the Provinces meant he had too many friends in the Craft for the outraged hierarchy to be able to take any further action against him. As he still effectively remained the power behind the magazine he may well have felt that he had in fact escaped unscathed.

Oliver whole-heartedly approved the advocacy of a more open attitude to public discussion of the aims and teaching of the Craft. The first letter he wrote to Crucefix expressing his approval has not survived, but it seems to have been unusually frank about the state of freemasonry in Lincolnshire and his own hope of being able to put matters to rights; he had only become D'Eyncourt's Deputy in the previous October, but was already well known as a masonic writer and his letter would receive attention. He became a regular contributor and much of the material on which his later works were based appeared first in the magazine's pages and was avidly devoured by the readership. At the Provincial meeting at Spilsby in the autumn of 1837 a proposal by Oliver that the Asylum project be supported had been carried, and in 1838 as DPGM he had sent an official letter to each lodge in the Province referring to the Grand Lodge resolution in its favour and asking them to contribute to the fund for building it. D'Eyncourt had authorized his own name being put on the list as subscribing £2, clearly not appreciating the strength of the views of his Royal patron. Crucefix attended the next meeting, at Grantham on 21 November, where he met Oliver for the first time, and £20 was voted in support of the project, with a promise that it would later be increased to £50. In fact, many Provinces supported the Asylum and opposition was in general centred on London; it was not the last time that English freemasonry would be divided in this way on an important question affecting the charities.

When the quarrel with the Grand Master came to a head, Oliver wrote to Crucefix (14 July) expressing his regret at the 'persecution' (the term ingeniously used by Crucefix) but that all would be well 'for the cause was good'. Yet in October his Provincial Grand Master would be taking a leading part in supporting the motion for Crucefix's expulsion. Oliver, being in touch with Crucefix, must have known by October at the latest that D'Eyncourt was involved; but there is no indication that he discussed it with his PGM, or that D'Eyncourt issued any instructions to his Deputy about it. In fact, D'Eyncourt had if anything led Oliver to think he approved of the Asylum by subscribing to it. The most probable explanation is that he saw no harm in the project and it was only when the matter became a personal issue between Crucefix and the Grand Master that he took a definite line and began actively to oppose both Crucefix and his proposals. But it does seem that he failed to give Oliver any indication of his change of mind.

It is true that some unrest had appeared in the Province in which Oliver had been indirectly at odds with D'Eyncourt. There had been considerable dissatisfaction with the PGM's failure to hold the annual Provincial Grand Lodge. To Oliver, who held strongly that such meetings were beneficial and wished them to be held twice a year instead of the more usual single meeting, this failure would be a disappointment, though there was nothing he could do about it, since the PGM had indicated such meetings were not to be held unless he had indicated that he would be present. One excuse after another was produced; in 1839 D'Eyncourt excused himself from attending the meeting at Grantham because he was expecting the Duke of Sussex as a house-guest; when the visit did not materialize he wrote that he was 'far from well' and two days before the meeting told his Deputy in a letter that 'this very damp weather has kept me in an invalided state and I am now suffering severely from a Rheumatic affection of the arm and Shoulder and from an oppressive Cold, which would make it most imprudent if not impracticable for me to preside at the Festival'.

In 1840 D'Eyncourt showed marked reluctance even to allow any Provincial Grand Lodge to be held. It is possible that his hesitation had to do with the fact that the row between Crucefix and the Grand Master had become general knowledge and proceedings against the former were being taken; he would know by then, if he had not appreciated it before, that Oliver and Crucefix were on very friendly terms. By 30 October, when D'Eyncourt spoke in the Grand Lodge debate on the expulsion motion, it was already known in Lincolnshire that once again the PGM was trying to avoid holding the annual meeting. A Bro. Barton had written to Oliver on 15 September reporting that D'Eyncourt felt it would be adequate if Provincial Grand

Lodge only met every other year and from that letter it appears that Oliver had already written about the matter. On 18 October the PGM wrote directly to his Deputy postponing that year's meeting, already provisionally fixed for Boston, to the following year. In December, the lengthy and laudatory FQR article about Oliver was published.

When the news of this latest postponement reached the members of the Witham Lodge at Lincoln, they promptly rose in revolt and unanimously passed a resolution that 'the Brethren of the Witham Lodge highly value the annual assemblies of PGL as providing an opportunity to meet other Lodges in the Province and for the preservation of uniformity of usages; that the *Book of Constitutions* is most explicit that the PGL of each province is to be held at least once in every year: that they regret the decision of the PGM not to hold a PGL this year: that these Resolutions be entered in the Minutes of the Lodge and communicated to the PGM, DPGM and the WM of each Lodge in the Province'. Witham Lodge, now no. 297, considered itself to be the leader among the Lincolnshire lodges; the lodge at Boston, Lodge of Harmony, now no. 272, was senior on the register of the Grand Lodge but Witham, despite the fact that the register gave the date of its foundation as 1793, claimed by this time to have been in existence in Lincoln for almost 100 years. Though Lodge of Harmony has an earlier number, and its warrant was dated 20 August 1789, it had originally been a Northampton lodge and was only transferred to Lincolnshire in 1806, the date which is now given officially as its constitution. The action by the Witham Lodge would therefore carry great weight with the Lincolnshire brethren.

Oliver was not present at the meeting when this resolution was carried, but the news was conveyed to him privately at Wolverhampton whither he had returned with his new curate to attempt to stem the rising tide of opposition. The messenger was W.A. Nicholson who seems at this time to have been on good terms with both D'Eyncourt and Oliver; his efforts to remain so were to produce catastrophic results later and to lead to his being described as a 'snake'.[3] Oliver had, more or less by force of circumstances, held the two previous Provincial meetings on his own responsibility and knew that this had been, as he later said, 'anything but pleasing to the P.G. Master'. He now 'implored the PGM to call a meeting or to give me explicit directions to do so, and to attend it himself'. It was all of no avail and no meeting took place until September 1841 when, however, D'Eyncourt did attend.

In the meantime Witham Lodge was preparing to celebrate its alleged centenary in 1842. A new lodge-room was to be built and the 'levelling' of the foundation stone was to take place on 5 April 1841 at Lincoln. As part of the preparations, Oliver wrote the history of the Lodge and it was printed, with an account of the ceremony, by 'B.S. Oliver, 14 Long Row, Nottingham'. The main publisher was R. Spencer, London, who became the best known masonic publisher of his day and brought out many of Oliver's books. Beverley Oliver may also have had a bookselling business at 14 Long Row for his name appears with Spencer's as copublisher.

The pamphlet opens with an Introduction by the DPGM which in the circumstances contained some sonorous but pointed comments; 'The influence of a

P.G. Lodge in stimulating private Lodges to the practice of that regularity which alone can secure permanency and success, operates not merely towards the preservation of a just discipline, and the dispensation of honorary rewards to worthy and meritorious brethren; but by its periodical meetings, it introduces distant brethren to each other, promoting the interchange of mutual goodwill and fraternal courtesy and cultivating those great privileges by which Freemasonry is adorned and supported'. In less controversial tones it touched on other matters which are still relevant today: 'Mankind are too apt to entertain an unfavourable opinion of a society from which they are carefully excluded; and as suspicion generates envy, and envy, uncharitableness, so they do not hesitate to reduce evil surmises to words, and speak with bitterness respecting practices, of whose existence they do not possess the means of obtaining accurate information'; and 'It is a fact, confirmed by experience, that an indulgence in late hours cannot fail to injure the credit and respectability of a Lodge, because it introduces other habits which are not consistent with the gravity and decorum which ought always to characterize the proceedings of masonry'.

Oliver had given permission, by Dispensation, for a public procession in which members and visitors would wear their regalia on the way to the church service which would precede the ceremony. His son, Beverley, and almost certainly his father, the Reverend Samuel, were present. D'Eyncourt also attended for at least part of the ceremony. After the brethren had assembled in their lodge-room Oliver made a formal entry and started the proceedings by seeking confirmation that no one present had 'done anything contrary to the laws of masonry . . . Whereby (he) should be suspended?' or 'who, after open lodge, is guilty of drunkenness, common swearing or profane words', a formula he seems to have been fond of using on such occasions. This having been satisfactorily settled, the procession was formed and moved off in state to the Church of St Peter at Arches where the public were admitted to the service, at which Oliver preached a sermon in his highest style of oratory. It was, for the modern freemason, compound of much that with the growth of scientific knowledge has been rejected but much that we should still do well to heed. The following extracts illustrate both and throw light again on his wide conception of freemasonry as a system of universal morality. 'We . . . live in times when the human intellect rises above the prejudices which are the offspring of ignorance and bigotry . . . Freemasonry . . . becomes proportionately communicative, and lays aside the reserve which marked its proceedings while under the influence of a jealousy which a perpetual system of espionage was especially calculated to excite and maintain . . . The true mason's lodge is a building not made with hands, eternal in the heavens . . . co-extensive with the universe . . . Does it comprehend the solar system? It does; and a thousand other systems of equal greatness and grandeur. It comprehends all space—extends through all extent . . . Millions of glorious suns and planets moving through space without collision, each occupying a space equal to thousands of millions of miles. And this vast space, which it is impossible to put into figures, is only one small part of God's dominions, to which the extent of a Mason's Lodge indubitably refers.' The passage is an interesting commentary on the way in which the new learning was engrafting itself on the well-established accepted truth of the time with its certainties of religious dogma, the sanctity of every word of the

Bible and yet its ability to reach out towards a comprehension of the vast extent of the unknown universes in which this planet is set. But on that day in 1841 it must have sent the brethren back to their lodge-room and ceremonial with proud hearts and heads held high.

D'Eyncourt performed the ceremony of laying the stone and gave an oration afterwards which is dismissed in the account of the proceedings in three lines. The lodge was then closed 'after a few observations from the DPGM about the discipline of the Province'—something about which his PGM must have felt some of the brethren could well be reminded. At the subsequent banquet D'Eyncourt proposed the health of his Deputy 'of whom it is impossible to say how much he had done for the spread of masonry, who was known for the many excellent works on the craft, not only in the lodges in this country, but his name was familiar in those of the whole world'. The names of both were to become even better known, equally widely, in the near future; but for the moment the old harmony between them was restored, at least so far as public appearance went. It is probable that while Oliver might feel all was well, D'Eyncourt, who seems to have been more than worried by the pressure which the Duke maintained, regarded it as merely an uneasy truce, still hoping he could retain both the services of the man who was so effectively running his Province for him and the favour of the Grand Master.

But if a temporary truce had been achieved in Lincolnshire, trouble was again brewing in London. Those who had supported Crucefix, led by the two others who had particularly incurred the Grand Master's displeasure, Wood and Stevens, were busily scheming to turn their opponents' limited triumph into a Pyrrhic victory. Two years before, in 1838, a project had been mooted to present a testimonial to Crucefix in gratitude for his efforts in behalf of the Asylum; Oliver having circulated the appeal to the lodges of the Province, had himself subscribed. A committee had been set up in London to further the scheme and Stevens became its secretary; he was employed by the Metropolitan Patent Wood Paving Company and was a man of substance. Crucefix installed him as Master of the Bank of England Lodge on 9 January 1840, by which time the committee's efforts had reached the point where donations were being received from all over the globe. The presentation was to be made at a special meeting of the lodge on 24 November 1841. Oliver was asked to conduct the proceedings and readily agreed. He was elected an honorary member of the lodge and the stage was set. A last minute panic was caused by the illness of Crucefix, but in the end he was well enough to attend, having risen from his sick-bed only two days before.

Oliver fully appreciated that his action in accepting the chair for this occasion might not accord with D'Eyncourt's wishes and at Provincial Grand Lodge, held at Boston on 29 September, offered to resign as Deputy PGM. This offer D'Eyncourt refused and, according to Oliver's later statement, made an urgent request to him to continue in office.

The proceedings at the presentation were of course fully reported by the FQR and the report was later issued as a pamphlet.[4] Inevitably they began with an oration from Oliver. In fact, in alleged obedience to a recent ruling by the Grand Master that some part of the Constitutions (which included certain 'Charges' on masonic subjects of doubtful antiquity but greatly revered) should be read at every masonic meeting, the oration was 'Probably intended as a marked compliance with' that direction. If so, it did not succeed in averting wrath in spite of the 'powerful energy and pure oratorical dignity' of the reverend doctor, who then went on to propose the health of the guest of honour. Rashly, he attributed the recent growth of the Craft at home and abroad to the 'exertions and merits of Brother Crucefix . . . in each succeeding number [of the Freemasons' Quarterly Review] we perceive the Craft gradually advancing in prosperity and usefulness, until the Fraternity was at length aroused by the persevering exertions of one man to a full sense of its own responsibilities' . . . He referred to the fact that he had himself been a regular contributor to FQR and 'cheerfully and gratuitously gave to that periodical his utmost support'. To cap his indiscretion he referred to opposition: 'To his foes, did he say?—(hear, hear). Was it possible that such a man could have foes?—(hear). Yes, it was possible, he was sorry to say it—(hear, hear)—and not only possible, but a fact'. In the face of the Chairman's flights of oratory, Crucefix was unable to speak for 'a few seconds'.

There can be little doubt that the Review's gloating report (31 December) must have been largely responsible for subsequent events; and it put beyond all doubt that the meeting was a direct snub to the Grand Master by commenting, 'What words can we use to express the truly dignified conduct of the reverend chairman!—his energetic manner in delivering his addresses; the deep emotion, which was almost irrepressible, while vindicating the honour of his Masonic Brother; and, above all, his graceful courtesy. The occasion was most anxious and important; Dr Oliver knew this and he proved equal to his allotted task. Royalty might have conferred the advantage of its high station—nobility the advantage of its rank; but there was only one mason in the whole universe whose presence could shed such bright influence on the interesting meeting, and that one left his peaceful home, accompanied by his two sons, to impart lasting consolation where it was so much needed; and to teach the Masonic world a lesson of the purest morality while supporting his friend. He left that friend grateful and happy; and he returned like a shepherd to his flock— rewarded by the consciousness of having done his duty'.

We can be certain that this would be brought to the Duke's attention. He had, as it were, only won his last brush with Crucefix on points, if indeed he had won it. The proceedings at the Bank of England Lodge had verged on the defiant, and Oliver's eloquence could be construed as criticism. There was no question, after the previous debacle, of bringing the matter to the Board of General Purposes, and so inevitably to the floor of the Grand Lodge again. Matters would have to be more circumspectly arranged. The obvious course was to press D'Eyncourt to act; it seems certain that the Duke ensured that it was made clear to his former equerry that by presiding at the meeting Oliver had greatly displeased him.

Even so, there was a lull. The first move was apparently made by letter from D'Eyncourt to Oliver dated 4 March 1842—'apparently' because it was later alleged that D'Eyncourt had suggested to Nicholson, then Master of Witham Lodge, that Oliver should resign, and may have done so a second time. The letter was addressed from 5 Albemarle Place and marked 'Private'. Under pressure from the Witham Lodge, Oliver had written to him once again about the necessity for calling the annual meeting of Provincial Grand Lodge, and so forced him to write when he would probably rather have postponed action. The reply read:

'My dear Sir,

'I was at Gloucester when yours of 28th reached London. I confess I feel very uncomfortable on the subject of it. I do not know at this distance of time whether I can attend & if I do not you would have to officiate for me. Now it will probably have occurred to you that I am placed in a very painful situation in consequence of your having presided at the dinner given to Dr Crucefix. I have not seen the Duke of Sussex & have avoided waiting on him because I think when I do so I may have to deal with this subject, but I cannot postpone my visit beyond a few days. I *know* that H.R.H. has expressed a *very strong* opinion with regard to your presidency on the occasion I have referred to, and if you were now to be seen on a great public occasion officiating as my Deputy he might consider me a party. I came up to Town above a year ago when the case of Dr Crucefix came before the G.L. in order to be present at the hearing, & took a prominent part myself in the course of it.

'Under these circumstances it may be better to postpone my reply to the Witham lodge until it can be seen whether I can attend.

I am Dear Sir
Yours truly
D'Eyncourt.'

Oliver clearly understood what was expected and sought the advice of Stevens, who wrote a long letter to him on 26 April from London, a letter which would be balm to Oliver but the advice in which was to be overtaken by events:

'My dear Sir and Brother

'Your value in the masonic community is not estimated by the collar you wear [i.e. masonic collar, denoting status in the Craft]. There lies not a Provincial Grand Master certainly, and I dare to believe no higher office-bearer in the craft, whose value can be estimated, in freemasonry, at any standard approaching your own. The masonic historian and expositor of our day, is elevated far above the level of Deputy-provincial-grand-masterships. One George Oliver would be divisible into a dozen masonic D'Eyncourts, Ansons and Lewis's, and have enough to mould a right good mason out of afterwards . . . *Take no hints.* To resign would be to admit yourself in error, at such a stage. To resign would be to give the PGM an excuse for filling the office with an inferior substitute. And where is he to find your equal with whom to super-cede you? No! No! *Never resign.* He has the right to change his officers every year. Let him exercise his right. Everybody will understand and know how to appreciate such an act. And if he *should* be silly enough to consummate his (or his Master's) wishes, for every ounce of dishonour you receive at his hands, we will make you up an hundredweight of honours elsewhere. . . .

'Stand your ground. Descend not to the inferior altitude of these (?hinters). And when certain that, in Pr. Gd. Lodge assembled, you will have to retire into the honoured rank of *Past* Grand Officers, let us know in time, that *somebody* may be there to see.

'I shall break this to the Doctor in a day or two. . . .' [This last reference is presumably to Crucefix.]

Before Oliver could well have digested this, another letter from D'Eyncourt ended the uncertainty. Dated on 28 April from Bayons Manor, Market Rasen, and appropriately written on black-edged notepaper, it was not received by Oliver, who had apparently been away from Scopwick, until 3 May.

'Dear Sir and Brother

'You are aware of the circumstances which have influenced my judgement when I feel myself called upon now to declare Vacant the Office of Deputy P.G. Master for Lincolnshire held by you.

'In communicating this my determination to you, I beg to express my best acknowledgements for the Service you have rendered to the Masonic body in this my jurisdiction during the time you have held the Office, & my great regret that the Interests of Masonry should require me to deprive myself of your valuable assistance.

'This separation gives me personally as much pain as the cause of it & not the less because my decision is one which I have thought it right to make on my own responsibility, without reference to or suggestion from any other party.

'I am Dear Sir and Brother

Your fraternally
Charles Tennyson D'Eyncourt
P.G.M. Lincolnshire.'

Was it formality, or a recollection of the close friendship they had enjoyed and the research from which both had derived so much pleasure that influenced him in signing his letter in this way instead of the simple 'D'Eyncourt' which he seems habitually to have used?

Among Oliver's papers is a draft letter to 'The Lodges of Lincolnshire' dated 3 May in which he repeats the first paragraph of D'Eyncourt's letter and adds only 'It may be necessary for me to add that the reason which the PGM assigns for my dismissal is that I presided at a meeting of the Bank of England Lodge in November last, convened for the purpose of presenting a Testimonial to our worthy Bro. Crucefix'. Whether the letters reached their destinations is doubtful, as will be seen.

This was not the only setback for the Oliver family in 1842; as curate for an absentee incumbent at Whaplode, Samuel Oliver had no security of tenure, and when the incumbent died at about this time, the new vicar terminated the curacy and left Samuel, who in a few weeks would be 86, with neither home nor income. On 8

July he and his wife wrote to George and Mary—the letter is in two hands, the first half apparently written by him and the second by her; it begins 'Our very dear children' and after comment on the aftermath of George's dismissal continues:

'*My very worthy vicar* has now paid me off, and I am very uncomfortable, being something like a Fish out of Water or at least in very shallow water, for I have been appointed one of Dr Busby's lecturers for the current season; which if it should please God I should live to accomplish the course will entitle me to twenty pounds after the first of April next ensuing, so that you will see I am not entirely without the means of bodily support, though nothing will prevail upon me to think that I have not been very scurvily treated by the Lord Chancellor for after having been so powerfully informed of both who and what I am which constitutes in my opinion an irresistible claim upon his Lordship, if he had not thought proper to give this benefice either to you or to me which perhaps he could not do having pre-engaged it before it was vacant, he might have given me some small Living which I know he had an opportunity of doing shortly after this became vacant, and not have quartered me upon a very prevaricating, narrow souled fellow, so *very intimately* connected with "*Quirk, Gammon and Snap*" as we find him to be, affording me another proof of what I have frequently remarked, that some people are too conscientiously religious to be honest, for I am not willing to consider them as confirmed idiots.

'There is no intimation of a [Provincial] Grand Lodge being held at Spalding this Autumn, perhaps we may have an opportunity of seeing you upon that occasion and if it happens to take place on an early day of the week you may then spend a few days with us.

'We expect your brother Saml: here in the course of another fortnight for the purpose of exhibiting his son and heir, but we are not sure to a few days when he will come for Betty Harris being there he cannot come till she goes.

'We are in very good constitutional health, thank God for it but bodily infirmities cont[inue] to be painful.

'That you may all be in good health both of body and mind is the daily prayer of

'Your affectionate Parents
S & E Oliver.'

It would seem that, although 'paid off' Samuel still for a while performed some parochial duties; and soon after this letter was written he stated 'Whilst going on my parochial rounds, I met a lawyer who periodically came down from London as an Estate Agent. "I say, Oliver, would you like a living?" "Should I like a living?", replied the Curate. "Why I've not lived for over 60 years; I have only existed". "Well, I can offer you the living of Lambley, near Nottingham, if you like to take it".[5] It is hardly necessary to add that Samuel took it. He was still at Whaplode in September, for a letter to George from Crucefix dated 22 September in which he promised to visit Spalding for Provincial Grand Lodge includes the sentence 'I see that *Whaplode* is within reach perhaps your kind wife has a wish to visit the patriarch'.

On 26 November Crucefix wrote 'I have been gladdened by a slip *from Moran* announcing your venerable father's promotion to tithe and glebe'; and Samuel was duly inducted at Lambley on 2 December. A newspaper report of the appointment suggest that the living was worth about £1000 a year: riches indeed for one who had lived on £100 plus any fees from his school for so many years.

The reason why he was offered the living was of course to allow it to be advertized for sale with a note that the incumbent was nearly 90 so that an early vacancy could be expected,—what was called 'a warming pan job'; but Samuel was made of stern stuff and took delight, when potential purchasers were seen prowling round, in appearing in the grounds, sometimes in his shirt sleeves with a spade on his shoulder; and when on one such occasion the prowler accosted him and enquired after his health is reported to have replied 'I never felt better in my life. I am just going to have some bread and cheese and porter, and shall be delighted if you will join me'. He lived there for some six years, so whoever bought the reversion of the living had a lengthy wait before possession was obtained. His wife, Betsy, died there on 4 November 1844, having lived less than two years to enjoy relative affluence for the first time in her married life.

Chapter Eleven

REACTIONS (1842)

(Scopwick, London, Lincoln)

When Oliver received D'Eyncourt's letter of dismissal his immediate reaction after writing to the Lincolnshire lodges was one of pique; he drafted a letter (and may have sent it) in which, after acknowledging 'your letter of the 28th ult. which only reached me yesterday', he continued 'As our masonic connection is now dissolved, I shall feel obliged if you will make me a remittance for 50 Sermons preached at Louth, and delivered to you by Mr Jackson, and for the Theocratic Philosophy of Freemasonry, delivered by my son, none of which are paid for, amounting to 2..18..0.' He periodically had trouble over debtors; in a letter written to Crucefix at this time about a Dr Senior who had made some request of him he writes 'I found the inclosed on my return (with another letter of great importance which I shall trouble you with soon). What am I to do? I only know Dr Senior as a defaulter in payment for the Theocratic Philosophy. What *can* I do?'. The 'letter of great import- ance' was presumably that from D'Eyncourt; it would seem Oliver needed time to gather his thoughts before he was prepared even to consult his friends about his own position, and from Stevens' earlier remark about breaking the news it is possible that Crucefix had been struck by one of his periodic attacks of sickness. He did write on 5 May, and we have Crucefix's reply (7 May):

'My kindest and Best friend—I have vainly attempted to reply to yours of the 5th and the last post finds me as incapable as in the morning when yours reached me—Indignation and contempt are sad subjects in a masonic correspondence—In a few days I hope to write more composedly.

'May Providence direct us all in this unexempled difficulty—My wife adds her kindest wishes with my warm regards to you and yours—Yrs most sincerely Robt Thos Crucefix.

'The party you name is altogether *unworthy* of your notice—consequently I shall not direct Bro. Spencer to give him the book' [the last words being a reference to Dr Senior's request].

Stevens too was quick to sympathize, though he wrote:

'I cannot bring myself to pity you—it were more easy to envy, if I could dare to aspire to be on a level with you in anything. The *PGM* is the man to be pitied. Everybody will draw a comparison between you, and though dif- ferences of opinion will arise as to the degree, they will only affect the excess

Right Advertisement for consecration meeting, St Peter's Lodge, 1802 (supplied by Peterborough Public Library).

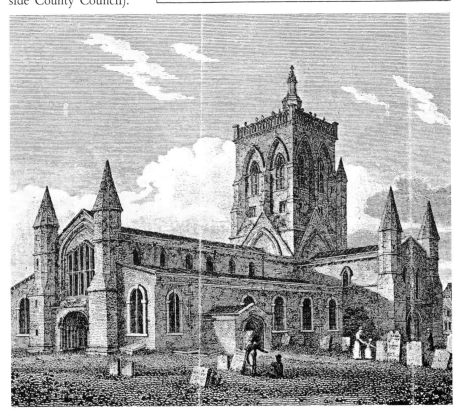

MASONIC MEETING AT THE

Angel Inn, *Peterboro'.*

L ODGE, No. 160, lately installed under the antient Constitution, assemble at the above Inn, on MONDAY the 26th Instant, at 11 o'Clock in the Morning, for the Purpose of confecrating the fame and celebrating ST. JOHN'S; where it is hoped the Brethren at a convenient Distance will attend.

Tickets to be had at the Bar of the above Inn, at 10s. 6d. each; & Dinner to be on Table at three o'Clock. By Order,

S. STEVENS, Secretary.

PETERBOROUGH, 13th July, 1802.

Below Parish Church of St James, Great Grimsby (supplied by Humberside County Council).

Left The 'Antients' pedestal in the Lodge Room at Peterborough.

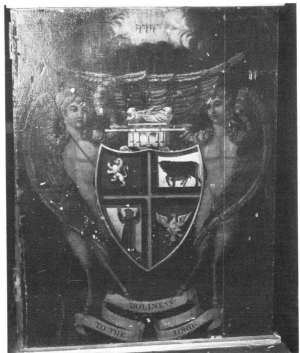

Above and Right Detail of the side panels of the pedestal.

Left Thomas Ewart, first Master of (Present) St Peter's Lodge and later DPGM of Province.

Below Clee Church, Lincolnshire mid 19th century.

Above The Apollo Lodge Building, drawn by Bro. A.E. Wade.

Right Notice of sale of furniture from the Apollo Lodge.

TO BE SOLD
By Auction,

BY MR. JUDD,

At the Apollo Lodge, Grimsby,

THIS AFTERNOON.

FRIDAY, JULY 19, 1833,

THE FOLLOWING

MASONIC
Furniture ;

VIZ.—

Four Mahogany Arm Chairs, 4 Forms with backs, 2 long Deal Tables, Portable Writing Desk, Pair of Globes, 3 Cushions and Boxes, Pulleys and Weight, 2 Brass Chandeliers, 3 Candlesticks, 16 Tin Candlesticks, Balloting Box and Balls, 5 Boxes, Stove, 4 Pictures in Gilt Frames, Copper Boiler, Pedestal, Piece of Painted Canvas, 14 Punch Glasses, Punch Bowl and Ladle, 2 Bibles, 4 Swords, 4 Spittoons, 9 Silk Collars, Drawing Board, 7 Mallets and Hammers, Ebony Inkstand, Waiter, 30 White Wands, Emblems, &c., &c.

☞ Sale to commence at Four o'clock.

SKELTON, PRINTER, GRIMSBY.

This page Scopwick: *Above* the village; *Left* the 'Royal Oak' public house; *Below* The church.

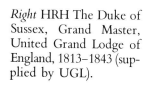

Right HRH The Duke of Sussex, Grand Master, United Grand Lodge of England, 1813–1843 (supplied by UGL).

Above The Collegiate Church of St Peter, Wolverhampton.

Below Freemasons' Hall, 1840; Grand Temple.

Right Tennyson d'Eyncourt's letter dismissing Oliver as DPGM for Lincolnshire (from Grand Lodge Library)

My Kindest & Bestfriend — I have vainly attempted to reply to yours of the 5th and the last post finds me as incapable as in the morning when yours reached me — Indignation and contempt are sad subjects In a masonic correspondence — In a few days I hope to be able to write more composedly —

May Providence direct us all in this uncoupled difficulty —

My wife adds her Kindest wishes with my warm regards to you and yours — Yr: most Sincerely

Robert Crucefix

May 7/42

The party you name is altogether unworthy your notice — consequently I shall not advise Bro: Spencer to give him the Book —

Left A typical administrative letter in Oliver's hand (from UGL Library)

Scopwick Vicarage June 25. 1844

Sir

I have just procured a good pencil drawing of Metheringham Church in this neighbourhood. I beg to ask whether it would answer your purpose to have it engraved if you received a written account of the Church & its Monuments?

I am Sir
Your obedient Servant
Geo. Oliver DD

[Gents Mag. Correspondence]

Right The Rt Hon. Thomas, Second Earl of Zetland, Grand Master of England 1844–1870.

Below A portrait of an older Oliver.

Left The Rt Hon. Charles Gordon, Earl of Aboyne (later Marquess of Huntly), PGM of Northamptonshire and Huntingdonshire, 1841–1863.

Right Peter Gilkes.

Below Parish Church of St John, Peterborough (from Peterborough Museum).

The portrait of Oliver commissioned by the Northern Lodge of China, No. 570, with its distinctly Oriental look (original in UGL Library).

of your magnitude contrasted with his own insignificance . . . Pitiful is the act itself, and with the most unblushing falsehood it is consummated . . . Lay your hand on your heart, my dear Sir, and tell me, are you a fit person to be the Deputy of *such a man?* Why my dear Sir you have been to him what the parabolic reflector is to the common lamp—you have made his diminutive light shine afar off—you have given strength and beauty to it. Now you have retired men will see it flicker. . .'

Balm in Gilead!

It was not in Gilead however that the next step was taken. Crucefix took advantage of the first Provincial meeting of the new Province of Northamptonshire and Huntingdonshire (the latter had been with Cambridgeshire until 1840) to intimate that Oliver's dismissal was to be the subject of a public crusade.[1] The meeting was held on 10 May 1842 at the George Hotel, Northampton, with the Provincial Grand master, Lord Aboyne, later Marquis of Huntly, in the chair. The Province, in common with many others, had supported the Asylum project and Crucefix was present as a guest with his brother, and at the subsequent banquet proposed the toast to the masonic charities. There were many other toasts and more speeches than would be readily tolerated at a masonic banquet today; they were also a good deal longer than would be acceptable. But when, late in the proceedings, the health of Dr Crucefix was proposed as 'a brother whose zeal in the cause of Masonry was only equalled by the services he had rendered to the Craft', the doctor 'after briefly but very energetically acknowledging the compliment' asked for permission before sitting down to propose 'The health of the Historian of Masonry, the Reverend Dr Oliver'. There was no difficulty from the Chair and he went on to describe 'that gifted brother' as 'unapproachable by any other brother in the order, as to the majesty of his intellect, the refined cultivation of his mind, his charitable construction of the errors and failings of others, or the readiness with which he brought all the sympathies of natural benevolence of feeling and of thought, to bear on cases where they were necessary to foster and protect; yet was he gentle as a child, wielding his great moral power with the mildness of a Christian minister'. FQR reported that the toast was drunk with unmixed gratification and delight.

It is indicative both of the popularity of Oliver and of the extent of feeling in favour of the Asylum project in the Provinces that permission for this unusual toast should have been given at an official gathering, and that it should have proceeded without any attempt by the Chairman, who as PGM was after all the appointee of and responsible to the Duke of Sussex, to damp the exuberance. Oliver was not present and was not a member of the Provincial Grand Lodge, though many there (and certainly Crucefix, who had reconstituted St Peter's Lodge at Peterborough in 1837) would be aware of his connection with it; but the proposal seems to have been Crucefix's own idea and it is doubtful to what extent Oliver would have approved it even though he was deeply resentful of the abrupt manner in which, without warning (as he maintained), he had been dismissed.

On 6 June Crucefix wrote again to him from London in sympathetic terms but did not refer to the exploit at Northampton. On the same day Bro. Watkins, Master of the Bank of England Lodge, also wrote: 'Although I had intended to await the meeting of the Bank of England Lodge . . . before I trespassed upon your time by giving utterance to the thoughts suggested by the disastrous Masonic Intelligence which has reached us from your Province—yet I meet on all sides with such evidence of intense excitement caused by the late events that I cannot resist troubling you with a few lines for the purpose of assuring you of the boundless sympathy felt by my Masonic friends, for the Martyrdom to which your singleness of purpose has exposed you'. After the meeting a letter from the Lodge Secretary conveyed the 'unfeigned regret' and 'indignant feelings' of the brethren of the lodge together with 'their very grateful acknowledgements for the high gratification afforded to them by the admirable manner in which you presided' at the dinner to Crucefix. Adjectival hyperbole was having a field day.

But it was in Lincoln that the battle lines were to be drawn up. The Witham Lodge centenary celebrations which had been planned the preceding year were due to take place on 9 June and Oliver was to be present. The PGM did not attend and Oliver took the opportunity to put his case. Later, with Beverley's help, he published an account of the proceedings including 'a narrative of the circumstances attending the writer's dismissal from the Deputy Grand Mastership of the Province'. Beverley, having offered to charge no more for the printing than could be recouped from sales, distributed 194 copies on a wide basis. Spencer published the final version, so this may have been a preliminary print run.[2]

It is obvious from the 'Narrative' that Oliver had expected to preside over the Provincial meeting for 1842; and this is confirmed by a common-place book of his (now in the keeping of the Supreme Council 33° for England and Wales), which contains the draft of the address he intended to give; in it he states his wish to have one of the masonic catachisms known as 'lectures' worked at each such meeting; in the event this was never in fact proposed, and the manuscript has been gone through in pencil with alterations to convert it into a statement of what would have happened. It seems clear therefore that it must refer to a meeting he did not hold and therefore to that he had anticipated having to conduct in 1842.

Having written in the 'Narrative' that 'Freemasonry is an Institution where science and philosophy are inculcated, and morality and virtue enforced; its activating principle is benevolence, and its cement is brotherly love'—statements which accurately state the attitude of the Craft—he describes the advantages of Provincial meetings. He emphasizes in particular those likely to accrue from the public seeing that great masonic meetings are conducted with dignity and decorum, all classes of society being present; only then does he mention what today freemasons tend to see as their main purpose, that they enable brethren of different lodges to become mutually acquainted and so help to establish the identity of the Province. He believed firmly that freemasonry should show a more open face to the world, something which is enjoined on every Master at his Installation but which, by its hankering for secrecy instead of privacy, the Craft in the years which followed the death of the Duke of Sussex largely rejected, for which action it is now suffering what it is nonsense to refer to as anything but a persecution.

Oliver then goes on to outline the circumstances leading to his dismissal. The Witham Lodge celebrations, at which he records that the opinion in his favour was not only unanimous, but most enthusiastic, had been completely overshadowed by it. He states that only a desire for temperate and unanimous conduct prevented further action—a strange statement but perhaps justified by the turbulence of the meeting and possibly meant as an indication that the matter was not finished and D'Eyncourt could expect trouble. The support he was receiving was making him more belligerent than was normally his nature and the insult he felt he had endured had marked him deeply. The indignation of his friends must have fuelled this, and Crucefix in particular seemed determined on a confrontation.

Oliver referred to the PGM's praises at the time of his appointment and protested his zeal, research and industry, and then swept into oratory: 'How is it then that the confidence of the Grand Lodge has been withdrawn from me! I have violated no obligation—I have broken no law—I have not infringed any Constitution of the order. I am not charged with any such transgression. I have, on the contrary, applied all the talents which nature has bestowed on me, in an earnest endeavour to increase the interest, and extend the usefulness of the Order; and not, I venture to affirm without success . . . It will be perceived, throughout the whole current of affairs, that though I have perhaps exhibited little worldly wisdom, yet I have always determined to do what is right, without regard to consequences . . . I patronised the Asylum on its own intrinsic merits alone, being certain that it could not fail to meet the approbation of our Masonic rulers, and the Craft at large. Alas, for the erring judgment of short-sighted mortals? I little knew what envy and jealousy were capable of effecting'.

It is clear that he regarded the Duke of Sussex as the force behind his removal from office, and elsewhere he said 'I was the instrument through which the Craft presented a testimonial to Dr Crucefix, because he is a benevolent man, and has succeeded by a great sacrifice both of time and money in establishing a noble Institution. The PGM proposed in Grand Lodge that this man to whom the Craft is under such weighty obligations should be expelled. Now, brethren, which do you think is most to be commended? I who was the instrument in rewarding virtue, or the PGM who would have punished it?' It was difficult to rouse him, but when roused he could match the best orators that the religious and political arenas of the time could produce.

He recounted the history of the testimonial fund in Lincolnshire, not omitting the facts that D'Eyncourt had contributed and that his own offer to resign on being invited to chair the Presentation ceremony had been refused; made much of the peremptory way in which he had then been dismissed; and concluded 'When the Duke of Sussex "expressed a very strong opinion" on the subject, he [i.e. D'Eyncourt] conceived it necessary to make an example of me, that he might avert the Grand Master's anger from himself'.

He also made it clear that his complaint was about the manner in which D'Eyncourt had exercised his power, not his right to do so—something which was to become of importance in the light of later developments about the part played by the Master of Witham Lodge, Bro. Nicholson. 'I do not question Mr D'Eyncourt's power to remove his Deputy at his discretion. The laws of Masonry distinctly confer that power. It is the wanton exercise of it that I complain of. Throughout the whole transaction there appears a want of delicacy—a want of courtesy—a deficiency of straightforward dealing, which renders it in the highest degree arbitrary and unjust . . . No reasons having been assigned . . . the most absurd rumours soon got into circulation. Disgraceful practices, and even crimes were imputed to me.' There was some justification for this outburst; as his letter to the lodges had never reached them, they knew nothing officially about the reasons for the dismissal and unfortunately men will always seek for a discreditable reason to explain a fall from high office; D'Eyncourt should have been aware of the likelihood.

The centenary celebrations themselves began with the dedication of the new hall whose foundation stone had been laid with such pomp the preceding year. Naturally this started with an oration from Oliver. In it he expatiated at length on the origins of freemasonry and on the need for discipline and integrity in its practice. It had recently been necessary to exclude (i.e. expel) a brother from the Craft and apparently in an oblique reference to this at the end of the oration he returned to a favourite theme which was too advanced for the masons of his time and which has only been seriously considered in recent years, the effect of too much secrecy: 'The public are not satisfied with a single victim, and his delinquency will not fail to be imputed to a society, whose proceedings, being secret, are suspected'. Later in the speech he pleaded for the repeal of a Grand Lodge edict forcefully supported by the Duke of Sussex, which forbade any publicity being given to lodge proceedings; the ban did not apply to the semi-private banquets that often followed great masonic occasions and where the attendance of non-masons was not unusual, so Oliver can be acquitted of resenting it as limiting his defence; he had in any case protested about it on other occasions. His objection was that it arose from the same preoccupation with secrecy which he saw as harming the interests of freemasonry in the eyes of the general public. 'I have no hesitation' he said on this occasion 'in saying that this law ought to be erased from the Statute Book, along with many others which are at variance with the steady progress of knowledge that distinguishes the present times, and the increasing liberality of opinion and facility of research from which such inestimable advantages have been derived to science and philosophy . . . What is there in Freemasonry, except the landmarks and peculiar secrets that we ought to be anxious to conceal?' This was very far from the view, already noted, of Lord Zetland, Pro Grand Master to the Duke and so second in the hierarchy of the Craft.

After the ceremony a most extraordinary informal meeting took place at which the brethren of the Witham lodge and their visitors gave full vent to the violence of their feelings. A vote of no confidence in the PGM was passed—an incredible and probably unique act of masonic rebellion, which is possibly why its operation was postponed to allow its validity to be determined. Instead, and as a temporary expedient, a resolution of regret at Oliver's dismissal was put and confirmed with an instruction that it be advertised in the newspapers of the Province and FQR.

At the subsequent banquet, when the usual toast to the PGM was proposed, it was greeted with 'a short and very significant silence' after which a senior brother on the dais rose and drank the health of the Provincial Senior Warden as the highest ranking Provincial Grand Officer present. In contrast, the health of 'the triangle of masonic charities, with the immortal memory of the founders of two of them, and the good health of Dr Crucefix, founder of the third and greatest' was greeted with loud and enthusiastic masonic cheers. Crucefix was present and replied.

Bro. Adams, of the Lodge of Harmony, Boston, and Mayor of that town where he controlled a newspaper, then proposed Oliver's health in a speech which was far from flattering to the PGM. It was extempore and when a copy was needed for the pamphlet reporting the proceedings there was no record available. Oliver wrote it from memory and sent the draft to Adams who replied (5 July 1842): 'I return the m.s. of the speech you have set down for me. Before the arrival of your letter I had tried but could not recollect even an outline of what I said at Lincoln. I generally speak very rapidly, and without any previous arrangement of my ideas, and although I can recollect any other persons' speech I never can report my own. Moreover I had not, until the moment of my rising, anticipated that the opening of the business would devolve on me, but had rather expected that some of the older and more distinguished of the brethren would have taken the lead. I have read your speech with much interest. It is quite clear that the movement which has commenced in consequence of your removal must go on and that all who usurp positions to which they are not entitled must be compelled to make way for better men unless the best interests of Masonry are to be sacrificed to gratify private and paltry feelings'. He would not be the first or last freemason to be called to propose or reply to a toast without much notice. At all events, he seems to have been content that the speech written by Oliver fairly represented what he had said!

Oliver was then called on for a reply, the third major speech he had made that evening. Even from a parish priest that was asking a lot, but he rose to the occasion and this time spoke less emotionally and with considerable logic, listing four errors in judgement which he claimed D'Eyncourt had committed:

'FIRST—he has dismissed me from my office at a moment's notice, after a faithful service of ten years' duration . . . As a matter of courtesy to one who has relieved him from all the toils, and burdens, and anxieties, necessarily attending the details of his office, for the above period, it ought to have been accomplished by a process less repugnant to my feelings: and particularly as . . . I had tendered my resignation . . . He urgently requested the continuance of my services . . . (He) might have favoured me with some notice of his intention, that I might have had an opportunity of taking leave of the officers whom I had myself appointed—that I might have taken leave of the Brethren of this Province, to whom I have been most affectionately attached; and one and all of whom I have ever considered not merely as my Brethren, but as my children. (Great applause) SECONDLY—the PGM has omitted to convene the Spring P.G. Lodge . . . THIRDLY—he has dismissed me on an alleged charge of insubordination, an offence, if it be one, which was committed many months ago, and out of the limits of his jurisdiction. FOURTHLY—he has broadly suggested that the interests of Masonry demanded my removal . . . out of the Province I cannot be responsible to him for my masonic conduct.'

It was an impressive indictment, recognizing the right of a PGM to dismiss his Deputy but directing the attack with all the force of wounded friendship against the 'former companion' who seemed heartlessly and publicly to have jettisoned him without warning after refusing him leave to go; it rang a knell which was to herald the end of D'Eyncourt's reign in spite of later revelations about the dubious activity, or inactivity, of Nicholson.

Oliver was capable of great indignation but he was above all a man of peace, and had there been an opportunity for discussion he might have realized that D'Eyncourt had not been as abrupt and discourteous as had appeared but had been led to believe that Oliver was being intransigent, as we shall see. As it was, Adams in Lincolnshire and Crucefix in London fanned the flames. The former may have felt, with others,[3] that D'Eyncourt was an unsatisfactory Provincial Grand Master and that it was only the appointment of Oliver as Deputy that had made his reign bearable; but the latter was of a more complex character and though feeling acutely for his friend's distress may also have seen how the situation might be turned to advantage, and this is a matter that must now be examined.

Chapter Twelve

THEORIES

(London, Lincoln)

At the meeting for the Witham Lodge centenary Oliver had referred to rumours that were spreading in the Province about the reasons for his dismissal and though he had characterized them as absurd they had upset him. The following day he wrote to the PGM about them:

'Dear Sir and Bro.

'I was yesterday informed that a report is in circulation at Market Rasen, that your reason for dismissing me from the office of DPGM, is (not what you yourself have assigned, but) that I am concerned in certain illegal and improper masonic publications. I shall be obliged if you will inform me whether such a report is authorized by you. And am Dear Sir,

Your obedient servant & Bro.
Geo. Oliver D.D.
Past DPGM for Lincolnshire

The letter was terse and to the point, but in a charged situation open to misconstruction. It elicited a firm reply dated 18 June from 5 Albemarle Street, the tone of which perhaps reflects the writer's training as a barrister:

Dear Sir and Bro.

I have just returned from the Continent & find yours of the 10th.

I had no reason for taking the course I did but that which was assigned & never made any statement with regard to yourself but that which was assigned & never made any statement with regard to your Publications which would authorize the report to which you allude.

I am Dear Sir
Your obedt. Servt. & Bro.
C.T. D'Eyncourt.

The decision to publish a pamphlet about the proceedings at Lincoln was taken almost at once. When Adams wrote from Boston on 12 June having been asked to provide a copy of his speech with results which have been noted, it is intriguing that he had found the latter part of the meeting 'desultory—in fact almost conversational, owing I think to the *timidity* of the brethren'; though it is difficult to imagine any meeting at which Oliver was in full oratorical flight and at which Crucefix was present in all the panoply of indignation being other than lively. Certainly when the pamphlet appeared it gave an impression of active indignation.

Crucefix, now back in London, was pressing for further action. He had joined a Lincolnshire lodge to ensure he would have the right to speak in any debate but wished this to be kept from D'Eyncourt's knowledge. Of the proceedings themselves he had a very different recollection to Adams: 'I am grateful that the meeting was so gratifying to your feelings . . . Your after dinner speech is energetic—lucid—straightforward—and should be given *entire* . . . I agree with you that the publication of the PGM's letter can alone satisfy the *profane* as well as the *masonic* world as to the real cause of your dismissal'.

Other support was forthcoming. Henry Udall, who had spoken for Crucefix in the expulsion debate and was associated with him in matters relating to the Christian masonic Orders which must shortly be examined, wrote of his astonishment at hearing of the dismissal: 'your character stands far too high, and your Masonic virtues are too fully appreciated to be affected by the petty tyranny of one, whose Masonic rank has been attained merely from the accidental circumstances of birth and fortune'. Shakespeare Lodge of Warwick made him an honorary member. Doric Lodge of Grantham in his own Province sent a Memorial which had been sealed in Open Lodge on 1 July in which, though noting (unlike the hotheads of Lincoln and Boston) that the principles of the Craft precluded inquiry into the motives of the PGM, they expressed their regret at the loss of pre-eminent services always given with cheerfulness and received with gratitude. 'To your influence must be ascribed the favourable position of the lodges of Lincolnshire. Under your zealous care the Craft has advanced in the opinion of the world . . . Need we tell you—how ably—how kindly—how fully you have performed the duties assigned to you. Whilst thus appreciating your worth—according *only* to your merit, we regret that the PGM forgetting the true spirit has acted too strictly within the letter of Masonic Law. Whatever the cause—however correct the motive—the Brethren of the Doric are fearful as to the effect, and think your Successor cannot exercise his authority so beneficially, so satisfactorily, or so creditably as you have done, since there are few (if any) amongst us who have displayed sufficient vigour of mind or Masonic knowledge to take upon themselves the Office'. This was open rebellion, rendered the more effective by the mildness of its tone.

Newspapers all over the country reported the dismissal and many carried scathing leaders castigating D'Eyncourt. The foreign papers copied and letters came from many parts of the world to Scopwick. Other honorary memberships were conferred. The pamphlet was printed and on 2 July Beverley wrote from Nottingham with the list of lodges in Lincolnshire, Warwick, Birmingham and Northampton to whom the first copies had been sent. Fifty had gone to Richard Spencer. 'You say strike while the iron is hot,' Beverley wrote. 'I think we are doing that without any mistake.' And Oliver's father sent his congratulations 'on your powerful and appropriate speech at Lincoln' and (in rather robust language) stated that everyone knew Crucefix was disgraced because of the Review: 'it matters but little how zealously it was taken to and supported by the Craft at large, H.R.H. the G.M. had spit at it, therefore it is no wonder that his most attached adherents should adopt his opinions and imitate his practice; Tennyson has lost his seat in the Privy Council, and consequently he is not very comfortable; you may recall the old Anecdote of the King kicking the Lord Chancellor's backside, which went regularly through the intermediate gradations till it ended in a Cat worrying a Mouse!!!' and went on to advise sending a full statement to every lodge in the world!

Dixon in his History justly calls this time 'a most critical period for the craft in Lincolnshire' and continues 'the next Provincial meeting, which had been fixed to be held at Spalding, was looked forward to with great anxiety & apprehension. The publicity given in the local papers, the well-known character and ability of Oliver, his personal friendship with all the active freemasons in the Province on the one side, against the evident unpopularity of the PGM on the other, marked a serious state of affairs'.[1] On 11 August Bro. George Wriglesworth Hebbs, Mayor of Lincoln, with the support of Adams from Boston, convened a meeting about which not much is known but which Dixon says paved the way for a reconciliation by allowing D'Eyncourt to show appreciation without loss of dignity; but Oliver's correspondence now in the Grand Lodge library does not refer to this or seem to bear it out, as will be seen.

Crucefix, writing on 25 August from Jersey, whither he had gone for his health (he said later that on returning he had 'discarded my crutch-stick and surprised my friends') referred to reactions in London to the Witham Lodge meeting: 'The Autocrat is I *hear* somewhat vexed at the Lincoln proceedings—the explosion of the mine has been either premature—or the satrap may *not* have perfectly understood orders—no doubt they were *clear* in their nature'. It would certainly seem that D'Eyncourt had not expected that the storm he had raised would blow so long or with such fury. To calm his Province he was forced after all to call the annual meeting of Provincial Grand Lodge to meet at Spalding on 29 September. But before passing to that part of the story it will be as well to ask why the storm was so violent.

Oliver was well known and liked, his fame as 'the sage and historian of masonry' was world-wide. Crucefix was greatly revered in the Provinces and had a good following in London. Both made excellent martyrs. The Grand Master was failing in health and in the course of nature his reign was nearing its end, but there was no question of a fight over the succession in Craft or Royal Arch. Some of his policies had stirred opposition, notably the removal from the ritual of Christian references and the demotion of the two Saints John as the patrons of freemasonry. Oliver had probably been the most persistent thorn in his side in this and had, without even trying or intending to do so, made himself the centre of resistance to the policy. But to seek to punish Oliver for voicing sincerely-held views would not accord with what we know of the Duke's character; it was not until Crucefix openly, publicly and contumaciously defied him that the Grand Master had acted against him. There was at times an air of paranoia in the Duke's dealings with Crucefix, almost certainly arising from the reporting activities of FQR; but annoyance over Oliver's speech at the testimonial dinner would be unlikely of itself to cause him to press for the speaker's dismissal with all the attendant publicity which Oliver's reputation and Crucefix's support were sure to attract. Admittedly the Duke was now old and an invalid; he must have felt death was not far distant and it could be that he was anxious that his work for the Jews should not be undone after he had left the scene; but by now the changes had been in operation for nearly 30 years and were generally accepted; even in the breast of an old and failing man there was surely little thought of any opposition party gaining sufficient strength or even any coherence to justify such fears.

Sir James Stubbs, who came into the administration of English freemasonry in 1948 and was its Grand Secretary or chief executive officer from 1958–1980 has a great interest in and knowledge of the history of the UGL. In a comment on a paper the author read to Quatuor Coronati Lodge, no. 2076, the premier lodge of masonic research, Sir James remarked:

> 'I wonder whether we have really got to the bottom of Dr Oliver's brutal dismissal. It is, I think, generally ascribed to D'Eyncourt's acting on a wink or possibly something stronger from his royal master in pursuit of the latter's vendetta against Crucefix over the early days of the Royal Masonic Benevolent Institution. It occurs to me that this is over-playing the relationship of Oliver and Crucefix . . . it also suggests to me that there was a malevolence in the Duke of Sussex which I believe to be quite out of keeping with what we know of him: autocratic and sometimes headstrong, yes; but mean, no. In short, I do not believe that he would have involved the sins of Crucefix in the matter of the Royal Masonic Benevolent Institution, or any-thing else, in someone not directly connected with that quarrel. We know that the Duke of Sussex was greatly interested in "universalizing" the Craft: it has been made clear to us this evening, even if we did not know before, that Oliver rated his Christianity very high, indeed to the extent that Freemasonry was its handmaiden. He had made this very clear already, and his fame was widespread; is it not at least possible that the Duke regarded him as a dangerous, even perhaps the most dangerous, obstacle to his own grand design, and that like Henry II he said "who will rid me of this turbulent priest"—or at least who will take him out of his authoritative position?'[2]

Contemporary reports and comments all assume that D'Eyncourt was prompted to act by 'higher powers' but regard the cause as being Oliver's presidency at the Crucefix banquet. Nor does it seem likely that so experienced a political person as the Duke would have imagined that Oliver's authority as a masonic writer would be damaged by the fact that he was no longer a Deputy PGM; after all, he did not hold, and was never likely to hold, the rank of a Grand Officer, the highest masonic honour to which he could expect to attain; yet that failure had not held down his soaring reputation. But Sir James may well be right in feeling that there is more than we know and it is possible that the answer may lie in the question of the Christian Orders of freemasonry. A hint of such a theory appears in a paper read to the Quatuor Coronati Lodge in 1961 by P.R. James[3] and is worth exploring in greater detail.

For many years two principal Orders which purported to be both masonic and Christian had been known to and patronized by English freemasons. The oldest, the Knights Templar, had been practised in various parts of the country for some time before the Union of the Grand Lodges and some Craft lodges regarded it as a degree they were authorized by their Craft warrants to confer. Oliver himself had received it, probably in Hull when he was living in Grimsby. The 'Encampments' (today usually called Preceptories) of Knights Templar had a separate existence from any sponsoring lodges and membership could only be obtained by duly qualified freemasons. The Order was Christian and knights had to swear allegiance to the Trinitarian Christian Faith. It was, at least nominally, under the control of a Grand Master and the Duke of Sussex had been elected to that office and installed on 8 August 1812, the same year as that in which he had become Grand Master of the Premier Grand Lodge (the 'Moderns'). The following year was that in which the Union of the two Grand Lodges took place and saw his election as the first Grand Master of the United Grand Lodge of England.

Under the terms of the Constitutions of the new Grand Lodge 'pure antient freemasonry' was stated to consist of the three Craft degrees and the Holy Royal Arch (or 'Chapter') and no more. There was thus no place for the Knights Templar in the Craft although it was well known and respected and had long been regarded as an authentic masonic degree; this made the position of the Duke as Grand Master of the Knights Templar anomalous. Further, he at once set about the removal of Christian references from the Craft ritual, and such a stance was difficult to reconcile with his status as Grand Master of a Christian Order. The normal course would have been to resign from one position, but this he did not do; to give up the leadership of the Templars could have been to offer a power base to someone who disapproved of the dechristianizing process. Instead he delegated his authority for the Templar Order to two senior Knights Templar and refrained from calling any meeting of the Grand Conclave, its governing body. The executive needs of the Order were then for some years controlled by Dispensations granted as required by his deputies until about 1830 when the Duke unexpectedly resumed control. Whether this was due to a feeling that opposition to the dechristianizing of the ritual was growing cannot be known, but it is worthy of note that Oliver had published *The Star in the East* in 1825 and *Signs and Symbols* in 1826, both overtly Christian in thinking and both popular. *The History of Initiation* published in 1829 was designed to show that freemasonry had nothing to do with heathen ceremonies; it was clearly a precursor to an outright affirmation that the Craft was essentially Christian. The Duke must have realized that even after more than a decade of use his revisions were not universally acceptable.

Even after 1830 the Grand Conclave was not summoned in the Duke's lifetime though he endeavoured to maintain order by issuing charters to Encampments and appointing Provincial Grand Commanders to govern the respective Provinces. These were probably necessary measures to prevent anarchy, but he carefully refrained from any more public avowal of the existence of the Order, an attitude which, considering the antiquity it claimed and its generally accepted standing as a masonic body, must have been in some degree resented.

The other Christian degree was the Rose Croix, which is not rosicrucian but a masonic order whose origins are not exactly known and which by the time of the Union had achieved widespread popularity in many countries.[4] It has now in general been absorbed into the Order known as 'The Ancient and Accepted Rite' which acknowledges 33 degrees, the Rose Croix being the 18th; the first three are claimed to be the equivalent of the Craft degrees. The government of the rite is vested in Supreme Councils 33rd degree, on a territorial basis; not all are now exclusively Christian though the Supreme Council for England and Wales and the Chapters it controls firmly adhere to the Christian Faith. The Constitutions of the Order, as established in 1786 lay down that while a Supreme Council does not always exercise its authority in respect of degrees below the 17th, and can delegate them 'even tacitly' that authority cannot be waived; they require all Lodges, whatever their degree, to obey and submit to the demands of those who have received the 33rd degree. Provisions such as these have indeed misled many non-masons to assume that the claimed supremacy is effective; one such was the late Stephen Knight. Supremacy can easily be claimed but unless it is acknowledged it is ineffective. Mr Knight could easily have ascertained that the claim was certainly not acknowledged since the official statement on the 'Aims and Relationships of the Craft' states 'The Grand Lodge of England is a Sovereign and independent Body practising Freemasonry only within the three Degrees and only within the limits defined in its constitution as "pure Antient Masonry". It does not recognize or admit the existence of any superior Masonic authority, however styled'; while the statement agreed by Grand Lodge in 1929 on the basic principles for recognition of other Grand Lodges as regular requires that a Grand Lodge shall have exclusive jurisdiction over the lodges under its control within its jurisdiction 'and shall not in any way be subject to, or divide such authority with, a Supreme Council or other Power claiming any control or supervision over those degrees'.

A Christian rite with similarities to at least one degree of the Ancient and Accepted Rite was known in England and Wales before the Union and linked with the Encampments; but elsewhere control was exercised in accordance with the Constitutions of 1786 under which all authority was vested in Supreme Councils 33rd Degree. The Constitutions were said to have been promulgated by Frederick the Great and under them the method of establishing a new Supreme Council in a country where none existed was carefully laid down. The northern states of America were allowed two Councils, the Northern and Southern Jurisdictions respectively. In France there were two bodies claiming to control the order there and the antecedents of one and the behaviour of both had caused some of the other Supreme Councils to regard them with wariness or downright hostility. To be recognized as such, a new Supreme Council had to obtain a patent from an existing recognized Supreme Council and only one Council was in general allowed to operate in any one country. The situation was further complicated by a quarrel between the Northern Masonic Jurisdiction and the French. The importance of England in the masonic world of the early 19th century cannot be exaggerated, and the facts that the Rose Croix there did not conform to the accepted pattern and that as there was no Supreme Council established there it was open territory under the constitutions of 1786, made it a tempting prospect in more ways than one.

In 1819 a French Rose Croix mason, Joseph de Glock-d'Obernay, was making approaches to prominent freemasons in London with a view to establishing a Supreme Council; his motives were doubtful and almost certainly venal, but he appeared to have the authority to offer a patent from one of the French Supreme Councils. He approached the Duke of Leinster, who apprised the Duke of Sussex of what had been proposed. The latter at once took steps to have d'Obernay brought to him. Their negotiations concluded, after the passing of a cash sum, in the grant to Sussex of a patent authorizing him to form a Supreme Council for Great Britain. This was a skilful move on the Duke's part since by virtue of the 1786 Constitutions it precluded the grant of another patent for England (as part of Great Britain) during his lifetime and so, as in the case of the Knights Templar, he was able to stultify the growth of a body which could be expected to oppose his work on the Craft ritual. He appointed the Duke of Leinster and another to make up the numbers of the Council, and then took no further action under it for the rest of his life.

The new Supreme Council had the grandiose title of 'The Supreme Council for the Kingdom of Great Britain, Ireland and its possessions in America and the Indies', but as it was not intended by the Duke that it should meet or be active in any way it remained in limbo. It would not however, affect Rose Croix Chapters already meeting in England, which generally would be held under the auspices of the Knights Templar Encampments and so far as there was any control would be subject to the Grand Conclave. Long before the Duke died in 1843 his policy of inactivity would have become clear and those who would relish the opportunity to obtain a fresh patent and flaunt their new status under it in the face of the United Grand Lodge would certainly be thinking about the possibilities that would open on his death. The nearest source for obtaining a patent would be France, but the unsatisfactory situation there made this a course that could give rise to difficulty elsewhere, and some eyes began to turn to the United States of America.

Crucefix was an ardent supporter of both the Knights Templar and the Rose Croix. The Duke died on 21 April 1843, and a Conclave of Knights Templar was summoned for 22 December. Crucefix had written in FQR about lack of discipline in the Rose Croix, 'each Templar Encampment controlling and regulating the material of the higher degrees amongst its own members, and the regalia is not uniform'. In 1845 it was rumoured, with some foundation, that an English freemason, Dr Leeson, was in fact making an approach to a French Supreme Council for a further patent and Crucefix decided to act. On 26 October 1845, he wrote to the Secretary General of the Supreme Council, Northern Masonic Jurisdiction (NMJ), asking them to issue a patent authorizing him to form a Supreme Council for England of which he would thereby become Sovereign Grand Commander for life. At some stage he informed the NMJ that Oliver would be his Lieutenant Grand Commander, the second office in the hierarchy; it was an astute move because Oliver was well known and respected in the United States and was about to be offered a patent as Past Deputy Grand Master of the Grand Lodge of Massachusetts. Any lingering doubts arising from Crucefix's somewhat flamboyant masonic career and ebullient character would surely be put to rest by the association of Oliver's name with the proposal. The NMJ decided, rather hesitantly and probably mainly in order to forestall the French, to grant a patent and a new Supreme Council for England was thereby authorized and in due course established.

The question which arises from all this is whether, at the time of Oliver's dismissal in 1842 there was any thought in Crucefix's mind of the possibilities for the Rose Croix that would arise on the death of the Duke of Sussex. Having an acute political sense, he would know of the organization of the Order under its Constitutions, and of the Duke's suppression of the patent granted to him. To a man who was unlikely to advance further in the Craft and was still regarded in high quarters with some suspicion the prospect would be tempting. Crucefix enjoyed the limelight and after his experience of repression would no doubt welcome authority which would enable him to rule an Order in spite of the UGL.

It is known that the NMJ were in touch with Oliver at the beginning of May 1845, five months before Crucefix wrote to their Secretary-General, and their letter, dated 1 May, is addressed to 'Illustrious Brother George Oliver, D.D.', which implies that Oliver had already received promotion in the Order. It will also be recalled that among the letters received by him shortly after his dismissal was one dated 15 July from Henry Udall, who became first Grand Treasurer-General in the new Supreme Council.

The furore created by Oliver's dismissal would probably have died down had he been left to follow his normal bent. There would have been a revolt in Lincolnshire, of course, but it is not likely that much more than sympathy would have been offered elsewhere. That this did not happen was largely due to Crucefix's ardent campaigning. He was very conscious of his friend's support in time of need and was inclined to be emotional. A scheme for a Testimonial to Oliver had occurred to him but not been actively pursued; soon after the dismissal he launched it. He also goaded Oliver into taking positive action to vindicate himself. The question has to be asked whether he had any ulterior motive? P.R. James, in the paper already mentioned, asserts that 'Though it did not appear on the surface, there was another, and perhaps more vital, cause of the conflict between Dr Crucefix and Masonic authority, and that was the Higher Degrees'—a description which does not attract universal approval but when used is generally taken to refer particularly to the Christian Orders. He suggests that Crucefix, Oliver, Udall, and others must have been practising the Christian degrees for some time prior to the application for the new patent. Certainly there is evidence that the Knights Templar Encampments, together with the Rose Croix Chapters they controlled, had continued to meet throughout the period of the Duke's Grand Mastership of the Craft. The evidence is thin and all is supposition; but the theory would go far to explain the Duke's annoyance at an alliance of Oliver and Crucefix. On the other hand there is no hint of any such interest in any of Crucefix's letters which have survived including many of those to Oliver written at the time of the dismissal furore; it seems almost certain that others which have been destroyed were first carefully examined, and it is unlikely that anything bearing on this would not have been preserved. It is on the whole probable that Crucefix initially acted as he did simply because being by nature a fighter he was disposed to throw his glove in the face of the rulers of the

Craft by whom he felt he had been unfairly treated. But if he had already formed the ambition of establishing himself at the head of a Supreme Council 33rd Degree, he would certainly be alive to the prestige which Oliver's support would be worth, particularly if negotiations were to be with NMJ. It is therefore arguable that it was also with an eye to this possibility that he carried Oliver along in his tempestuous wake, preventing him from flagging by the project for the testimonial, which would be gratifying to the wounded pride of the sacked Deputy.

Oliver's reputation at home and abroad, particularly in the United States, and his respectability and known belief in the essential Christianity of freemasonry would make him an ideal partner in the application. The possibility of a French patent being obtained would greatly concern NMJ and add urgency to the request. The hesitancy of the NMJ was overcome and the patent issued, though events were soon to show that body that its misgivings had not been without foundation.

Chapter Thirteen

TESTIMONIAL (1842–1844)

(London, Lincoln, Spalding, Peterborough)

The proposal for a testimonial gift to Oliver was mentioned to him for the first time by Crucefix in a letter of 16 June 1842. From a later letter (5 July) we learn that the possibility had been canvassed with Nicholson as early as January. Nicholson had 'replied in a very friendly way and intimated that the greatest delicacy would be required with regard to the PGM', an interesting remark as it indicates that Nicholson had already been informed of D'Eyncourt's concern over Oliver's presiding at the Crucefix Testimonial dinner, a fact which will be seen as important in considering later developments. Crucefix had answered, dealing with all Nicholson's points but heard nothing for some time. Eventually Nicholson had written to suggest that the matter should be left in abeyance until the Provincial Grand Lodge.

The letter of 5 July was written in reply to a confidential communication which Oliver had sent him about Nicholson, the text of which has not survived; in the light of the opinion Oliver must have expressed in that letter, Crucefix now suggested that any proposal should emanate from the Provincial meeting rather than be left to Nicholson. This would suit Crucefix, who was at that time intending to retire and leave London.

In spite of his honeyed words at the Witham Lodge meeting it began to look as though Nicholson was playing a double game. At a meeting of that Lodge in June or July it had been proposed that he, as Master, should write to all the Lincolnshire lodges requesting the Masters to support the proposed testimonial. Instead of this he wrote to the new DPGM, the Reverend George Coltman, Rector of Stickney. An emergency meeting of the Witham Lodge was called to hear Coltman's reply which was dated 16 July and 'though it may appear harsh' refused sanction, not to the suggested letter but to the testimonial proposal; Coltman wrote 'under the present circumstances I have no choice' and went on to tell the Lodge that such action could 'only be regarded as a mark of their disapprobation of his [Oliver's] removal from office, and consequently as a condemnation of the PGM's conduct. To give my authority therefore to the originating of such a testimonial would he highly indecorous as well as unjustifiable'. He suggested that the matter should be deferred until a Provincial Grand Lodge in September at which D'Eyncourt would preside. This was in spite of the PGM's 'best acknowledgments' for Oliver's services in the letter which had dismissed him; but the new Deputy was aware of what lay behind a seemingly innocent suggestion and was probably wise in seeking a respite for passions to die down. Nevertheless, a little effort at compromise and enquiry by Coltman at this point might have served his PGM better than the bare refusal which he issued.

Oliver's eldest son, George, was by chance in Lincoln at the time the emergency lodge was held and attended it. He described the proceedings in a lengthy letter to his father dated 21 July:

'Nicholson received a regular reprimand from Harvey for proceeding in the manner he had done but he excused himself by referring to the Book of Constitutions which says no resolution shall be published without the consent of the PGM or his deputy—a copy of his letter to Coltman was called for but he could not produce one nor could he recollect of it All the snake in the grass could say was that it was a *regular business letter* (I have no doubt of that) A motion was made that the Lodge be adjourned to next Tuesday & a copy of that letter be obtained from Coltman Now do not you think it very doubtful whether we can get a *true copy* I never heard any man so eloquent as Harvey was on the subject he said if the copy could not be obtained or if headquarters put their veto on the proceedings he would take it on himself to call a meeting of the Masons of the County at Sleaford or some other central place in the county in such a manner that neither the PGM or the DPGM could interfere and there forward the matter for he said he knew full well if they did not give the affair a start the Bank of England Lodge would & he considered it a disgrace to the Masons of Lincolnshire to allow it to emanate from any other place—he continued if he should be so unfortunate as not to succeed in his plan he would attend any meeting which might be held in London to convince the Masons there that the Lincolnshire Masons were not indifferent about it— I had a conversation with Harvey after the Lodge he is very much annoyed at Nicholson's conduct—Goodacre said if the PGM would not allow any proceedings to take place in Lodge he shd consider it his duty as chairman at the dedication dinner to write to those brethren who proposed the matter there requesting their co-operation in the business Old Whitehouse gave Nicholson such a rap he will not forget for some time I never saw a man cut such a miserable figure he spluttered & stammered & really did not know what to say for himself—he [Nicholson] wanted very much to beg of the Brethren to allow it to stand over to the Spalding meeting but no one would hear of such a thing—Nicholson never mentioned Dr Crucefix's letter—was that a private letter or directed to him as Master I did not know whether I shd be doing right in mentioning it so I said nothing about it—I shall attend next Tuesday if you would wish any particular motion to be made I will either do it or get it done whatever you want doing you may depend on Harvey—but as to Nicholson as Harvey says he can see what he means that is I believe to support D'Eyncourt let the consequence to you be what it may the less you say to N the better for I believe he would not hesitate to tell Coltman everything . . . he is a regular double faced fellow.'

Punctuation in letter writing was not something young George believed in.

Further surprises about Nicholson's previous conduct were to come at the Provincial meeting; but meanwhile Crucefix, writing on 22 July on the back of a notice of the seventh annual festival of the Asylum because 'my dear wife has been putting as *she* thinks all to rights during my absence and consequently—I have not a sheet of paper at hand', announced that the Oliver tribute had begun. London had after all provided the launch pad. From another of his letters (26 July) we know that there was to be a meeting to appoint a committee of management for a 'General Masonic Testimonial to Dr Oliver' at the City Arms Hotel, Lincoln, at noon on 11 August; the notice is signed by Goodacre, and Crucefix economically wrote this time on the back of it—perhaps he was still looking for paper; Oliver would certainly understand his friend's problem judging by his own opinion of spring-cleaning.

Not all the lodges in the Province were ready to set the Witham on fire. In the minutes of the Shakespeare Lodge at Spilsby which Oliver had constituted in 1835 and of which Coltman had been Master in 1838 and 1839, the following entry appears in the records of the August meeting: 'Communications from the Lodge of Harmony, Boston and the Hundred of Elloe Lodge, Spalding, having been read by the W.M. respecting the removal of the Revd Dr Oliver from the office of DPGM, the members present after due consideration came to the resolution that they could not consistently entertain any discussion on the subject'.

The matter of the Testimonial went ahead; Crucefix toured the country, pressing the cause wherever he went and setting up local committees; at Wolverhampton Slade reported a 'tolerable contribution' from St Peter's Lodge and grumbled about playing second fiddle to 'Mr C . . . a miserably incompetent leader' (the reference was probably to the Vicar of the new Church of St George); he reported that the town was in a sadly depressed state, full of soldiers and with hordes of miners wandering about begging; and took the occasion to ask for a bigger increase in pay. Only in Lincolnshire did the organization of the testimonial drag; the wrong men were chosen to forward it and the chairman died. Though all was well in the end there was considerable worry lest Oliver's own county should not make a good showing.

Attention now turned to the forthcoming meeting of the Provincial Grand Lodge which Crucefix and Stevens expected to attend though the latter had to withdraw at the last moment. It was eventually summoned for 29 September and Goddard, the Provincial Secretary, wrote to Oliver with advance notification on the 14th.[1] The shortness of notice for such meetings is in sharp contrast to the present practice when many weeks' warning would be given and is a reminder of the efficacy of person to person communication in those days. Adams had submitted a motion highly critical of D'Eyncourt direct to the PGM. Goddard had of course previously helped Oliver to run the Province and the two were on good terms: he was later an executor of Oliver's will. He was neither a timeserver nor a turncoat and was not going to be a party to any attempts to stifle debate. Now, knowing of Adams' action, he wrote to D'Eyncourt asking for copies of all motions for the meeting which had been submitted to him or the Deputy. He had also told Oliver that a motion had been received 'That the Prov Gd Lodge be subscribers of £2.2.0 to the fund for presenting a Masonic offering to Dr Oliver'. He said Bro. Nicholson was 'much better but I think (to avoid the P G Master's thumbscrew) he will plead indisposition & thus abstain from going to Spalding'. Later, on 17 September, sending Oliver the formal circular calling the meeting, he enclosed 'a score for friends of yours'.

From the same letter it appears that letters from Oliver to the Lincolnshire lodges had been sent to Goddard for distribution but had got no further than his office. Goddard wrote: 'With regard to your communication to the Lodges, I deeply regret to say that I neglected to send them. This circumstance arose from your letter reaching me at the office with many others during Mr Nicholson's illness, and was placed by one of our Clerks amongst the "Answered Letters" by mistake in which condition I have just laid my hands upon it . . . What atonement can I make? Would it be out of place to send them now?' The likelihood is that this would be the letter Oliver had drafted to announce his dismissal.

With the imminence of the Provincial meeting for which he had been hankering and the prospect of action, Crucefix was in his element. 'The steam is up', he wrote on the 22nd, 'and if the Engineers and Stokers do their duty—the "offering" will have a good fair sum. I propose with my Lance Corporal JLS to be at Spalding on Wednesday evening'.

The Spalding meeting was indeed being looked on as a confrontation. Both Oliver and D'Eyncourt had engaged rooms at the White Hart Hotel—on opposite sides of the entrance, and a letter from a Bro. Williamson to Oliver on 24 September shows that the local lodge, the Hundred of Elloe, now no. 469, was looking forward to welcoming him. The Reverend Samuel was also there to support his son. But the expected fireworks were never set off. There seems to have been a meeting between D'Eyncourt and Crucefix before the Provincial Grand Lodge was opened, at which matters were so arranged that the motions in support of Oliver put forward by Adams would be passed and a sum voted for the Testimonial, PGM and former Deputy would give a show of harmony and D'Eyncourt would give his account of events leading up to the dismissal.

However, the first public reference to the dispute came at the customary Church service which preceded the meeting. The new Provincial chaplain, the Reverend W. Muckler, somewhat daringly preached his sermon upon the text 'Behold how good and joyful a thing it is, brethren, to dwell together in unity'. To those who listened and did not know of the negotiations behind the scenes, his boldness would seem amply justified by the event.

The resolution passed at the subsequent meeting was in the following terms (the words in square brackets were omitted in the later 'official' version; those in italics are in the 'official' version only):

'That this P.G.L. entertains the warmest feelings of gratitude towards Brother the Rev. George Oliver, D.D. late D.P.G.M. for Lincolnshire, for his unwearied and successful efforts to promote the best interests of freemasonry in general and in this Province in particular—and for the unequalled talent, research and industry displayed by him as a Masonic Writer.

That being duly impressed with [a sense of] his great public, private and social virtues, this P.G.L. cannot but deeply lament the loss of the very valuable services of Brother Oliver as D.P.G.M., the duties of which office he for many years discharged so as to gain the veneration and esteem of the Brethren generally, and to call forth repeated marks of approbation from the P.G.M.

That the sum of Five Guineas be paid from the funds of this P.G.L. in aid of the subscription now raising for the purpose of presenting to Bro. Oliver a Masonic Offering, as a mark of fraternal regard and of the grateful acknowledgement of his invaluable services in the cause of Masonry.

At the suggestion of the D.P.G.M. it was expressly understood that the P.G.L. in agreeing to this resolution do not intend to pass any censure upon the P.G.M. for his dismissal of Dr Oliver from the position of DPGM, or to express any opinion upon the propriety or impropriety of such a step.'

Later Crucefix was to complain of a breach of the agreement reached at Spalding, stating that even Oliver did not know its full details. But for the moment all was specious accord and a newspaper[2] was able to report 'we are happy in announcing what we are certain will be received with unqualified gratification, that such explanations were made as led to the restoration of amicable union between the Provincial Grand Master, Mr D'Eyncourt, and his late deputy, the Rev. Dr Oliver'.

The general relief felt at the time was reflected at the dinner which followed.[3] Dixon writes;

'One is scarcely prepared for such an exhibition of true masonic spirit as was witnessed at the banquet which followed the Lodge . . . Could any Brother who attended . . . have imagined that . . . the force of the preacher's text . . . [would] be exemplified in such a forcible manner as probably had never been experienced by those hundred brethren who had the good fortune to be present?

'And moreover, that the health of the PGM should be proposed by Dr Crucefix . . . ; that the PGM in returning thanks should say "that [Dr Crucefix] had repaid unkindness by charity, and a too hasty judgement by the most benevolent construction of human error". Yet all this took place.'[4]

But the meeting had not been without its surprises, and it is clear from what happened that these words of D'Eyncourt's did not refer to Oliver's dismissal, but to the part that the PGM had played in the attempt to expel Crucefix from the Craft; they are as much a tribute to Crucefix's personality as to the speaker's magnanimity, but they would hardly sound well in the ears of the Grand Master.

D'Eyncourt's record as a politician shows he was well able to handle hostile meetings. He had prepared carefully and his bombshell came during his address which lasted two hours; the stamina of our ancient brethren was greater than ours, both in making and listening to speeches. It gradually became clear that he had agonized for some time about the position of his friend and deputy and had more than once tried to give him the opportunity to resign gracefully. He read a letter, possibly two letters, which he had written to Nicholson explaining the difficulty in which he felt he was placed by Oliver's presiding at the Crucefix dinner and suggesting that Nicholson should press Oliver to resign. As the main thrust of Oliver's campaign had been that the dismissal had been unheralded and unexpected, this was serious. Nicholson, as Goddard had expected, was not present. Oliver was obviously taken aback and though he does not seem to have made any direct contact himself, his friends saw to it that Nicholson was made aware of the depth of his anger. On 1 October Nicholson wrote to him:

'To my great surprise I have learned that you have denied your recollection that, in a conversation with me relative to your dismissal, you never gave as your reasons for not resigning, That the dinner to Dr Crucefix being independent of this province your presiding at it could not be construed into an offence to Mr D'Eyncourt: that you were unconscious of any breach of masonic discipline: that at the dinner no offensive allusion was made to the Duke of Sussex: that you had stipulated that such should be the case: and that when you proposed his health, the toast was received with the warmth that accompanies it at other masonic festivals.

I cannot doubt that you will recal [sic] all this to your recollection & will do me the justice to say so.'

Oliver felt this was dangerous ground and that his reply might 'be brought before the world'. He promptly sent the letter to Stevens with a hastily drafted reply. The draft, as amended by Stevens, survives with a note by Stevens that he had shown it to Crucefix and though they both approved he proposed 'a few trifling changes' saying 'There is no necessity for hitting N. so hard. Depend on it he has a good case against D'E. At all events it is enough for you to *weigh him down*—you need not sink him'.

The draft is long and the following only an extract; words in square brackets were deleted by Stevens:

'In your letter you have omitted the real point, which as I understand it is this. Mr D'E—wrote two letters to you in March and April saying that if I did not resign he shd be under the necessity of dismissing me from office, owing to the peculiarity of his position with the D. of Sussex; and authorizing you to invite me to resign by communicating to me the contents of those letters. Mr D'E— exculpated himself from the charge of harshness towards me, by stating that he had actually proposed to me the alternative through you—thus giving me an opportunity of avoiding the more invidious step. *And he read your Letter in evidence of this very important fact.*

'The points stated to me in your letter of 1 Oct are subordinate and of no manner of importance, for they are most of them mentioned in my speech at the Centenary dinner. They [no doubt] occurred in many conversations on the subject both with you and others, and I make no secret of them. But I had no idea you were in official correspondence with Mr D'E—on the subject; nor had I any idea that any [casual] conversation between us would have been communicated to him. This makes all the difference. For the question at issue was whether Mr D'E had or had not dismissed me without [preparatory] notice. He stated that he had given me notice thro' you, I read your letter in [reply, as] evidence of this fact; I stated on the contrary that no such communication [as that described] had taken place.

'[Instead from the many disrespectful allusions to Mr D'E—which I have so frequently heard to drop from your lips, I must confess I was not a little surprized when I heard your Letter read by him in G. Lodge. And this surprise was not diminished when I was told by a Friend and Bro. that he heard Mr D'E—say in private on the same day, that he felt indignant, after what you had said to him respecting me, that you should have attended "the Offering" Committee on 11 Aug. & propose (sic) a Resolution in my favour.]

'[But to the point.] The conversation to which you allude was probably one which took place in Lincoln street, after my return from WHamton, for I can find no other that is at all applicable to it. It appears in my memoranda as follows. "Lincoln. Saw friend Nicholson in the Street. Said he had seen Mr D'E—who is in a d——l of a funk about my presiding at the Crucefix dinner. I said I am sorry for it, because he had no reason to be so, for the dinner was held outside his Province, & nothing occurred which could displease the most fastidious critic, and therefore Mr D'E—ought not to take offence. He sd the D. of Sussex is displeased. I replied—He cannot be so justly, for he was treated with great respect and his toast was received with cheers. He then sd some of the Brethren think you ought to resign. I replied, that as Bro. D'E— had refused my resignation at Boston, I saw no necessity for increasing his difficulties by such a course; but I would consult my friends about it. He answd—*Well, I neither can nor will give you any advice myself, for I am determined not to mix myself in the matter.* And he said further that Mr D'E—must inevitably resign himself, under the circumstances. . .

'Again—you say, if I remember your Letter correctly, that you advised or invited me to resign—when in fact you declared most explicitly "that you neither could nor would *advise* me—nor mix yourself in the matter". . .

'Now, my dear Sir, I beg leave in candour to add, that although you have certainly misstated the circumstances . . . I am still inclined to believe business may have driven the main points from your recollection; for I cannot think you capable of a wilful misrepresentation of facts although that misrepresentation alone appears to have produced all the mischief. . .'

Nicholson's reply on 10 October was to deny that he had ever received any such letters from D'Eyncourt or that he had ever been authorized by him to propose resignation; nor could any communication of his to D'Eyncourt 'be understood as a contumacious and insubordinate reply from you'.

A reconciliation of sorts between Nicholson and Oliver seems to have been achieved at a special Lodge meeting on 24 October but no details have survived.

The collection for the Testimonial continued throughout 1843, the year in which the Duke of Sussex died. Nearly three weeks after his death Oliver was the guest of the Provincial Grand Lodge of Northamptonshire and Huntingdonshire, as Crucefix had been the previous year just after the dismissal. Crucefix was also present. Oliver's health was proposed by the PGM, Lord Aboyne. The meeting was appropriately at Peterborough, though this was by coincidence since it had been changed to suit the Senior Warden. It was held under the auspices of St Peter's Lodge, the lodge in which the PGM had been initiated and the successor to that in which Oliver had first been received into the Craft.

In reply to his toast Oliver of course referred to his early association with the city, and 'standing in the presence of a venerable parent who gave me masonic birth'—which was only symbolically accurate but 'good theatre'—said he felt a degree of hesitation which almost precluded him from expressing his ideas. He made a short but powerful and emotional speech; the dejection of his spirits was shown by his closing remarks: 'I am grateful to the Lodge of St Peter, for having conferred on me the title of Master Mason; I flatter myself I have never disgraced the confidence reposed in me. I have ever considered Freemasonry as the best and kindest gift of heaven to man—subordinate to our holy religion. It is an opinion I have founded by mature deliberation that I have arrived at the time of life when I ought to retire from the active business of Masonry; and as I began my masonic career in St Peter's Lodge, it is highly probable that I shall close it in the same place by my appearance among you today. It is extremely probable that this is the last open lodge that I shall see in this world. May we all meet together in happiness in the world beyond the grave'. He then at once proposed the toast of the DPGM, Bro. Ewart, the man who had resurrected the lodge in 1836. But there was a little prospect that he would be allowed to retire from active freemasonry; Crucefix would surely see to that.

Charles Wellington Oliver, his third son, was initiated in the Witham Lodge in 1843 and his eldest son George had become a Provincial Grand Steward in 1841.

On 24 April 1844 the second Earl of Zetland was installed as Grand Master of the United Grand Lodge of England. As already indicated, he was not well-disposed to 'the historian of masonry'. The Testimonial presentation had at last been fixed for 9 May 1844. Crucefix may have hoped such an event could take place in London where freemasons from all over the world would have gathered for the Grand Master's Installation a fortnight before, but Oliver, never fond of travel, would surely feel Lincoln to be the proper venue. At any rate, Lincoln it was, at the City Arms Hotel again, and again Witham Lodge were the hosts. Oliver proposed 'the memory of our late Grand Master, HRH the Duke of Sussex' whom he praised as evincing 'a most laudable activity, united with learning, talent, and zeal, in the execution of his high office from which the institution derives the most essential benefit' and then continued:

'You, Brethren, who know me well, will be surprised to hear that I stand accused of offering a premeditated insult to this useful and illustrious individual. I am surprised at it myself. And the report has been propagated in quarters where its contradiction appears impracticable. I am sure that you—at least—will believe me, when I say, that the knowledge of this fact has given me extreme pain; because it is a charge so perfectly improbable—so perfectly at variance with my habits and disposition. You all know I am incapable of insulting any—even the very meanest of God's creatures; much less could I make up my mind to violate a solemn obligation by the most indirect slight upon one whom I have been bound, by the ties of Masonry, to honour and obey, and for whom I ever entertained the highest possible respect. I am glad to have this public opportunity of solemnly asserting that there is not the slightest foundation for the report . . . Freemasonry has taught me Prudence, it is true, but she has also taught me Brotherly Love, and Gratitude, and Truth. She has taught me that hypocrisy and deceit ought to be unknown among Masons; that sincerity and plain dealing ought to be their principal characteristics; while the hand and the heart ought to unite in promoting each others welfare, and rejoicing in each others prosperity . . . It is solely on account of Freemasonry being the vehicle of such invaluable lessons of morality, that I have ever held it up as the best and greatest of all human institutions'.

From this he passed on to the question of instruction in the principles of freemasonry. In the absence of printed rituals, the lectures formed the accepted mode of instruction in ceremonial as well as in the Craft's traditions and morality; but in fact when they had to learn the ritual many brethren seem to have had recourse to the better-informed of the 'exposés' which had appeared in the early part of the century, and to have neglected or shortened the lectures in order to have more time for refreshment. Oliver now related how, in his early years in the Craft, he had found the lectures in normal use to be short and common-place and continued: 'On inquiry, I found that that the lectures were, in reality, much more comprehensive; and that they embraced a more extensive view of the morals and science of the Order than was contained in the meagre portions which were periodically doled out to the Brethren in the county of Lincoln. In fact, I am afraid that the majority of the Brethren thought more of the convivialities than the science of Freemasonry. A very short section of the lecture was usually considered a sufficient sacrifice to Masonic labour, while refreshment was commenced with avidity, and often continued to a late and unseasonable hour . . . Still I could not divest myself of the idea that Freemasonry contained some further reference than what appeared upon the lectures, even in their most extended form. But of the nature of that reference I was perfectly ignorant. I communicated with my Masonic instructor on the subject, but he was equally at a loss. I consulted other eminent Masons, but without success. I remained in this state of doubt and indecision for several years'.

Not all his address was on this high plateau. He referred for instance to some of his work on ceremonial; he was by this time acquiring a reputation far beyond Lincolnshire, and even beyond these islands, as an expert on such matters; and he relates how, when he became DPGM he remodelled the procedure for receiving the PGM into Provincial Grand Lodge and for his departure from it 'which had been very loosely and inefficiently conducted before my time', and laid down new rules for public processions of freemasons 'so that regularity and decorum succeeded carelessness and disorder . . . Thus Masonry became respected; and, instead of continuing to be a by-word and reproach, it is now considered a title of distinction'.

Many of his arrangements had indeed been adopted in other Provinces. He also saw to it that the system of lectures was once again practised in lodges, but lamented that his dismissal had cut short the completion of his plans. All in all, it was an account of a very good stewardship and the reception it received showed that its truth was accepted. He acknowledged that his interest in masonic ceremonial and ritual had been 'a kind of monomania which I have never endeavoured to suppress', and paid tribute to the approbation and zeal with which the brethren of his Province had supported him; he ended by referring again to his intention to withdraw from the active arena.

The Testimonial of a silver cup and five groups of pieces was then presented, though as has already been noted the cup was retained by the committee for a less formal occasion at Scopwick. The inscription on the cup read:

To George Oliver,
Doctor in Divinity and
Fellow of the Society of Antiquaries, Edinburgh,
Vicar of Scopwick, Incumbent of Wolverhampton,
Lately in the County of Lincoln
of Freemasons
Deputy Grand Master,
Also of the Witham Lodge 374 a member and Chaplain,
A Philosopher & Archaeologian
Second to none,
In Historical subjects most learned,
An Orator whether in Church or in our Councils,
Both in Knowledge and in Eloquence most excellent,
Of the Mystic Union Founded in Brotherly love and Truth
For 40 years the most Erudite Expositor,
A Brother of Reverence unceasingly most worthy,
The Brethren throughout the whole surface of the Earth
Celebrating the Rites of Freemasonry
For the sake of Honour and love
Have given this
Offering

A.D.1844   A.L.5844

A toast to 'Mrs Oliver and Family' was drunk to which George Oliver junior replied and the proceedings were over. The five groups which comprised it were intended to be on the basis of one for each of the doctor's children since, when viewing the enormous gift presented to Crucefix (now in UGL Museum) he had remarked that it would be nice to have a testimonial which could eventually be divided among the family—something his friend had remembered. It had been a very happy evening and must have done much to restore Oliver's spirits. From then on we hear little of a withdrawal from active freemasonry and his reputation, already high, was to increase beyond measure.

Chapter Fourteen

THE SAGE OF MASONRY

(Scopwick, Wolverhampton, London)

Although the years 1840–1844 were full of incident and anxiety for him, it was then that Oliver resumed his writing. Since the publiction of *The History of Initiation* and editing Preston's *Illustrations of Masonry* in 1829 he had published no major work, but only a number of minor pamphlets on ecclesiastical, social and historical subjects. The ecclesiastical works included several addresses (his farewell to Grimsby, pastoral addresses for Wolverhampton, the *Candid Statement*, and his reply to his churchwardens there), as well as the *Letters* to his curate and the pamphlet on the apostolic institution, the missing letter to the Archbishop, and a number of sermons. The social works included the Wolverhampton *Hints* and *Scopwickiana*; while the historical publications were those on the Holy Trinity Guild at Sleaford and St Peter's Church, Wolverhampton, with local histories of Beverley, Clee, Ratcliffe and Castor (sic). His masonic writing had effectively been limited to a new edition of *Signs and Symbols*, and articles for FQR to which he remained a regular contributor, so keeping his name before the masonic public and establishing a considerable reputation with them as a historian in preparation for the time when he would be able to press further with the Grand Design. His parochial duties and difficulties in Wolverhampton, his preoccupation with the sorry state of the masonic Province of Lincolnshire and his work at Scopwick must have left him little leisure, but in 1840 he published the next book of the Design under the intimidating title of *The Theocratic Philosophy of Freemasonry*. Hamilton, Adams & Co., R. Spencer and B.S. Oliver are named on the title page and there is a long list of subscribers, mainly from the masonic Provinces of England and including Lord Aboyne and Crucefix.

The intention of the new book was, as he expressed it later, 'to elucidate the true philosophy of the Order, to show it as it is, and not as it ought to be . . . and to enquire whether it has any correspondence with practical religion'.[1] The Concise Oxford Dictionary defines 'theocracy' as 'government or State governed by God directly or through a sacerdotal class &c' and in the Preface to the book Oliver claimed that 'it is the THEOCRATIC PHILOSOPHY OF FREEMASONRY that commands our unqualified esteem, and seals in our hearts that love for the Institution which will produce an active religious faith and practice', showing once again that he regarded the Craft as intensifying a man's devotion to his religion. The 'lectures' into which the text is divided are arranged historically. Following his acceptance of the literal truth of the Bible, and belief that a system of morality to complement the religion ordained from the Creation had been laid down from the beginning of the world and had developed into freemasonry, he plunged straight into his thesis: 'Freemasonry, in its primitive and ineffable state, was an institution of pure, ethereal light. But light was Heaven (Col.1.12), the eternal seat of the divinity, and a place of absolute perfection and happiness. It follows therefore that Freemasonry is synonymous with eternity, undefiled charity or heaven'.[2] It was a logical development of the arguments that had proved controversial in *The Star in the East*. He traced the traditional growth of operative masonry and the way in which a 'spurious freemasonry' (that is, paganism) had developed in heathen countries while 'true freemasonry' was in all ages 'veiled in allegory and illustrated by symbols'. The historical summary lingered over the building of King Solomon's Temple and then turned to the form of the masonic lodge of his own day and its 'working' or 'labour'. His practical advice shows a typical mixture of abstract idealism with downright common sense, referring to the Master's duty 'to lead the brethren, by degrees and prudently, into all the depths of masonic research . . . Above all, the expert Master carefully avoids the frequent repetition of dry technicalities and monotonous forms of speech'[3] and he rightly claims that 'many a brother who has sustained a subordinate part on the great theatre of the world, has had his dormant powers called into operation in a masonic Lodge; and abilities have been elicited where they were not previously supposed to exist'[4]—something that is still true today.

In assessing these arguments it is necessary to recall once again the constraints on accepted Christian thought in the pre-Darwin era. Much that today seems ridiculous—as much of our thinking today may seem ridiculous in a hundred years—was taken as literal and God-given truth. Oliver was in fact arguing from settled principles which are quite contrary to what we feel we know to be true. If the world had been created in 4004 BC and guided from the Fall in accordance with a divine plan which had in due time been revealed in the Gospel of Christ, whose Second Coming would end it, then it was logical to assume that both religion and a code of morality had been given to mankind from the beginning. Oliver considered freemasonry, properly understood, to be a moral code comprising all that was best in philosophy and morality, the 'Wisdom' of Solomon, and considered that in his previous work he had shown that the man who conscientiously investigated and learned from freemasonry must inevitably be drawn to or confirmed in a belief in Christianity as the only true religion. The general acceptance of Darwin's logic today must mean that this argument cannot be sustained historically but that is no excuse for ejecting baby and bath-water together, and many freemasons will know of cases where men have been led to a deeper study and practice of their religion as a result of their association with the teachings of the Craft. Oliver was probably the first to analyse this potential and to seek to explain the relative juxtaposition between freemasonry and Christianity. This is what is behind his frequent references to the one as the humble hand-maiden of the other.

Today the Craft insists that freemasonry is a system of morality and is not linked to any religion in particular, though the legends and symbolism of the ritual are based on the Old Testament. To be accepted into the Craft a man must have a religion since, as we have already seen, before he can be initiated he must admit in

Open Lodge to a belief in a Supreme Being; and he will thereafter be expected to practise his religion. It is difficult for masons to understand why they are sometimes accused of worshipping some masonic god when it is a prerequisite to acceptance into the Craft that candidates must confess an existing religious belief, something which few other societies require. Obviously, admission into the Christian masonic orders is only available to those who have been accepted into the Craft and who openly profess the Christian faith; and though since the Union only the three degrees and the Royal Arch are acknowledged as 'pure antient masonry' a progression from the Old Testament based degrees to the Christian orders is often regarded, in the masonic Provinces particularly, as normal for Christian freemasons.

One of Oliver's works, which was only published eight years after his death but was written about 1840, is concerned with inconsistencies in the masonic ritual. This is *The Discrepancies of Freemasonry*. It records conversations which had taken place some years earlier between a group of freemasons, including at least one of distinction, Peter Gilkes, well-known and respected in the early years of the 19th century for his knowledge of masonic ritual and ceremonial. While the contents may help satisfy the curiosity of freemasons with an interest in older methods of working, its importance for his biographer lies mainly in the Introduction, which shows not only his attitude to critics but a realistic approach to ritual and ceremonial which others might well copy.

As might be expected, his view of those who would criticize freemasonry was tolerant; but that did not mean he would not be forthright in expressing it: 'I do not condemn my friend the agriculturalist, after he has failed thrice on as many good farms, for becoming a theorist and instructing other to do what he has signally proved himself incapable of effecting in his own person: because every practical farmer will judge for himself, and will scarcely be prevailed on to follow the directions of such a teacher, if they differ widely from the results of his own experience. I do not condemn the politician for fixing his eye with a steady and undeviating gaze on the sweets of office, because his enthusiasm cannot fail to rebound to the good of his country in some shape or other. Let all those, therefore, who consider freemasonry a trivial and frivolous pursuit, apply the same rule to me, and I ask no more'.[5]

Strange comparisons indeed.

Of the ritual he said: 'The system of freemasonry undoubtedly contains anomalies, difficulties and inaccuracies ... some of these antiquated senilities are absurd, and others are not only antagonistic to the truth, but absolutely irreconcilable with it',[6] and urged that it be updated to keep abreast of modern knowledge lest it 'degenerate in the scale of social institutions, and take its place beside the Oddfellows, Foresters and other societies ... Still the system goes on without improvement, and men submit to the propagation of error because some are indifferent, and others are not agreed about the correct mode of rectifying it'.[7] Those who consider Oliver as totally wedded to the masonic practices of the 18th century might well ponder whether in fact he was not well in advance of the 20th.

This danger of obsolescence was the reason he gave for preparing the book for publication, even though it was not in fact published in his lifetime, as it probably would have been had Spencer been consulted. Why it was withheld can only be surmised; he clearly felt deeply on the subject as the following passage shows: 'It would be a wise policy to revise the Lectures of Masonry more . . . I have taken the liberty of pointing out its anomalies, that the attention of the Craft may be fairly attracted to the subject, in the hope that all will unite in a simultaneous endeavour to place Freemasonry on such a foundation, that it may constitute the unmixed pride of its friends and defenders'.[8] But it was not to be, and many freemasons will feel that the Craft is the poorer for the failure to keep the lectures revised and relevant.

After his normal castigation of the revisers of the ritual at the time of the Union he returned to the failure to alter the lectures: 'The inevitable question again recurs—Shall we rectify or retain them? The old laws of Masonry are averse to any change. "Alter not the ancient Landmarks" . . . But what if the ancient Landmarks be erroneous or untenable? . . . Men will not always be satisfied with the same dull round, like a blind horse in a mill, confined in trammels which he can neither alter nor destroy'.[9]

The passionately-held devotion of so many freemasons to the ritual and their anger at any suggestion of revision led the Rulers of the Craft to shun any review for many years lest harmony be disturbed. The present Grand Master, HRH the Duke of Kent, has never been afraid to speak out to the Craft for its own good and now changes are indeed being considered, partly perhaps in reaction to criticism from theologians who may see some relief from their internecine quarrels in trying to read into the masonic ritual weird meanings it could never bear. It may be that in due time a new library of brief talks on masonic subjects by which brethren may be instructed in the tenets and history of their Craft will emerge: the suggestion has already been made and is practised in some other masonic jurisdictions.[10] Oliver saw the dangers 150 years ago; only now is he appearing as a prophet rather than a devotee of things past.

The discussions in the book are conditioned, as was everything else, by the fundamentalist beliefs of the Christians of the period; but when it breaks with that straightjacket it contains much of interest of which a few examples may be given. To a question 'In what part of the Pentateuch do you find the name of freemasonry mentioned?' the reply given is, 'A name! What's in a name? I am not speaking of words, but of things, not of names, but of principles. The term Freemasonry is comparatively modern, and its derivation doubtful. I speak of the institution as a science of LIGHT, founded on the practice of moral virtue, or if you prefer the name bestowed on it by our Grand Master Solomon, WISDOM, the same quality is implied. And this, I contend, is as old as creation; and its divine principles will continue to illuminate mankind with beams of celestial light when time shall be no more'.[11]

Oliver reports himself as answering another question, 'How can Freemasonry be considered Christian when it originated with the Jews at the building of the temple?' '. . . in the first place, the Jewish religion was the type and forerunner of the Christian dispensation; and in the next, because the Lectures of Masonry are so full of Christian references, that if any of them were withdrawn, the blood, muscles and vitality would be gone, and nothing would remain but a skeleton of dead, dry bones'.[12] This links with a tale he told in his speech at the Oliver Testimonial dinner, of a lodge which, about 1813–14, appointed a committee to revise the lectures by deleting from them every Christian reference; they began with great zeal, but found that they could not achieve their objective without 'reducing the noble system to a meagre skeleton, unpossessed of wisdom, strength, or beauty'. The attempt was abandoned and the episode made a deep impression on Oliver as showing the extent to which freemasonry could be 'made . . . of great actual value to the moral and religious institutions of the country'.[13] It was one of the factors which led him eventually to write the works of his Grand Design. It is also possible that such attempts were behind the reluctance, if not refusal, of the Duke of Sussex to contemplate the revision of the lectures; both Oliver and another masonic writer, George Claret, noted a reply by the Duke in Grand Lodge to a question by Peter Gilkes as to what was to be done about the lectures following the revision of the ritual; it was to the effect that the lectures would find their own place and no special action was required;[14] something which ensured their collapse and brought about the present situation where they are regarded as interesting survivals to be brought out and 'worked' when there is nothing else to do or when it is desirable to involve junior members in the work of the lodge.

In 1840 Oliver resumed work on the Grand Design. Preston's *Illustrations of Masonry* (for the new editions of which he had been responsible since 1829) contained a history of freemasonry on the traditional lines. So that the future works of the Grand Design might be based on an up-to-date account of the Order, he prepared a supplement, *The History of Freemasonry, 1829–1840*. At about the same time a new edition of *The Star in the East* was published 'long called for' but delayed 'owing to other and more pressing avocations'[15]—an understatement which covered his attempts to run the Province of Lincolnshire while coping with his problems in Wolverhampton and his activities connected with the Crucefix Testimonial. The reappearance of a book by a recognized masonic writer, which roundly and categorically asserted the essential Christianity of the Order in spite of the efforts of the Duke of Sussex, was hardly the best preparation for averting the wrath of the Grand Master over the Testimonial affair.

In 1843 a reprint of *The Antiquities of Freemasonry* appeared, as well as his edition of a masonic classic, *The Spirit of Masonry* by William Hutchinson, which it is doubtful if he would have felt worth producing without pressure from Richard Spencer, who had a good sense of what would sell and no doubt saw the commercial advantage of linking two of the famous names in freemasonry.

The relative pause in literary output over these years happened in part because he was hard at work on the most monumental book of the Grand Design, *The Historical Landmarks of Freemasonry*. He wrote of this period 'my thoughts, wishes and aspirations were all on masonry, and nothing but masonry . . . during the two long years it was in hand, from the Introduction to the Index; occupying a space of nearly fourteen hundred pages'.[16] It was in two volumes, published in 1845 and 1846 respectively, after appearing as usual in parts over a period. Perhaps with Lord Zetland's rebuff when approached for permission to dedicate a work to him in mind, Oliver wrote in the Introduction that it was an error of judgement to discountenance publications on the origins of freemasonry and its philosophy, and he claimed that 'the moral influence of Masonry would be much more powerful and efficient—its funds would be increased, and its charities better supported, if its sources of intelligence among the fraternity were augmented . . . For a century Freemasonry has been advancing gradually in public opinion, but its progress has been slow and uncertain'.[17] He then argues for a greater exposure to public scrutiny—clear evidence that he was now determined on his own course and would no longer be fettered by those whom he regarded as responsible for his dismissal. None of which explains why the second volume is dedicated (by permission) to 'the Earl of Zetland, G.M.'.

It is difficult to explain to readers who are not freemasons just what the word 'landmark' means in the Craft. It is more a mental concept than something capable of rigid definition. The analogy is of that which must not be moved ('Cursed be he who moveth his neighbour's landmark'[18]), and so it becomes a principle or object which is so essential to freemasonry that it must not be altered. In recent years analytically-minded brethren have striven to define it more closely and in doing so have reduced its meaning to nonsense, by claiming that a landmark must be something physical and have existed from time immemorial. At the risk of starting a vitriolic private correspondence, the writer would claim that most masonic landmarks are not physical and that the landmarks in fact do change from time to time. Every brother believes he knows an ancient landmark when he encounters it, and every brother's list would differ, though there would be many similarities; but while the argument about them can sometimes be used to stultify all development and change, the concept is of great use in providing a check on capricious and inadequately-considered alterations.

Oliver's view was that the landmarks 'constitute the foundation of our faith in the system'[19] (though he did admit that so-called landmarks were susceptible to change from time to time) and he listed many different categories.[20] But the new book was concerned with history, and what he regarded as historical landmarks were the incidents of biblical history from the Creation. This was something he regarded as basic and there could be no question of changing these landmarks. Throughout the work runs once more the conclusion he considered established by his earlier works, that freemasonry is consistent with the Christian religion rather than with any other. So, in the second of the 50 lectures into which it was divided we find 'It is a mistake, however, to suppose that Freemasonry is a system of religion. It is no such thing. It is but the handmaiden to religion, although it largely and effectively ilustrates one branch of it, which is *practice*'; and, in the preface to the second volume, 'Freemasonry . . . forms no part of the national religion, although it comprehends and teaches the genuine principles of Christianity'.[21]

He was nevertheless careful to avoid vouching as established truth all the traditions he recorded; he saw his task as being to report them faithfully 'while leaving their credibility to be determined by the reason and judgement of my readers'.[22]

It was an enormous labour, and it enhanced an already great reputation. Further, it established him as an authority on all aspects of the Order, because it was of the essence of freemasonry to venerate practices for which the approval of antiquity could be claimed, and the further back in antiquity, the better. He had become in the opinion of freemasons throughout the world, except the hierarchy of the English Craft, the sage and historian of masonry.

If it is reasonable to presume that Crucefix and others were now directing his attention to the Christian masonic orders and in particular to the Ancient and Accepted Rite, it is hardly surprising that he should finish this monumental work with a firm statement about the link between Christianity and freemasonry:

> 'The principal object I have had in view has been to deduce from the science of Freemasonry a series of proofs, in corroboration of the fact contained in the sacred writings, that the design of God . . . was to prepare the minds of men for the development of the great plan of human redemption by an atonement for sin, to be wrought out by the sacrifice of the word of God, the Messiah of the Jews, and the founder of the Christian scheme of salvation . . . It has therefore been shown that the Historical Landmarks consist of certain prominent facts recorded in the Jewish Scriptures . . . as typical of the Redeemer of man, and of him only.
>
> 'The conclusion is therefore obvious. If the lectures of Freemasonry refer only to events which preceded the advent of Christ . . . and if those events consist exclusively of admitted types of the Great Deliverer . . . it will clearly follow that the Order was originally instituted in accordance with the true principles of the Christian religion.
>
> 'I have been anxious to establish this great truth, because, if Freemasonry does not contain any direct reference to our holy religion, its morality, beautiful though it be, would not be sufficient to save it from the effects of public obloquy in this Christian country'.[23]

It is a strange irony that a Christian challenge to the Craft should be mounted in a country now far from Christian but in which every freemason who professes the Christian faith—and there are many, all finding no conflict between their religion and freemasonry and not a few of them priests and ministers—is strongly urged by the Craft to support and practise his professed religion.

Chapter Fifteen

THE CHRISTIAN FREEMASON

(Scopwick)

Oliver's dismissal as Deputy to D'Eyncourt was by no means the end of his masonic career, whatever his own immediate feelings or the intentions of the masonic hierarchy in England. It had been a great disservice to the Craft in Lincolnshire but it provided a focal point for those who were becoming restive under the autocratic rule of the aging Duke of Sussex. It also effectively freed Oliver from constraints of loyalty which may previously have inhibited his writing; he would now be free to pursue his goals guided by his own conscience and knowing that he had support even where his views differed from those of the Grand Master and his advisers. The authorities would have to be very careful before they took any action against him, for the storm that had been brewed by Crucefix and his helpers had brought Oliver before the Craft of the English Constitution, which was widely spread over the globe, as a deserving martyr. It had also attracted the powerful support of North American freemasons for whom the dismissal drama had all those elements of fight for freedom of expression, rebellion against autocracy (particularly as a son of an English monarch was involved), and tyrannical exercise of power against a subordinate which would appeal to those who had so recently and forcefully established their own independence.

It is improbable that Oliver himself saw the situation in such terms. He was secure in the support of his friends and did nothing to embarrass D'Eyncourt after the reconciliation at Spalding. While matters in the Province rapidly deteriorated and those friends were maintaining an aggressive attitude of armed peace, he attended to his priestly duties and his masonic writing; not that he did much for Wolverhampton—he had seen enough of that town, and the unpopularity which the trouble between him and Messrs Parke and Thorneycroft had aroused still lingered in some quarters. He metaphorically shook its dust from his feet and left it to the care of his curate; it was not in character and not a matter of which to be proud, but others had treated both his father and him in this way and he did not relish conflict. Crucefix on the other hand seemed to thrive on it, though, as has been seen, it is debatable whether he at once appreciated the possibilities opened up by the dismissal. The tone of his letters to Oliver at that time show only shock and concern. The Grand Master's attempt to disgrace him had now rebounded onto someone for whom he had a deep regard and who by nature was unfitted to fight back; his own health was declining but his energy for a cause would overcome that, and he still had a secure power-base in the FQR, even though he had technically ceased to be its editor.

The value of that power-base was apparent after the Spalding meeting. The delay in providing a copy of the resolution thanking Oliver for his work was probably due to the usual difficulty in getting replies from D'Eyncourt; but it aroused the suspicions of Crucefix and others. When it became known through a letter from Goddard dated 15 October that Coltman was redrafting the minutes, their concern increased. The resolution drafted by Adams had been passed without amendment except for Coltman's addition and a reservation about the legality of the proposed contribution to the Testimonial. Adams wished to publish it in the Boston paper, but Coltman refused to allow this as he and D'Eyncourt had agreed it was a private matter, having taken place in lodge and 'the PGM and myself have thought it better to conceal the whole from the uninitiated'; he added that he proposed to pay an early visit to the Boston lodge (which Adams, writing to Oliver on 23 October, said he took as a threat of surveillance). In the same letter Adams also 'regretted that the distance from our fishing ground at Boston being too great for an evening walk in this time of year' a proposed visit to Scopwick would have to be a 'purpose visit'. The distance is some 25 miles.

Though Adams abandoned the proposed Boston publication he maintained that as the resolution had been his, he could provide copies if he wished. So, borrowing a copy from Oliver without explaining why it was wanted, he forwarded it to Crucefix; it was then published in the FQR as well as in the *Sunday Times* and *Sun* newspapers in London, which meant it would be copied in provincial and overseas publications. Coltman, though angry with and suspicious of Adams, could prove nothing; he tried to blame Oliver for the publication but had to withdraw in a letter of 7 November. Crucefix, writing to Oliver on 8 November, described Coltman's letter as 'written in the style of a sophist that would entrap' and without actually admitting his own responsibility, wrote that he knew who had been responsible (though he did not want this generally known). He claimed that the attempted suppression was 'a violation of the compact sealed and delivered on the 29 September' (i.e. at the Spalding meeting) and threatened to meet Coltman at Spilsby and disclose the terms of that compact 'which even you scarcely know (*this is private*)'. On 23 October Coltman had sent Oliver a copy of the resolution as originally drafted— presumably this was the copy that found its way to Crucefix, but it was 7 November before he sent the certified copy. He and the PGM had clearly not appreciated that delay would breed doubts about their good faith, and the mistrust created between the Lodge of Harmony at Boston and Coltman was to last for the rest of D'Eyncourt's reign. The Rector of Stickney was not finding his introduction to high masonic office easy.

A different sort of attack was launched against Oliver in 1844 by George Claret, already mentioned, and who produced unauthorized masonic works, something he had started doing when his application for charitable relief from the Grand Lodge funds had been rejected. In a work entitled *Masonic Gleanings containing a Disquisition on the Antiquity, Extent, Comprehensiveness, Excellence and Utility of Freemasonry. With Moral and Sublime Elucidations for the Advancement of the Craft. With Anecdotes etc. etc.,* he referred to a comment on his work by Oliver in the *Historical Landmarks of Freemasonry*, then being published in parts (the first volume of the full work appeared the following year). Oliver had written 'What harm have the publications of Pritchard, Lambert, the author of Jachin and Boaz, professor Robinson, Finch, Carlisle or Claret, done to British Freemasonry?'[1] A zealous brother mason had paid a special visit on Claret to ask why his name should be mixed with such authors. Claret expressed his indignation at length:

'It is well known that all of them wrote against masonry, but where did Dr Oliver obtain his proof that I had ever done so, if he had taken the trouble to have enquired of his most intimate London friend and brother, he might have been satisfied that I never had, but having (as I suppose) jumped to that conclusion he thought proper to assert a falsehood. Again he says at page 13 note 28 "The detached pieces published by Claret are *I believe* merely a trade speculation, they are very expensive, and of very little value". This is certainly very kind of our clerical brother, but sounds *rather* unlike what ought to emanate from a minister of the Gospel towards one whom he has sworn "*that I will not injure him myself, or knowingly suffer it to be so done by others, if in my power to prevent it, but on the contrary will boldly repel* THE SLANDERER OF HIS GOOD NAME ETC". Well, gentle reader, how he can reconcile this I certainly don't know, but I shall leave him to his own reflections, and proceed to dissect the paragraph as regards the first "detached pieces". This is not true, there are no detached pieces in any of my works, they are all complete in themselves. 2ndly "I believe they are a trade speculation" to this I plead guilty. Having contributed largely towards the support of the order for a quarter of a century, and being at length obliged (from circumstances over which I had no control,) to apply to be assisted with *part* of what I had so contributed, I was refused, which refusal was the sole cause of the publication of my masonic works, as being denied the protection of those laws I had so long supported, I was compelled to do the best I could for myself. But the assertion "Trade speculation" comes with rather a bad grace from Dr Oliver. What are the whole of his masonic works but Trade speculations? I am of opinion that if he did not receive a benefit from them; he would soon cease their publication. Now for the 3rd part "and of very little value" in these few words, Dr Oliver has made a most egregious blunder, I must tell him (if he does not already know it) that my masonic works are (to the practical mason) worth the whole of his, Yes! and have done more good to the cause of masonry, having effected what his cannot do, however learned they may be, mine have enabled the zealous mason, to discharge the duties of his lodge properly, they have created a spirit of emulation in the order which never before existed, and instead of being of *little value* they have in many cases, proved to be most invaluable, having been the means of affording instruction, where otherwise, it could not be obtained, and caused many brethren to be very anxious to learn and practice [sic] *Genuine Modern Free-Masonry*. Let us therefore have no more gratuitous attacks. I never gave any offence either by word or deed to Dr Oliver, then why, I ask, did he give publicity to that which he knew to be untrue? I have been driven to the necessity of making this statement to the brethren having done all I could to avoid it. About a month since I wrote to Dr Oliver requesting him to make the *amende honorable*, and to let me know his intentions, informing him of the consequences of his not doing so, but he has not thought fit to make any reply, as such the blame rests with himself.

'Now for a word or two about Dr Oliver's Historical Landmarks, on the title page it is as follows "A Series of practical Lectures . . . Arranged on the system which has been enjoined by the Grand Lodge of England, as it was settled by the Lodge of Reconciliation, at the Union in 1813". This statement is not true, the Lodge of Reconciliation *did not* arrange, settle, or at all interfere with the lectures in any way . . . A question was put by the late Bro. Gilkes . . . "What in future is to be done respecting the lectures?" to which H.R.Highness replied, let the new ceremonies be combined with the old lectures: nothing more, as they will soon find their level . . . After this explanation perhaps the brethren will be at no great trouble to discover which of the two, viz. Dr Oliver or myself, is most entitled to that dignified epithet, he, in the plenitude of his wisdom has been pleased to bestow on me "CHARLATAN".'

It is hardly necessary to add that there is no record of a reply.

After his dismissal Oliver in general confined his masonic activities to his Lincolnshire lodges and his writing. The Grand Master and the masonic hierarchy might not approve of what he was doing but he was so well and so widely known, with (thanks to Crucefix) all the popular sympathy appropriate to a well-publicized martyr, that to take overt action against him might even have split the Craft since he was regarded as the champion of those who considered freemasonry to be essentially Christian and still, 30 years on, resented the alterations to the ritual. The publication of *Landmarks* enhanced his reputation still further and letters reached him from many parts of the globe, some of them couched in terms that would have turned the head of a lesser man; it is to his credit that he remained 'the recluse of Scopwick' as a reviewer in FQR called him.[2] Honours were showered on him from many quarters; but he refused to allow his name to be proposed as head of the Royal Arch in Lincolnshire ('Grand Superintendent'), saying he was too old and too infirm. This preoccupation with his health appears from time to time though reports that have survived suggest he was in excellent health for almost the whole of his long life.[3]

In 1845, while still in the throes of publishing *Landmarks* he brought out a small volume of sermons, *Jacob's Ladder; the ascent to Heaven plainly pointed out. In 18 practical addresses delivered in familiar language from the pulpit*. It was published by Spencer and the name of Beverley, living in Nottingham, appears on the title page as one of the distributors. The book is remarkable for two reasons: first, the difference in tone that has already been noted between the introductory addresses to his two congregations, in Wolverhampton and Scopwick; and second for the difference in style between its content and that of many of his other works. It bears out the statements in the 1840 article in FQR that his preaching was in a plain and simple style, quiet and persuasive; and the explicit advice he gives to those who might wish to use the addresses in the pulpit shows he was fully alive to the arts of presentation:

'These addresses would not be suitable to a rapid delivery. If the interrogatory sentences were not propounded slowly and distinctly, and accompanied by judicious pauses, to afford the hearers an opportunity of deliberating seriously on their propriety and importance, the effect would be entirely destroyed . . . I am not apprehensive that any fault will be found with the doctrine . . . Every thing necessary to salvation has been plainly stated. I have not indulged in any metaphysical subtleties, which are above the comprehension of unlearned men; because I conceive it to be the duty of a Christian minister to instruct the people in their obligations to God, their neighbour and themselves, in language which they may easily understand. St Paul observes, with great propriety and truth, that he had rather preach ten words that his hearers can understand, than ten thousand words in language that is above their comprehension. (1 Cor, xiv, 19.) Indeed, what benefit could they possibly derive from hearing his words, if they were unable to understand his meaning? They would derive none whatever; he might as well not preach at all.'[4]

There may perhaps be those who would feel diffident about quoting St Paul in this particular context.

The plan of the book has masonic overtones. In the Craft 'lectures' Jacob's ladder reaching from earth to heaven is described (following the teaching of some theologians) as symbolically resting on the Bible and being 'composed of three principal steps or rounds'. The sermons start with an Introductory Address about the ladder itself: 'The number of staves or rounds comprising this ladder, which constitutes the way to heaven, though they may justly be termed innumerable, as embracing every minute point of the faith and practice of a Christian, have been reduced by theologians to three principal ones; by some termed Repentance, Faith, and Obedience; and by others Faith, Hope, and Charity'. The second sermon is an 'Address on the Basis of the Ladder, The Holy Bible' based on the text 'Search the Scriptures; for in them ye think ye have eternal life (John.v.39)'. The three principal steps, Faith, Hope and Charity, are each covered in five intermediate steps or sermons.

The sermons themselves are written clearly and with a realist's eye to effect as in these passages:

1 'And now, my brethren, before I proceed further, I am desirous of asking you one simple question. At this moment, when all is silent around you; when you are seated in devout attention to the exposition of God's word; and feel conscious that you ought to act like good and faithful Christians— to foresake your sins, and make your peace with God—may I ask—how long will these impressions remain after you have left this holy place, and mix with the world again? This is a question you may easily resolve. And I appeal to your experience, whether the impression is not soon effaced by "the cares of the world and the deceitfulness of riches", leaving very slight

traces of its appearance? This is the effect of Satan's temptations, and requires a steady faith and a strong resolution to overcome it.'[5]

2 'But you are young and healthy; and therefore you are inclined to think that the solemn warning may be deferred to some more convenient part of your lives. Is it so? Let me try to destroy this fatal argument. You say you are in perfect health. How long shall you remain so? In the course of my ministerial experience, I have attended the dying-bed of many young persons, who, only a short time previous, were as healthy and strong as you are now, and thought as little of death and judgment. I have seen the pale cheek and the brow bedewed with perspiration. I have seen the lip quiver with agony, and the whole frame enfeebled by disease. And I have seen the remorse of conscience exhibited in all its terrors. Seriously contemplate such a subject, my brethren. Death is about to strike the trembling victim; and while he grieves to leave this beautiful world, in which his imagination had painted so much pleasure to come, he dreads to enter on another, for which he feels himself quite unprepared.'[6]

Unlike many preachers, however hard he struck at the sins and errors of his hearers, he ends each sermon on a note of hope; he never left them without solace.

The teaching was direct and simple; in the fifth step ('Trust in God') he says: 'Do you ask, what will Christianity do for us? It will make us happy, both in this world and the next, if we receive its precepts with humility, and sincerely obey its commands; trusting in God for our reward; and it will accelerate that happy period mentioned by the prophet, when "the knowledge of the Lord shall cover the earth, as the waters cover the sea" '.[7] It was uncompromising in its doctrine:

'In the earliest ages of the world, animal sacrifices to atone for sin were used by all nations . . . We learn from the text ['It is blood that maketh an atone-ment for the soul: Lev.17.11'], that in the Jewish religion, which was intended as an introduction to Christianity, sin was atoned for by the shedding of blood. An animal was slain in the name of the offender; and his blood, ceremonially offered, was accepted as the punishment of sin; and the sinner, having been sprinkled with the blood, was reputed clean.

'In Christianity a similar doctrine prevails. We do not, indeed, sacrifice animals, but our sins are pardoned by the blood of Christ . . . And St Paul assures us that they who do not believe the doctrine, or—which is the same thing—refuse to profit by this blood-shedding, will be exposed to the burning wrath of God. . .

'This, therefore, is the chief truth of the Christian religion, it is the groundwork of our faith, the foundation of our hope. It is not necessary to call on you to believe it. You cannot disbelieve it. You are followers of Christ—then the blood of Christ must be your chief dependence, if you hope for happiness in futurity.'[8]

In spite of the care for the oppressed and weak which was so strong a feature of his pastoral philosophy, he warned his younger hearers against the 'deceivers who miscall themselves Socialists', apparently because he considered their 'visionary schemes' allowed no room for a faith in God which relied on the merits of Christ's atonement. But these partisan matters apart, the sermons breathe sincerity; he preached a simple creed, but behind it is a breadth of reading and of experience, and above all compassion, which command attention even when they cannot compel agreement.

Another example is of interest in the particular context of this biography because the quotation it contains is from masonic ritual, though not acknowledged as such:

> 'But if you allow your impure thoughts to triumph over your good resol-utions, and to become prolific, bringing forth a series of evil deeds, you will no longer be in a condition to perform the duty of self-government "by such a prudent and well-regulated course of discipline, as may best conduce to the preservation of your corporeal and mental faculties in their fullest energy; thereby enabling you to exert the talents wherewith God has blessed you, as well to his glory, as to the welfare of your fellow-creatures". If once you allow the floodgates to be opened, it will scarcely be in your power to prevent the waters from overwhelming your soul. And even should your better dis-positions at length prevail, when you behold the wide and wasteless ruin which your imprudence has occasioned, and you should succeed in stemming the torrent, your repentance will be bitter, and your return to Christian habits and virtuous propensities will be over a rough and thorny path.'[9]

He ends in pastoral terms reminiscent of his farewell sermon at Grimsby: 'My brethren, I am extremely anxious that my flock should escape this punishment. I hope better things of you, and things which accompany salvation. I hope to present you for acceptance at the throne of judgment, purified from your sins; that I may be able to say to the Judge—Of those whom thou hast committed to my charge, have I lost none'.[10] Whether confronted by success at Scopwick or failure at Wolverhampton he was at all times conscious of his responsibility to God for those entrusted to his care.

Chapter Sixteen

CHALLENGES (1846)

(Wolverhampton, South Hykeham, Scopwick)

Since Oliver had left Wolverhampton in the care of Slade, the pressure there for reform of the church establishment had been growing. This was hardly surprising as ecclesiastical matters had become of public concern in the wake of political reform, and the Wolverhampton arrangements were clearly both inadequate and inappropriate. Hobart would certainly be the last Dean of Windsor and Wolverhampton, and though reform in his lifetime was unlikely, his death would signal change. A letter from Crucefix to Oliver on 22 May 1843 suggests that even in the Dean's lifetime concern was being shown by the Church of England hierarchy: 'I think it is not difficult to understand the *suggestion* of W. Cantuar. And from what I can gather from the papers you are made to *feel* all the effects of the venom that has been spouted against the Collegiate Church—the resources of which are I verily believe as mis-directed as any place of church emolument—others who enjoy the sinecure are I dare say exculpated by the mitred superior—the Incumbent alone must sustain the wrath of all—Could you renew the proposed treaty with *Slade*, who appears to be generally liked?—but in so doing I should consult the proctor as to the manner in which Slade *could give* securities—At any rate you must gain a little time'. In fact nothing did happen until 1846, when Hobart died.

On the masonic side, the new Supreme Council came into existence in 1846, and set about organizing the Ancient and Accepted Rite (including the Rose Croix) in accordance with the Constitutions of 1786. Crucefix was the senior member (*primus inter pares*) as Sovereign Grand Commander; Oliver held the second post as Lieutenant Grand Commander; Udall was Grand Treasurer-General. They had to tread carefully in establishing exclusive control of the Rose Croix and avoid upsetting the Knights Templar who had hitherto dominated it. Crucefix had been prominent in that Order and had acted as Director of Ceremonies in 1846 at the second Grand Conclave after the death of the Duke of Sussex, when a new Grand Master was installed. An olive branch was offered in an article in FQR which if not written by Crucefix would certainly have been approved by him, and the terms of which were hardly likely to appeal to the UGL:

'It is hardly necessary to remark that, in the exercise of these important functions, the Supreme Council do not intrench on the privileges of the Grand Conclave, which is constitutionally limited to the degree of Masonic Knights Templar. The jurisdiction of the Grand Inspectors General commences with the Sublime Grand Lodge, and ends with their own, including all the inter-mediate degrees.'[1]

In the same article some account is given of the disorganized state in which the neglect of the preceding years had left the Rose Croix, the reference to 'Haut Grades' being to the degrees controlled by the Ancient and Accepted Rite because it regarded itself as conferring higher degrees (up to 33rd) than the three and the Royal Arch over which the UGL and Supreme Grand Chapter respectively ruled:

'The Haut Grades in this country have hitherto had no rallying point—no governmental discipline; but this is not the worst part of the subject. To seek for diplomas without the attainment of knowledge was not considered unbecoming—to grant them without sufficient discrimination was not held to be infra dig. Consequently in these piping days of railroad speed and economy, it is not to be wondered at that the mania has extended to Masonry and that many a mason, scarcely fledged from the nest, has taken wing and returned home a full grown 33°. Not but that there are very honourable exceptions but we fear that they only prove the rule. It has long been a desirable point that English companions should be trained to find in their own country the means of attaining the highest possible qualifications. . .'[2]

The NMJ patent appointing Crucefix had been backdated to 26 October 1845, the date of his application for it and this is taken as the date of the foundation of the new Supreme Council (now known as The Supreme Council for England and Wales and its Districts and Chapters Overseas). It first met on 30 June 1846.

The usefulness of FQR as a power base was now demonstrated again. Publicity was easily achieved on a country-wide basis and interest led into the intended chan-nels. Without it, the establishment of order could have been difficult and prolonged, particularly in view of the official attitude of the UGL and the traditional position of the Knights Templar. It is clear that, even 30 years after the assault on the overtly Christian-based ritual of the 18th century, there were still many who would support a body which was established to control a Christian masonic order if only they could be assured of its regularity. Barely four years had elapsed since Oliver had become the centre of the dismissal controversy, and Crucefix, already well known and also qualified as a martyr, had been much before the masonic fraternity at that time. Both had been in the public eye in the intervening period and Oliver in particular had attracted much goodwill at home and overseas. When in 1845 he had accepted the offer of the high rank of Past Deputy Grand Master from the Grand Lodge of Massachusetts, Crucefix became a Past Grand Warden of that body. The patent granted to Oliver, dated 1 January 1846, is in the possession of the Dr Oliver Lodge, no. 3964, at Peterborough. A newspaper report said 'This compliment comes with greater force from the circumstance of its being the first occurrence of the sort on the part of the Grand Lodge referred to; and affords very conclusive evidence of the great and moral effects which these eminent and exalted brethren exercise, even in a distant hemisphere. Their names run parallel in masonic history, the one as the unrivalled expounder of doctrine and illustration, the other as the most accomplished proficient in discipline and practice'.[3]

In acknowledging the honour Oliver wrote 'It was with no common degree of satisfaction that I received your Diploma, because it conveys an assurance to my mind that my continued labours in the cause of our noble Science have had the good fortune to secure your approbation. The sole object I have had in view has been to place freemasonry in its legitimate rank as a genuine institution, and to extend the influence of religion among all ranks of society by means of a right understanding of its beneficial tendency. That I have partially succeeded is evidenced by the testimony of eminent masons in every quarter of the globe, and none has been more gratifying to my feelings, than the unequivocal expression of esteem with which I have been favoured by the Grand Lodge of Massachusetts'.[4]

Volume 2 of *The Historical Landmarks of Freemasonry* having been published in 1846, the way was clear for the preparation of the final work of the Grand Design; but other matters now claimed Oliver's attention. The death of Dean Hobart brought matters in Wolverhampton to a head, and Parliament stepped in to rearrange the ecclesiastical establishment of the Collegiate Church. Oliver was offered an exchange with the Rector of South Hykeham, a small and charming village south of Lincoln and reasonably close to Scopwick. The Rector, the Revd J. O. Dakeyne, M.A., was a freemason and had been prominent in arranging the Lincolnshire end of the Oliver Testimonial fund. He fared badly in the exchange, for having accepted the office of sacrist or perpetual curate in accordance with the provisions of the first part of the reforming Act (11 & 12 Vict. cap. 95), he found its later clauses abolished the office and he could not claim the fees appropriate to it; not the first time nor the last that the apparent bounty of Parliament has proved to be an illusion at the careful hands of the Treasury.

The exchange took place on 10 April 1847. Meanwhile, in 1846, while all this was going on, Oliver managed to write two pamphlets on the antiquities of Lincolnshire; *The existing remains of the Ancient Britons, within a small district lying between Lincoln and Sleaford*, published by Spencer in London and C. W. Oliver in High Street, Uppingham, and *History of the Religious Houses on the Banks of the River Witham*. Beverley, in Nottingham, now described as a bookseller at Long Row, Nottingham, was present about this time at a dinner given to his grandfather, the Rev. Samuel, now aged 90, by the Archdeacon, local clergy and his churchwardens which the old man drove into Nottingham to attend. The death of his wife in 1844 had not robbed him of his zest for life.

But the main factor which interrupted the Grand Design was Oliver's decision to answer charges against freemasonry which had originated in India and which have a strangely familiar ring. He thus later described them:

1. That a true Christian cannot, or ought not to join in masonry, because masons offer prayers to God without the mediation of a Redeemer.
2. That masonry inculcates the principles of brotherly love and charity to those peculiarly who have been initiated into the Order; whereas such acts, to be acceptable to God, should proceed from a love of him reconciled to mankind through the sacrifice of Christ; any other motive being not only not acceptable, but sinful.

3. That the mention of the Lord's name in the lodge is a contravention of the third commandment.

4. That the Protestant Church of England knows nothing of the Society of Freemasons, and therefore it is a desecration to suffer any section of that society to appear in the character of masons within the walls of its sacred edifices.'[5]

To combat these he wrote a series of articles in FQR and later published them as *An Apology for the Free and Accepted Masons* which he 'respectfully submitted to the consideration of those clergymen who doubt the propriety of allowing the use of their Churches for Masonic celebrations' and who as usual did not want to listen, let alone hear. Stating that 'the times in which we live are distinguished by a rigorous severity of profession, accompanied by a laxity of practice, both in spiritual and temporal matters, which, I believe is without precedent' he went on to point out that from time to time the same objections appear, are refuted, and re-occur; but now a new set had relieved the monotony, plausible but not founded on truth. 'They . . . allude to a presumption that the character of Freemasonry is anti-Christian . . . Such charges display a profound ignorance of the plan on which freemasonry has been framed'.

The arguments he advanced will be obvious from what has already been noted about his views on freemasonry as typifying a system of morality, 'lux', or 'wisdom', established from the Creation; and he does not forget to point out the debt the Church owes to the operative freemasons of the Middle Ages with whom speculative freemasonry traditionally claims a tenuous connection. What is new is that he now regards the Craft as the first stage and the 33rd degree of the Ancient and Accepted Rite as the ultimate or *ne plus ultra*, an attitude still very prevalent today, particularly in the Provinces, though not the official policy of the Craft. Even of the Craft he declares 'the whole system is essentially, though not professedly Christian', a proposition which he would regard his earlier works as having proved.

While post-Darwinians are unlikely to accept arguments that rest on the sanctity of the books of the Pentateuch as true history, there is still point in the argument. The Christian Church's Sacred Book is the Bible, comprising both the Old and New Testaments; and the view that the old covenant of God with His people, as disclosed in the former, no longer has any validity, though it might have been accepted in Oliver's day, is likely to be challenged today when a greater understanding of Judaism and other religions has at last permeated the Christian conscience. The legends on which the Craft and the Royal Arch rely for their allegorical teachings are founded on the events of the Old Testament; in the Jewish Scriptures a Messiah is promised, and the central feature of the Christian religion is that Jesus is that Messiah. He was a Jew and in His life on earth spent much time interpreting the Scriptures, correcting glosses which had been foisted onto the earlier writings. Freemasons may perhaps be forgiven for asking whether their Christian critics do not accept the Old Testament and its messianic prophecies as part of the Christian Bible.

Oliver's final summing up is still valid today: the criticisms 'originate in a mistaken idea of the nature and design of Freemasonry. It is assumed to be a system of religion . . . The premises, therefore, being unsound, the conclusions will necessarily be false'[6] and includes a broadside—'It is freely conceded that Freemasonry is not Christianity. Neither is the Church of England'.[7]

Chapter Seventeen

AN INTERIM PERIOD

(Scopwick)

Research for *The Landmarks of Freemasonry* had led Oliver to explore many by-ways, and it seems as though he was unable to proceed with the final stage of the Grand Design until he had first purged his memory of the knowledge so acquired. He wrote two short publications in the form of letters to Crucefix; one dealt with the history of the quarrel between the two Grand Lodges and the other with the insignia of the Royal Arch. The latter formed the basis for a much fuller exploration of that Order and its history at a later date. It was a subject which was to continue to attract him for many years and a revised and consolidated version in book form was probably the last work he sent to the printers, and one which is of importance as showing the final development of his views on the compatibility of freemasonry and religion. The letters seem almost like interim reports by comparison.

The effect of recent events is vividly shown by the difference which appeared about this time in the description of the author on the title pages of his books. Hitherto this had been limited to Deputy (or Past Deputy) Provincial Grand Master for Lincolnshire, usually with a reference to his Church preferments at Scopwick or Wolverhampton and his (somewhat mysterious) appointment as domestic chaplain to Lord Kensington. After his dismissal and his transfer from Wolverhampton to South Hykeham, he is usually described by reference to his office in the Supreme Council and as Past Deputy Grand Master of Massachusetts, and 'honorary member of numerous lodges', sometimes also as Past DPGM for Lincolnshire (modern usage would be 'of Lincolnshire').

In January 1848 his next work in connection with, though not really a part of, the Grand Design, *A Mirror for the Johannite Masons*, appeared. This also was in letter form and from the dating of the letters they were written at Scopwick between November 1847 and January 1848. At the start is a quotation from Sir Walter Scott, whose 'inimitable novels' Oliver admired (as he felt everyone must in her Majesty's dominions who possessed the slightest pretensions to taste[1]): 'From the time of Chaucer to that of Byron, the most popular authors have been the most prolific'; Oliver offers no comment, though in the first letter he writes 'it appears to me that I shall display my gratitude [i.e. to his brother masons for their approval of his efforts] more effectually by continued efforts to promote their amusement and information than by retiring from the field ... There is something within which urges me forward with irresistible force'. He refers also to the quips of friends at his expense, saying 'they frequently asked me how my combat with the windmills was likely to terminate'.[2]

The rather ponderous title was a reference to the 18th century masonic pre-occupation with the two Saints John, the Baptist and the Evangelist, and in the letter dedicating the work to 'the Right Hon. the Earl of Aboyne, Prov. Grand Master of Masons for Northampton and Huntingdon etc etc etc', Oliver says it is 'intended to explain a doctrine which in those days [i.e. when he became a freemason] had never been questioned; and all Masonic Lodges were opened and closed in the name of God and Holy St John', and the object of the book was to 'determine how far the two St Johns are, or ought to be, legitimately connected with the order'.[3] But in fact he also discusses in the earlier letters matters connected with the reform of the ritual and the removal of discrepancies, a theme well ventilated in *The Discrepancies of Freemasonry*. He affirms his own view that the removal of all mention of either St John is of doubtful authority, being 'the unjustifiable alteration of a landmark',[4] and blames it primarily on the Reverend Dr Hemming, a member of the committee which dechristianized the ritual. He then makes it clear that so far as he is concerned the foundation on which to build is always the system of practice as it was in 1717 when the first Grand Lodge was founded. Inevitably he pleads that the observance by freemasons of the feasts of the two saints should be restored, but without 'expensive banquets or public parades'.[5] Inevitably also the plea would fail, as, being a visionary who always retained a firm contact with the ground, he clearly realized it was likely to do: 'I am not one of those bold and unquiet spirits, who would dictate to the fraternity what they are to believe, and what they are to reject ... I regard Free-masonry as a grand machine, in the hands of Omnipotence, for promoting the bless-ings of peace, harmony and brotherly love amongst all orders and descriptions of men ... We are all fallible; nor will I go so far as to assert that Masonry is perfect';[6] and he arrives at the conclusion that it is 'an institution calculated for the observance of every nation and people in all ages of the world, however much they may be dis-tinguished by a dissimilarity of manner, customs, education, or climate'.[7]

This book was probably written because of a compelling sense of need rather than to further the argument and, coming at a time when the resurgence of the Christian orders was in clear prospect, may well owe more to Oliver's growing preoccupation with the Ancient and Accepted Rite than to any hope of reforming the Craft. He ends it with an unaccustomed diffidence: 'I am no system maker, my Lord, but am anxious for the discovery of the truth. If my arguments be inconclusive, or my authorities untenable, let the inference be rejected ... I shall not be disappointed ... However they may decide, my object is attained'.

Another project had also occurred to him, the republication, with notes, of articles and sermons by masonic writers of the 18th century. Crucefix was consulted and approved; Spencer was agreeable and set about setting the original works for Oliver.[8] The result was *The Golden Remains of Early Masonic Authors*, published in five volumes over the period 1847 to 1850, which also covers the time when he was writing the final and key work of the Grand Design, *The Symbol of Glory*. In his late sixties, his output was prodigious.

Each of the five volumes of the *Remains* deals with a particular subject:

1. Masonic Institutes.
2. Masonic Principles.
3. Masonic Persecutions.
4. Masonic Doctrines.
5. Masonic Morality.

The dedication this time was not directed to any individual but 'To the Fraternity of Free and Accepted Masons in every part of the globe'; Oliver was described as:

'the Rev G. Oliver, D.D., Author of *The Historical Landmarks*, *The History of Initiation*, *Antiquities of Freemasonry*, *Star in the East*, etc etc etc, Past DGM of the Grand Lodge of Massachusetts, US and Past DPGM for Lincolnshire. Hon. member of the Bank of England Lodge, London; the Shakespeare Lodge, Warwick; the First Lodge of Light, Birmingham; the St Peter's Lodge, Wolverhampton; the Witham Lodge, Lincoln; the St Peter's Lodge, Peterborough; Light of the North Lodge, Londonderry; Royal Standard Lodge, Kidderminster; Lodge Rising Star of Western India, Bombay; St George's Lodge, Montreal, etc etc etc'.

In the preface Oliver wrote that 'the weapons used by our ancient Brethren have been cleared from the rust, and newly polished; and it is hoped that their brilliancy has been restored, without any deterioration of their primitive virtues'.[9] The whole had a pronounced Christian bias; many of the works reprinted were sermons; but their content is matter for a history of freemasony or of masonic literature, and for present purposes it is Oliver's copious notes that are of importance, together with his introductions and prefaces. In the first volume he proposed to bring under notice, as a 'standard of reference from which there can be no appeal', great names of the past—Anderson, Martin Clare, Desaguliers, Dunckerley. The inclusion of Clare is interesting as Anderson was in the early 18th century minister of a Presbyterian Chapel in Swallow Street, Piccadilly and the author of the first book of 'Constitutions' adopted by the Craft, a work which can almost claim to have invented masonic history in every sense; Desaguliers was a professor of Experimental Philosophy at Oxford, an admirer of Issac Newton, and the third Grand Master of the Premier Grand Lodge; and Dunckerley, usually believed to have been a natural son of George II when Prince of Wales, was one of the greatest characters of 18th century freemasonry in England, particularly in regard to the Royal Arch; while of Clare little is known, though Oliver in several places refers to him with approval as having revised the neglected lectures.

In one Introductory Essay Oliver refers to early campaigns against freemasonry saying that the Craft nevertheless 'kept on the noiseless tenor of its way, uninjured by occasional volleys of small shot from the pop-guns of its feeble opponents; and not affected even by the heavy ordnance of more potential adversaries' and mentions almost with glee the public burning of a pamphlet (not to be confused with one of his own bearing an identical name) *An Apology for the Free and Accepted Masons* which 'attained, as it well deserved, such an extensive circulation, both in England and in the continent, as alarmed the Holy See, and produced a papal decree, by which it was censured, condemned, prohibited and ordered to be burnt publicly by the minister of justice in the street of St Mary supra Minervam',[10] a fate which today would have ensured its rapid rise to the status of a best-seller.

Many of the notes stress the moral, beneficial and charitable aspects of freemasonry and illustrate Oliver's constant claim that its tenets must be made clear to the public. He emphasizes too the reasons why discussion of religion and politics is forbidden in lodge, as in this note: 'The very foundation principle of Masonry is the exclusion of religion and politics; because the lodges ought to admit men of all religious and political opinions. To exclude them would be a species of intolerance as bad as that which promoted the papal persecutions of the Order'.[11] The third volume, dealing with persecutions, is that which provokes the most direct discussion of the relationship between freemasonry and religion and in one note he points out that although the Craft has been persecuted by bigotry in all ages of its existence, it has never itself been the persecutor 'which speaks volumes in favour of the purity of its principles, and the correctness of its doctrines and disciplines'.[12]

It is true that Oliver was greatly prejudiced against Roman Catholicism, as were many Englishmen of the early 19th century; and he reacted to that Church's prejudices against freemasonry with a violence of rhetoric and spleen that showed less than his usual charity, yielding (though not to the extent that many others have thought it necessary to go in defence of a particular belief) to the hurtful pride that has disgraced much of the history of Christianity, as it has that of other religions, and which there are at last some grounds for hope that love, grace and a sense of humility may yet overcome. Now, just as when, some years later, he defended the Craft against a Papal Allocution, he indulged in vituperative language that did not become him:

> ' . . . whence then arises such bitter hostility, and why does popery dread the progress of freemasonry? It is because the two systems contain antagonistic principles. The pure doctrine of freemasonry—its principles of universal beneficence—its charity and brotherly love, and the truly Christian duties which its practice inculcates, are utterly at variance with that system of superstition and bigotry which, under the denomination of Catholicism, seeks to perpetuate ignorance and error, fetter the conscience, and enslave the mind. Protestantism cherishes and promotes Freemasonry—popery would persecute and suppress it'.[13]

That final sentence is of interest as showing how attitudes have changed in recent years. Christianity and freemasonry have not altered; yet the Church of England seems prepared to label archbishops, bishops and clergy as heretics at the least because they were freemasons and perhaps wishes to forget that 'monarchs themselves have been promoters of the art, have not thought it derogatory to their dignity to exchange the sceptre for the trowel, have patronized our mysteries and joined in our assemblies',[14] some of those monarchs having been also Heads of the Church of England. Strange.

He is on better ground when he confines himself to the defence and does not confuse the issue by the bitterness of inter-church quarrels:

'Is Freemasonry unconnected with Christ? Does it reject the Lord Jesus, as some would intimate? I deny it firmly, zealously, truly . . . [The Old Testament is] useful to the proper understanding of His infinite grace and man's great salvation. The science of Masonry stands in the same relation to Christianity.'[15]

In the Preliminary Remarks which he prefaced to the fourth volume ('Masonic Doctrine') he made some very perceptive statements about the appeal of freemasonry to possible candidates, some of which are still valid today:

'They first perceive its rank and estimation in the eye of the world; they observe that it contains a brilliant reputation; and curiosity induces them to enter a lodge, that they may ascertain the process by which this reputation has been attained. The emblems of the craft attract the candidate's attention, as the stars of heaven invite the admiration of the beholder. He contemplates their form—he enquires their meaning, symbolical and moral—and having ascertained this, he seeks no farther; thus losing the true beauty of the application, and remaining ignorant of the manner in which the sublime lessons which they embody operate to promote the influence of Freemasonry, and the benefit of the fraternity at large. Like a boy blowing bubbles from a tobacco-pipe, and pleased with the beauty of the colours which they display as they rise gradually into the air, but totally ignorant of the science they display, and of the recondite problem which he is unconsciously working out. Yet these symbols frequently embody the very essence, not only of freemasonry, but also of the worship of the Deity. . .

'Such superficial Masons reflect very little credit on the institution, whatever their rank in life may be; for it is the internal, and not the external condition of a man that Masonry regards. Our late Grand Master the Duke of Sussex pursued a different course. He tells us himself, "When I first determined to link myself with this noble institution, it was a matter of very serious consideration with me; and I can assure the brethren that it was at a period when, at least, I had the power of well considering the matter, for it was not in the boyish days of my youth, but at the more mature age of twenty-five or twenty-six years. I did not take it up as a light or trivial matter, but as a grave and serious concern of my life. I worked my way diligently, passing through all the different offices of Junior and Senior Warden, Master of a Lodge, then Deputy Grand Master, until I finally closed it by the proud station which I have now the honour to hold. Therefore, having studied it, having reflected upon it, I know the value of the institution; and I may venture to say, that in all my transactions through life, the rules and principles laid down and prescribed by our Order, have been, to the best of my faculties, strictly followed. And if I have been of any use to society at large, it must be attributed, in a great degree, to the impetus derived from Masonry".

'And this is the course which every brother should pursue from the moment of his initiation, otherwise his masonry will be useless to himself, and of no value to those whom his example ought to influence. It is but too true, however, that there are many who know little more about the real nature of the institution than the cowans themselves; and this is not a complaint that applies exclusively to the present period, for it has characterized all time. Nor does the masonic society stand alone in having incurious and careless members; the charge applies equally to all other public bodies of men; and even Christianity—blessed Christianity—all powerful to the salvation of the Christian soul—is inundated with apathetic believers (if believers they be, notwithstanding their baptism) who make shipwreck of their faith, and live as though they had no responsibility. nor any souls to save . . .

'Added to the credit of being a member of such an institution, some superficial Masons attend the lodge for the sake of its refreshments, to which they are inordinately attached; when in fact refreshment is only intended as a subordinate item in the practice of masonry. I am quite ready to admit that the hour of refreshment is very attractive, which is probably the reason why so many people prefer it to the graver business of the lodge. It has been said that man is not by nature a working animal; and the proposition is illustrated by the disinclination of those who have fallen desperately in love with masonic refreshment, to participate freely in its labours. For such brethren as these, a certain portion of masonic knowledge, as a test to secure their admission to the lodge in all its degrees, becomes indispensable. . .

' . . . The entire system of Masonry is contained in the Holy Scriptures. The Old Testament presents us with its history and legend, its types and its symbols; and the New Testament with its morality, and the explanation of those allegorical references which were a sealed Book until the appearance of the Messiah upon earth, and the revelation of his gospel.'[16]

Oliver, now in his mid-sixties, was probably at the peak of his abilities. He had been through a great deal in the ten years between his presentation to Wolverhampton in 1834 and the Testimonial banquet in Lincoln; to some degree his experiences had caused him to withdraw into the background as 'the recluse of Scopwick'[17] and only come before the public outside his parishes as an author. His Christian faith was as firm and fundamentalist as ever, but his attitude to freemasonry seems, not unnaturally, to have changed. He now had no reason to support the Grand Lodge in ignoring the Christian degrees, and in particular the Rose Croix; and Crucefix had seen to it that he had every reason to support them. It would suit his own beliefs to feel that masonic progression led naturally from the Old Testament world of the Craft to the Christianity of the self-styled 'Higher Degrees'. Further, the progress of the Grand Design was drawing him nearer all the time to his final argument on the essentially Christian nature of freemasonry; his certainty on that subject had by now become absolute and so free from doubt that he was, with rare exceptions, able to take a balanced view of the relationship between freemasonry and Christianity. The notes to *Golden Remains* show how much the subject was occupying his mind as the final plans for *The Symbol of Glory* took shape, though always subject to the caution he gives in another note that 'with religion, whose sublime doctrines it cannot increase, whose noble precepts it cannot improve, and whose sanctions it dare not judge, Masonry does not interfere'.[18]

The notes to *Golden Remains* also shed light on his thoughts about other, more mundane, matters. Two of them deal with Christmas: 'I am a friend to old customs, and would have Christmas kept as it used to be in the most social times of Merrie England, because I do not think that this country has gained anything by that prudish and sanctified demeanour which would exclude all rational amusements from the practice of the people';[19] and 'True Christmas mirth is of a very social nature. It rivets love, and cements the sweets of acquaintanceship. For instance, the Christmas dinner is a gathering together of generations—an assembling of age, manhood, youth and infancy. Contrast this with the dreary picture of a Christmas dinner under the stern prescription of the Puritans'[20] and quotes Pepys' description of the Christmas he and his wife endured in 1668.

One of the lectures in the second volume attempts to explain why the order is exclusively male, and as Oliver did not approve the rather chauvinist attitude of the original author, his notes are pointed: 'Some men are equally as unqualified to keep a secret, as the women are here represented to be'; 'females are possessed of as much stability and moral courage as men'; 'the mind of the female is frequently more refined than that of the rougher sex'; 'nothing is so worthy of being loved and honoured as a good wife'.[21]

By 1848 he was working simultaneously on four major masonic works; *The Symbol of Glory* was being prepared; the *Mirror* was being finished; volume four of the *Remains* was in hand, as was an entirely new enterprise *The Book of the Lodge*, an account of the symbolism of the Lodge Room, the work of the officers and much of the ritual. It was produced because of the large number of requests he was receiving for guidance on ritual and ceremonial matters in the Craft, subjects on which he had attained a reputation that spread far beyond the boundaries of England. It is a fascinating book, and though parts are now dated or outmoded, there is much in it that is still both relevant and useful. It is probably his best-known work and there were to be two subsequent editions each considerably enlarged; the third edition (1864), the last published in his lifetime, has recently been reprinted (Aquarian Press, 1986). With the later editions he included *A Century of Aphorisms*, a hundred guides on conduct for the freemason.[22] Though called aphorisms some were rather too long to deserve the title and others would today seem too much like platitudes. But there is still good sense in many and one (number LXIX) has already been quoted in connection with the dissolution of Apollo Lodge.

In spite of the prohibition on discussion of religion and politics in lodge, the third aphorism was emphatically Christian: 'As you are a Christian Mason, you must on all occasions study to perform the duties of Christian morality, which are comprehended under the triple category of God, your neighbour, and yourself'. Even though the vast majority of English freemasons would be Christians, and even though the Bible must lie open on the pedestal all the time that the lodge is open, this is somewhat strange as a general statement from one who elsewhere, discussing the presence of Jews in lodge said 'I cannot throw odium or even doubt on the cross of Christ; nor can I allow any contempt to be cast on that sacred atonement by which I trust to inherit the kingdom of heaven, either by my silence or my connivance. I will admit my Hebrew brother into a mason's lodge . . . but as he will not abandon his faith at my command—neither will I'.[23]

An aphorism which deserves the name, being short and pointed, is number LXXXIII: 'A young Mason should never pretend to a knowledge which can only be gained by experience. The higher the ape climbs, the more effectually he discloses his posterior deficiencies'. Two others worthy of note are number LXXI, 'He is a wise Brother who knows how to conclude a speech when he has said all that is pertinent to the subject', and number VIII, 'An incompetent person in the Chair of a Lodge is like a hawk on the wing, from which all the inferior birds hasten to escape, and leave him sole tenant of the sky. In the same manner such a Master will cause the Lodge to be deserted by its best members, and be left alone in his glory'.

Given the ingrained reticence of freemasons about their ritual, it is at first surprising to find an ardent supporter of the Craft speaking as openly about its ceremonies, ritual and equipment as Oliver does in this book. It has already been pointed out that when he wrote there were no printed rituals officially countenanced, much less sanctioned; and many members must have relied either on unofficial exposés, of which several were used despite their inaccuracies (about which senior brethren would be only too willing to correct their juniors); or on the writings of brethren like Finch or Claret who plied a trade in such things. Oliver was certainly prepared to go further than many of his contemporaries in writing about the Craft and though he was reticent about some parts of the ritual and ceremonial (particularly in regard to the third degree and the Installation of the Master), he was too forthcoming for the liking of some—including, as we have seen, Lord Zetland. He seems to have felt that uniformity and regularity would suffer unless someone recognized as an authority by the brethren, even if not by the masonic hierarchy, was prepared to offer guidance to them; and although some of his admonitions were deeply embedded in the traditions of the 18th century, in general the experiment worked. Each successive edition was extensively revised and not, as fresh editions of his works sometimes were, a mere reprint. It is clear that the early success of the book led him to disclose ever-increasing detail so that even today a freemason reading the third edition may find himself surprised at the extent of that disclosure.

In the 'Address to the Fraternity' which began the work, Oliver described himself as a champion for the purity of masonic forms and ceremonies and went on to rejoice that in his lifetime he had roused freemasons to feel that the dignity of the movement required some exertion on their part. He referred to the receipt of many enquiries 'respecting the proper arrangement of Masonic ceremonials' which had suggested to him that general advice on such matters would be 'hailed as a boon by the Fraternity at large' who would 'gladly adopt a uniformity of practice on points where they have hitherto been at a loss to determine whether ceremonies of constant recurrence are, or are not, in accordance with ancient usage'.

The first edition must have provoked even more queries, for the preface to the second starts 'In exemplifying the science of Freemasonry, an author is bound in fetters from which the professors of other arts and sciences are free' and laments that 'the fraternity are apt to expect more information than can consistently be imparted'. The somewhat self-satisfied tone of this preface mirrors the author's pride in his achievement and there is no suggestion that some may have felt too much had been revealed. The dedication of the second edition to his son Charles has already been noted.

The preface to the third edition went further; it contained an implied criticism of the official view of such disclosures. Earlier editions had been republished in the United States among other places and had clearly been of use 'to relieve the embarrassments which must necessarily be felt in the absence of an authoritative guide'; Oliver comments that 'this desirable information has not been furnished by the authorities', a statement which was not likely to help heal the breach that had opened up between him and those authorities. He adds that as in view of his age this was likely to be the last edition he would supervise, he was anxious that it should be as perfect as possible. It is interesting to note that there are still lodges which pride themselves on working the ceremonies in accordance with the methods he prescribed.

The final work of that busy year was the climax of the Grand Design, *The Symbol of Glory*.

Chapter Eighteen

THE GRAND DESIGN (1850)

(Scopwick)

George Oliver's father, Samuel, died on 9 August 1847, aged 92, at the house of another son, the Reverend Samuel Pierpont Oliver whose benefice of Calverton adjoined Lambley. He was buried in Lambley Church where his wife had been laid three years before. The Latin inscription on the tombstone translates into familiar words, 'We are not worthy so much as to gather the crumbs under Thy Table'. Three generations of the family attended the funeral.

His will is dated 28 June 1847. It recites that he was 'aged and infirm but sound in mind thanks be to God for it and all his mercies' and directs that his burial be 'with as little ceremony as possible' in accordance with directions in a 'Loose paper in the first volume of Mants Bible'.

The legacies began with £20 to a grandson, Samuel Oliver Crosby, a student at Codrington College, Barbados; this was stated to be 'residue of a certain sum which I agreed to allow him by payments every half year'. George Oliver, his eldest son, was given his portable writing desk, Mants Family Bible and Prayer Book, 'the whole of my *Illustrated London News*', 12 volumes of Shakespere [sic], six volumes of Pope, five volumes of the *Anti-Jacobin Review*, three volumes of the *Christian Remembrancer* and the selection of ten other books. To another son, John, went 'my half pint Silver Drinking Mug', clothes, five volumes of Family Sermons, four volumes of *Saturday Magazine*, *The History of Beverley* (presumably that written by George) and a dozen silver teaspoons as well as two promissory notes for a total of £120, to be treated as a legacy of that amount. His son Samuel was given a silver tea service, a pair of silver table spoons, 'my Gown and Bands', the selection of 12 books 'with my unbound Typographical Sermons and Pamphlets of every description'. Two daughters are mentioned, Susannah Harris and Ann Fenton who each got some silver and shared the 'Linen, Calico and Muslin' except for two pairs of sheets which, with 'the Furniture in her own Room' and castors and silver butter knife were given to a granddaughter, Elizabeth Harris; she had presumably kept house for him after Betsy died and is probably the 'Betty Harris' referred to in the letter his parents wrote to George at the time of the dismissal drama. Minor legacies went to another grandson, Henry Harris, a son-in-law, Thomas Crosby and a daughter-in-law Charlotte Oliver. His servants received the balance of a full year's wage each.

The residue was divided into fifths, two parts going to George and one each to Susannah, Ann and Samuel; John was not included; the promissory notes suggest a tendency to anticipate his inheritance and their surrender must have been considered an adequate contribution to his welfare. John was however named as an executor as well as George and Samuel.

It will be apparent that of the nine children born to Samuel and Betsy, three sons, George, John and Samuel, and two daughters, Susannah Harris and Ann Fenton, were living in June 1847 when the will was executed; while another daughter had lived long enough to marry Thomas Crosby and have a child, Samuel Oliver Crosby. Assuming Charlotte to be the wife of John, there would be three who had died young, one having already been noted in connection with his father's astrological experiments.

The death was reported in FQR.[1] The lengthy notice referred to his birth as being 'according to his own account' in 1756 but suggested, without stating any authority that it might have been three or four years earlier; as he was baptized on 5 September 1756 in the church of St Peter, Mansfield, the supposition is unlikely.

In the following year, 1848, D'Eyncourt at last resigned as PGM for Lincolnshire. The state of freemasonry in the Province had deteriorated again and Coltman had not been able, or else had been unwilling, to prevent the decay. One can feel sorry for him. He had been appointed when feeling over George Oliver's dismissal had been high and he had to encounter resentment and bitterness from the start. As Provincial Grand Chaplain and a fellow-priest he had been on friendly terms with his predecessor and was well aware of the latter's popularity and of the pride with which the Province viewed his achievements and reputation. As Deputy to and spokesman for an unpopular absentee he was at once confronted by such aggressive and well-known men as Crucefix, Stevens and Adams who were out for blood. Only an exceptionally able man could have won the sympathy and support of the Province at that juncture. Had circumstances been different he might have succeeded; as it was, he failed.

Writing from Boston on 25 November under 'private and confidential' cover, Adams commented 'I fear that our Boston brethren will be considered a somewhat turbulent set, but we undoubtedly are very impatient under misgovernment, and have never settled down since we lost you'. He goes on to relate that in the previous week brethren from other lodges had gathered by invitation at the meeting of the Lodge of Harmony in Boston to discuss what were described as 'matters of great importance', which in fact were the indifference of the PGM and his Deputy to the progress of masonry in the Province and their lack of courtesy. Adams had managed to stop the proposal of a resolution calling for the immediate resignation of both, 'seeing that it would place us in a false position at once', and had suggested the PGM should be asked to call a Provincial meeting 'to consider the present state of Masonry in the Province'; a resolution to this effect was unanimously passed, the visitors undertaking to propose similar resolutions in their own lodges. Adams went on 'I stated in the Lodge that I should inform the DPGM and through him the PGM of the unanimous condemnation of their government by the Lodge of Harmony—and the next day I carried that resolution into effect, adding that we were resolutely bent on having a change. This morning I have had a *private* note from the DPGM informing me that he had communicated with the PGM and he has reason to believe he will immediately resign, if indeed he has not actually done so. Of course the Deputy falls with his chief—and so ends the D'Eyncourt dynasty'. D'Eyncourt did indeed resign and an attempt was apparently made to persuade Oliver to intimate that he would be willing to accept appointment as deputy, but he did nothing to encourage this, and indeed showed very little inclination to become active in office again, even in respect of the Supreme Council of the Ancient and Accepted Rite.

It was against this background that he at last began to write *The Symbol of Glory* in 1849. Published in 1850, it is a strange book; its object was to examine the purpose of freemasonry, to show it to be consistent with Christianity, and, as the 'handmaiden'[2] of that religion, its supporter in showing the way to eternal life. The title refers to a symbol in the lodge-room which is intended to remind each brother, whatever his religion, of his duty to his Creator. Although he felt he had already demonstrated the position of freemasonry as a system of morality and only a handmaid to religion, he felt it necessary to protest against the way in which this question was commonly over-simplified by assuming that 'either Masonry is a system of infidelty and excludes religion altogether from its disquisitions, or it is a religious sect which would supersede the necessity of Christianity and monopolize the office of procuring the salvation of men. The truth however lies between these two propositions: Freemasonry is neither an exclusive system of religion, nor does it tolerate the detestable principles of infidelity. It is a teacher of morality, and contributes its powerful aid, in that capacity, to the salvation of souls . . . And this course of discipline is perfectly consonant with the teachings of Christianity'.[3]

The process by which he came to this conclusion will be clear from what has already been said about the other books of the Grand Design; but there is much more in it than a simple restatement, and some attention must first be paid to the book itself. It is made up of three types of statement, a 'Valedictory Address', 'Epistles Dedicatory', and 13 lectures. The Address is partly autobiographical and partly explanatory of the nature of the Grand Design. Each lecture is dedicated to a masonic body with which he was connected by honorary membership and is preceded by a letter, the 'epistle dedicatory', in terms felt to be particularly appropriate to the addressee. The lectures are intended to lead step-by-step to an appreciation of the meaning and object of freemasonry as an adjunct to religion. Thus he writes of the book that it 'is intended to be a type of the masonic institution. It opens with a view of the science [i.e. of freemasonry], considered as a means of producing spiritual perfection. On this point I am anxious to avoid any misinterpretation. Freemasonry cannot accomplish this result single handed, but as contributing its aid in connection with other agencies. No one can become a Mason without a sincere profession of a belief in one God, the Great Architect or Creator of the Universe; nor can he give his assent to our ordinary lectures without an appreciation of the types of the Old Testament to the manifestations declared in the Gospel; or in other words, without an acknowledgement of the truth of Christianity'.[4]

Turning now to the 'Valedictory Address', it was so called because Oliver, in his mid-sixties and recovering from illness, felt he was unlikely to write much more; he referred to the book as 'my closing work' but though he also wrote that it was 'intended as the completion of a series, and the winding up of a masonic life',[5] either this meant only that either it was the final step in the Grand Design, or that he had underestimated his ability to lay down his pen. It is lengthy, covering 40 pages, and traces the course of his masonic writings from their inception, explaining why he began the series and stressing the methodical nature of its progress. The jibes which Claret had made about 'trade speculations' still rankled and in the first paragraph he states 'I have derived very little profit from my masonic publications . . . I have never been troubled with an ambition to accumulate riches; nor have I ever been overburdened with wealth, or greatly inconvenienced by its absence'.[6]

The next paragraphs merit quotation at length:

'Some authors construct their prefatory introduction as a programme of the book; some to conciliate the reviewers; and others, more venturesome, hurl at the critics their unmitigated defiance; like the sailor, who, having occasion to pass over Bagshot heath in a chaise, and being told that there were "hawks ahead", deliberately taking a pistol on each hand, he thrust his feet through the front windows crying out, "down with bulk heads, and prepare for action".

'I have been too long before you, and have received too many of your favours, either to dread a severe sentence, or to feel the necessity of flattering you into a good humour. It is well known that while a favourable review of any work passes unnoticed by the multitude, an unfavourable one is sought after with avidity, circulated amongst the author's personal friends with persevering industry, and frequently perused with the greatest unction. . .

'It is too late for me to entertain much apprehension for the fate of a volume which is intended as the completion of a series, and the winding up of a masonic life. Like the mosaic pavement of a masonic lodge, my pilgrimage has abounded in variegated scenes of good and evil; and success has been chastened and tempered by mortifiying reverses. Fast friends I have had many, and bitter enemies not a few; and honours and rewards on the one hand, have been balanced by vexation and trouble, and the basest ingratitude for essential services on the other.'[7]

The last paragraph of this extract may be compared with a passage in *The Book of the Lodge* where, again, in regard to the mosaic pavement of the lodge room, he refers to a view that the equal distribution of the black and white tesserae might seem to imply that virtue and vice are spread equally over the face of the earth and adds a note, 'A moral writer of the last century however disputes the fact, and I am inclined to agree with him. He says "Whatever be the sum of misery in the world, there is a much larger sum of happiness" '.[8]

To return to the Valedictory Address; claiming that his first ventures as a masonic writer were intended primarily for his private amusement, he says their popularity was unexpected and led to the plan for the Grand Design. The various steps in the design are then traced and explained, not without diversions.

Two personal items can be extracted; first, he refers to a recent severe indisposition;[9] and second, in keeping with his reputation as 'the recluse of Scopwick', he mentions efforts made to involve him in the literary round of society: 'By nature humble and unassuming, it is a difficult task to draw me out for the purpose of lionizing. The attempt has been made at sundry times, but with very little effect'.[10]

The bodies to whom the 13 lectures were addressed were:

1 The Grand Lodge of Massachusetts.
2 Lodge of Social Friendship, No.336, Fort George, Madras.
3 Bank of England Lodge, No.329, London.
4 Shakespere Lodge [sic], No.356, Warwick.
5 Witham Lodge, No.374, Lincoln.
6 St Peter's Lodge, No.607, Wolverhampton.
7 St George's Lodge, No.643, Montreal, Canada.
8 Bro. the Earl of Aboyne, P.G.M., and St Peter's Lodge, Peterborough.
9 First Lodge of Light, Birmingham.
10 Royal Standard Lodge, Kidderminster.
11 Rising Star of Western India Lodge, Bombay.
12 DPGM for Derry and Donegal and Lodge Light of the North, Londonderry.
13 Lodge Hope and Charity No.523, Kidderminster.

If the Valedictory Address details the history of his masonic writings, the epistles contain some general remarks about the conclusions he has reached.

To the Grand Lodge of Massachusetts he explained his division of the opponents of freemasonry into three classes: '1. Those who hate masonry because it is a secret institution, without being able to assign an adequate reason for their dislike. 2. Those who live in the neighbourhood of an ill-conducted lodge, and see the evil consequences which result from carelessness on the one hand, or intemperance on the other. And 3. Those who are desirous of admission, and do not possess the requisite courage to encounter the presumed terrors of initiation'.[11] In this, he shows perhaps less than his usual perception; he had spent considerable quantities of paper and ink in dealing with the arguments of those of his fellow clergy of the Established Church who either thought freemasonry a religion or an anti-religious creed, or otherwise felt it to be incompatible with Christianity, and who would presumably under this classification have to be counted under the first head though most of them would feel they had theological reasons for their doubts. He presumably felt that he had shown such doubts to be unfounded, but to classify them as having no adequate reason is surely to adopt a subjective rather than an objective view. Freemasons do, and must, respect the sincerity of opponents who are not motivated (as unfortunately many seem to be) by envy or bigotry and must deal frankly with their arguments, as elsewhere Oliver had done.

In writing to the brethren of the Shakespere Lodge, Warwick, he reveals something of the sense of wonder and pride which the early Victorians felt at the progress of science, something we share with them though for us it is not unmixed with fear. It is a useful reminder to those who today are perhaps intoxicated with our own achievements, of the advances that were then being made and of how quickly the world was changing for our ancestors; we do not have the monopoly in scientific discovery, and perhaps we too may learn to live with our discoveries and inventions.

'We live in strange eventful times. Were our forefathers to rise from their graves, they would hold up their hands in astonishment, and pronounce it to be a different world from that which they had left behind them half a century ago. The work of *locomotion* for which they were indebted to the power of living animals, is now effected by means of steam produced by a mineral dug out of the bowels of the earth; and even our artificial light, for which, at that period, a dead animal contributed various portions of its body, is also the result of a different combination of the same material . . . and by the aid of another science, *Electricity* we are enabled to hold familiar converse with friends at incredible distances, without any fear of interruption or disappointment by the miscarriage of letters, of the unfaithfulness or death of messengers . . . It behoves us . . . to consider whether the Order we profess and admire is in a progressive stage commensurate with the gigantic strides by which others are advancing . . . The Landmarks of masonry are necessarily stationary; for by a fundamental law of the Craft, they cannot be altered. To the lectures, therefore, we must look for an evidence of the progressive improvement of the Order. And accordingly between the years 1717 and 1817, we have had six different arrangements of the Lectures, each being an improvement on its predecessor. But from 1814 to 1849, during which period such vast and momentous discoveries in science have been accomplished our means of social improvement pursue the same unvaried rounds.'[12]

His anxiety was justified. Before a century had elapsed from the writing of those words, the lectures had virtually disappeared from normal lodge working; though when extracts are given in lodge today, they are heard with approval as marking the moral standards to which a freemason is expected to conform. Oliver was probably the first mason to appreciate how the failure of the Duke of Sussex to order the revision of the lectures at the Union would change freemasonry; and he may have been correct in suggesting that the reason for the failure was that they are so essentially rooted in the Christian faith that it would have been impossible to change them conformably with the Grand Master's intentions.

To the Witham Lodge, which, until he became an honorary member, had been his own Lincoln lodge, and which had been so closely involved in the débâcle that followed his dismissal by D'Eyncourt, he wrote 'Some of my happiest moments have been passed in a masons' lodge';[13] but in his letter to the brethren of St Peter's Lodge, Wolverhampton, he referred in agonized phrases to 'the hostile denunciations' he had encountered during his residence 'as the Incumbent of the Collegiate Church and the head of the Ecclesiastical Establishment in the town'[14]—a reference to the quarrels with his churchwardens and the incumbent of St George's Church, Mr Clare, who later seems to have asserted his own claim to that pastoral leadership of Wolverhampton against Oliver's last curate, Slade.

In the letter to St Peter's Lodge, Peterborough, Oliver referred to his first years as a mason: 'nothing can be more material than for a mason to feel a predelection in favour of the Lodge where he first saw light streaming from the east . . . My Alma Mater is St Peter's Lodge . . . I shall never forget the pleasurable sensations with which I listened to the first instructions I received from Bro. Stevens, who was then the Worshipful Master . . . I have ever considered Freemasonry as the best and kindest gift of heaven to man; subordinate only to our most holy religion.'[15] It has already been noted that the lodge to which he was writing was not in strictness that in which he had been initiated, but the link was there and was far from tenuous. It should be made clear that the Stevens here referred to is not the mason of that name in London whom Crucefix called his 'lance-corporal'.[16]

In the final letter, to the Lodge of Hope and Charity at Kidderminster, he wrote of his own attitude to those in the Craft who disapproved of his writings. 'I am sure I never intentionally penned a single sentence to wound the feelings or excite the wrath of any individual brother. Even when I have found it necessary to vindicate myself from calumnious attacks, I have invariably endeavoured to preserve a respectful tone towards my accusers, and am not conscious of having ever exceeded the bounds of a temperate and graceful style of controversy . . . and when that could not be done with propriety, I have adopted the mason's peculiar virtue—Silence'. He goes on to refer to the distinguished men and masons who have extended their patronage to him: 'the Dukes of York and Sussex; the Archbishops of Canterbury and York; the Duke of Leinster; the Earls of Zetland, Yarborough (late) and Aboyne; the Bishops of the dioceses where I reside . . . and many other distinguished personages in various parts of the world. The patrons of this my final work, which constitutes the cope-stone and crown of my masonic publications, are the brethren of those Lodges by which I have been more particularly distinguished; and the fraternity at large, wheresoever dispersed under the wide and lofty canopy of heaven'.[17] Finally, reverting to the theme of the book itself, the successful achievement of God's approval of the individual's course, and referring to 'those happy mansions . . . where they will be ever happy with God, the Great Geometrician of the Universe, whose only Son died for us that we might be justified through Faith in his most precious blood', he wrote 'This is our Hope, that we may all finally meet in that blessed abode of never-failing charity; and it has constituted the animating principle which has supported me through all the arduous trials of an eventful life; and still forms the sincere and only wish of him who has the honour of dedicating his closing lecture to you'.[18]

Sincerity is impressive however sententious the expression, and Oliver was here summing up the whole of his philosophy. His exhaustive efforts had earned him the title of 'sage and historian of masonry',[19] but he saw himself as the pastor who had laboured to save the flock entrusted to him and to establish that freemasonry as a system of morality was compatible with the doctrines of the Christian religion as propounded by the Established Church; and, as we shall see, it was to this same subject he returned on his last appearance at the Provincial Grand Lodge of Lincolnshire a year before his death.

The actual text of the lectures in *The Symbol of Glory* follows expected lines. He did not confine his survey to freemasonry. In the eighth lecture, 'The Theological Virtues and their application to Freemasonry', he touched on education: 'There is but one method of producing Hope in manhood, and Charity in old age, and that is, to educate children in the true principles of their faith, or in other words, of religion and virtue'.[20]

In the last lecture he discussed the state of the order at the time and particularly stresses one dilemma facing it—the question of what should and what should not be publicized.

'The English fraternity is divided into two parties, both powerful from intellect and position; one of which is impressed with a conviction that Masonry will be extended and ennobled by an open promulgation of those doctrines and practices which are peculiar, but not necessarily secret; while the other adopts the creed of those "scrupulous brethren" of the last century, who committed many valuable documents to the flames, lest they should fall into the hands of Dr Anderson when he compiled the original Book of Constitutions by command of the Grand Lodge.'[21]

He could not anticipate the revolution in thinking that was to follow the publication of Darwin's *On the Origin of Species* nine years later, and he wrote for the world he knew. His true subject was Christian salvation, and he saw freemasonry as supportive of the Church's role in bringing that about. In the course of summing up his previous work and drawing it to a conclusion, he adopted a very practical stance, giving advice which he felt his own observation warranted: 'The masonic experience which I acquired during my occupation of the Chair of a private lodge for eleven years in the whole, succeeded by the sole management of a large and populous Province for nearly the same length of time, enables me to speak with some degree of confidence, on all subjects connected with the details, as well as the general principles of the order'.[22] He refers also to 'having observed, with feelings of sorrow and regret, its sensible decline in my own Province since the period of my decadence from that high office',[23] and advised on practical measures to maintain standards and to inculcate and demonstrate the high moral tenets, particularly in regard to charity, to which freemasonry adheres.

The plea for a renewal of the practice of instruction in moral principles by means of a revival of the lectures has been noted and he constantly returns to the fact that these principles are those propounded by Christianity. One extract will suffice to show how the visionary and the practical freemason are linked in his thesis: 'In the present state of intellectual improvement, men do not meet together for the insane purpose of hearing repetitions of truisms with which they are already acquainted. Their minds reach forward to something new . . . Time is considered too valuable to be wasted without actual improvement . . . To Freemasonry, as in all other pursuits, the onward principle must be applied . . . If therefore we wish Freemasonry to be publicly esteemed as a popular establishment, let us boldly apply the active cautery, and expunge every questionable doctrine and practice from the system'.[24]

There is no doubt that though he regarded *The Historical Landmarks of Freemasonry* as a major work, it was *The Symbol of Glory* which he considered his masterpiece, and within the limits of the knowledge and beliefs of his time it was indeed a great achievement. It was greeted as such and its reception justified the effort and anxious thought that had gone into its compilation. Oliver, in the opinion of a majority of the freemasons of his time, had attained a summit of achievement that set him above all previous masonic authors.

Chapter Nineteen

LATER WORKS (1850–1860)

(Scopwick, Nottingham, Lincoln)

Apart from the final volume of *Golden Remains* which appeared in 1850, no major work emerged from Scopwick for more than two years after the publication of *The Symbol of Glory*. There is reason to think Oliver may at this time have been more concerned with his health than usual;[1] but the biggest blow must have been the unexpected death of Crucefix on 25 February 1850. This left Oliver as head of the newly formed Supreme Council which was not having the easiest of times.[2]

In forming it Crucefix had included as one member Dr Henry Beaumont Leeson MD, FRCP, FRS, who had been in communication with the French for a patent at the same time as Crucefix had been negotiating with NMJ. It has been seen that there was considerable animosity between the French and NMJ and that this was one reason why the NMJ patent was granted to him. He had however been explicitly cautioned against dealings with the French in a letter from the Grand Secretary-General of NMJ;[3] the letter stated the view of the Sovereign Grand Commander, NMJ, that of the two French bodies that might be involved, one (the Grand Orient) had been guilty of irregular and unmasonic conduct, and the other (The Supreme Council of France), though regularly constituted, had degenerated and 'become corrupted by French innovations, and it is not now in correspondence with the Supreme Councils in this Country'. It is clear that the trouble was serious and the warning emphatic. Nevertheless at a meeting of the English Supreme Council on 24 February 1847, when Henry Udall was acknowledged as the representative of the NMJ in England, Leeson was also acknowledged as representing the Supreme Council in Paris.

The Americans were furious and considered that there had been 'a deep-laid systematic plot' and that they had been 'circumvented in a most shameless manner'. On 3 September they resolved 'that all intercourse or communication with the aforesaid Dr Robt Thos Crucefix, or his Supreme Council has ceased'. It is possible that the link with Paris was the price for Leeson's support of the new Council; certainly it needed support for it was surrounded by enemies and non-friends and in any case had still to establish its position in relation to the claims of the Knights Templar. It was not a situation to bring joy to 'the recluse of Scopwick' who must have seen his peace endangered yet again and his harmonious relations with North America at risk.

This then was the position when Crucefix died and Oliver became titular head, though *primus inter pares*, of the Order. He seems rarely if ever to have attended its meetings and his age and inclinations, particularly if he was now seriously concerned about his health, were not likely to make him the driving force the new Council needed to expand its influence and establish itself as a coherent and responsible authority. On the other hand, it was not in Oliver's nature voluntarily to surrender a position; probably the struggles that fortune had thrust on him and on his father to obtain and retain an assured living had made him disinclined to give up authority once it had been obtained. At all events, he was unwilling to resign his new position, and it would seem that it was only under pressure that he agreed in 1851 to revert to his former post of Lieutenant Grand Commander and allow Leeson to become Sovereign Grand Commander in his place. He finally resigned from the Supreme Council in 1856.

It was 1853 before his next book was published, *A Dictionary of Symbolic Masonry*. He may well have been compiling it for some time. Whether it was really needed is open to doubt and he does not seem to have been enthusiastic about it.

In the same year D'Eyncourt died in London on 12 July after a brief illness. There is no record of any personal *rapprochement* between the two men, nor does there seem to have been any animosity. The long-standing intimacy had been shattered but, though Crucefix and Adams remained sceptical, the explanations given at Spalding may have satisfied Oliver that his 'friend and companion' had been misled by Nicholson and had not been guilty of the suspected discourtesy. ·

In 1854 or 1855 Oliver's voice began to fail, and eventually he felt unable to continue the personal oversight of his benefices, leaving even his beloved Scopwick in charge of a curate. On 25 March 1855, he preached a farewell sermon there. Dixon gives the following quotation from it:

> 'I have been preaching the gospel to you, my Brethren, faithfully and sincerely these many years, until my physical powers are exhausted; and as I cannot continue to discharge the duties of the Church with satisfaction to myself or benefit to you, I reverentially conclude that it is the will of my Divine Master that I should no longer abide with you.'[4]

He seems first to have retired to Nottingham where Beverley was a bookseller but in November 1855 the dedication of the second edition of *The Book of the Lodge* to Charles gives an address in Bank Street, Lincoln; and it was in a house at Norman Place, Lincoln, that his wife died on 13 October 1856. After her death he lived in Eastgate, nearly opposite James Street; there his widowed daughter, Mrs Pears, who acted as his secretary and for many years prepared his books for the printers, kept house for him till his death.[5]

He had retained many of his father's papers. A number of these related to visits Samuel Oliver had made to lodges in London in the late 18th and early 19th centuries; one of these lodges seems to have been the oldest lodge in the country, Lodge of Antiquity, now No.2. (Its original number was 1 on the list of the Premier Grand Lodge ['Moderns'], but at the Union numbers had to be reallocated and the order in which this should be done was decided by lot; the 'Antients' were successful, so their lodge no.1 retained its number while the much older lodge, which has no warrant but acts by immemorial constitution and had been a founder of the Premier Grand Lodge, had to be content with no.2).

The son now made use of his father's papers to write another book, *The Revelations of a Square*, to show how the lodges of that period worked and something of their history.

In the preface he describes how 'my lamented father . . . was very methodical in all his transactions, and being a masonic enthusiast, he noted down in a diary, expressly devoted to that purpose, under a vivid recollection of the facts, whether they were witnessed by himself or communicated to him by others, every event or conversation that struck him as being either singular, characteristic or important in the working of the Craft. By this process he preserved several interesting conversations of our distinguished Brethren in the eighteenth century, which would otherwise have been irrevocably lost'. It may be added that the historical accuracy of some of the matters is often open to doubt or can be proved wrong, but whether this is due to incorrect recording by Samuel Oliver or to the amount of masonic legend that was current at the time cannot now be determined. His son admits to correcting the language and in many cases extending and amplifying the dialogue, but 'is not aware that a single event has either been misrepresented or heightened in colour or perspective' and claims, with reason,that the result will show 'a true picture of the manners, customs, usages and ceremonies of successive periods during the eighteenth century, drawn from the active working of Lodges'.

As to his motive for undertaking the task, he says 'The three stages of initiation can no more make a man into a mason, than the indenture of an apprentice can make him a mechanic. He must read and meditate, study with care and attention the history and doctrines of the Order, and attend his Lodge with the utmost regularity that he may become familiar with its discipline by active personal observation. There is no Royal road to Freemasonry',[6] thus once again showing the extent of what he understood by freemasonry and the attention that in his view it required from its members. The preface is dated from Scopwick Vicarage, December 1854. He is described on the title page as Vicar of Scopwick; Past Deputy Grand Master of the Grand Lodge of Massachusetts; Past DPGM for Lincolnshire; Honorary Member of many Lodges and Literary Societies.

The book itself is odd in that he chooses a Square, the badge of office of the Master of a lodge, as the narrator and the story proceeds on the premise that Oliver is not to interrupt or the Square will have to stop talking. The tales include stories of fabled masons such as Sir Christopher Wren, whose membership of the Craft has never been proved though Lodge of Antiquity still counts among its treasures the 'Wren maul', which it sometimes permits to be used in connection with the laying of foundation stones of significance. The narrative also describes the Reverend Dr Dodd, the first Grand Chaplain, who in spite of his fame as a preacher and his many influential friends, was hanged for forging Lord Chesterfield's signature to a bill even though no loss had been suffered; it was a *cause célèbre* and Boswell records how Dr Johnson failed in his efforts to save Dodd from the gallows.[7] Many distinguished masons of the 18th century flit across the pages and however strange the method of telling the story and however inaccurate the detail, the object of picturing the lodge workings of those times and the characters of the men who became freemasons in them is achieved. Oliver was to use a similar conceit later, so he was no doubt satisfied with it, however it may jar upon modern sensibility. Richard Spencer, who published the book, advertised it as 'exhibiting a graphic display of the sayings and doings of eminent and accepted masons'. To the general masonic public it probably became one of the best known titles of all his works, second to *The Book of the Lodge* the third edition of which, as already noted, was printed in the following year.

In 1859 Oliver's *Institutes of Masonic Jurisprudence* appeared, again published by Spencer. It was an analysis of and commentary on the *Book of Constitutions*, which contains the regulations governing the English Craft and of which the newly installed Master is told 'scarcely a case of difficulty can occur within the lodge in which that book will not put you right'—if he can first find his way about it. The *Book of Constitutions* has nothing to do with ritual and in fact the word 'ritual' does not appear in it; it is a book of rules governing procedures and administration and so a fair target for such a book as Oliver now produced. In that more vigorously litigious age it may have had its uses, but no Grand Secretary was going to admit its validity or impugn his own authority by accepting its rulings and it would seem to have been doomed from the start.

Oliver indeed seems to have fallen temporarily into some sort of torpor. The death of Crucefix, the decline of his own health, the surrender of his pastoral responsibilities to another, and finally the death of his wife may well have left him listless and one may with reason speculate that he was only writing because Spencer was urging him on. It was not until 1862 that events brought him out of seclusion again and freed him to write his final works. In the meantime his reputation was sufficient to bring an approach from Grimsby to write a sketch of the town and port as a preface to *A New and Complete Directory of Great Grimsby and Cleethorpes*, a request doubtless originating from the *Monumental Antiquities of Grimsby* which he had published 35 years before.[8]

Chapter Twenty

THE LAST YEARS (1861–1867)

(Lincoln)

Oliver was responsible for the 17th edition of Preston's *Illustrations of Masonry*, published in 1861, but it was in essence merely a repetition of the 16th. It took the brilliance of a great masonic celebration to bring him once more to the fore—the Installation of the Duke of St Albans as Provincial Grand Master for Lincolnshire on 29 April 1862. This took place in Lincoln and Oliver was invited to conduct it. He was again in the midst of great ceremonial and a few years later the Duke would refer to the deep impression which the ceremony 'so impressively performed by the Reverend Doctor' had made on him.[1] Oliver was at his best on such occasions and it would be an auspicious start to a new reign as well as a public recognition that the troubles of the past were forgotten. The doctor's pen was triumphantly taken up again.

The Freemason's Treasury was published at the turn of the year. The preface is dated from Eastgate, Lincoln and the lengthy sub-title explained the author's objective: *Fifty-two Short Lectures on the Theory and Practice of Symbolical Masonry adapted for delivery in Open Lodge or at Lodges of Instruction in which obscure passages in the ritual are explained, errors corrected; the Landmarks classed; old traditions ventilated; and the whole system simplifed and made easy of attainment to any industrious Brother.* 'By the Rev. George Oliver, D.D. Past Grand Commander SGIG xxxiii Degree for England and Wales; Past DGM of Massachusetts, US; Past DPGM for Lincolnshire; Honorary Member of Lodges, No.48, Bath; 176, Newport, Isle of Wight; 191, New York, US; 319, Portsmouth; 326, Madras; 342, Rising Star, Bombay; 329, London; 348, Worcester; 356, Warwick; 374, Lincoln; 523, Kidderminster; 607, Wolverhampton; 643, Montreal; 646, Peterborough; 689, Birmingham; 690, Spalding; 773, Melbourne, Australia; and the Hiram, Londonderry.'[2] It was published by 'Bro. R. Spencer, 28, Great Queen Street, opposite Freemasons' Hall. 1863'. Oliver had no intention of having his light hidden under any bushel of masonic disapproval from Freemasons' Hall. Nor at this stage of his life was the 'modest and unassuming' mason of 1850 going to bow before any wind of change or any official snub. He had laboured in the vineyard and he intended that the wine should be properly appreciated. This was made apparent in the opening words of his preface: 'I am under no apprehension that my present well-meant endeavour to diversify the business and lighten the labours of a Lodge will either be rejected or treated with indifference. I have condensed an abundance of valuable matter in small compass'.[3]

It has been suggested that this book may be indicative of a change in Oliver's beliefs as to the origins and antiquity of freemasonry, and that in it he was correcting some of his earlier statements in the light of later knowledge.[4] But the motive behind it is so clearly to fill the gap left by the failure to revise the lectures, and Oliver's feelings about this had been so consistently and forcefully expressed that it seems wrong to ascribe any other reason as the primary purpose for its publication. It has already been noted that he had warned his readers against too literal an acceptance of early masonic myths and he was well aware that they would be prone to relish the myth and disregard the warning; in the preface he refers to his own researches into 'discrepancies' and 'sundry traditions in cognate subjects, which even at the beginning of the present century, amused some imaginative brethren, whose wisdom was eclipsed by their credulity, and whose curiosity blinded their judgment . . . A few of these traditional puerilities . . . I have omitted altogether, for I cannot consent that Freemasonry should be accounted a gigantic myth. The days are come when the real must supersede the ideal'.[5] As this book was to provide Masters with material for instruction, he would be particularly careful to keep historical matter of doubtful authenticity out of it. That he had not himself changed his earlier views as to the origins of the English Craft is apparent from a lecture he delivered later to the Witham Lodge in the same year and which will be discussed later. For these reasons the case does not seem to be made out and it is suggested that those who support it place a wrong emphasis on his warnings by seeking to turn an historical pulpit into a stool of repentance.

The Freemasons' Treasury was successful as a book but a failure in so far as it attempted to provide new lectures. This is not so much a comment on its content as on the altered approach of the fraternity to the work of the lodge. The moral and philosophical catechisms accepted as part of the lodge working in the 18th century had not always been practised with zeal even in those days,[6] and had often been curtailed or even abandoned either on grounds of time or because of laziness. In the 19th cenury the degree ceremonies and Installations increasingly came to dominate every meeting and lodge rooms were no longer arranged with a central table around which the brethren could gather for the lecture period. Scientific discoveries made it necessary to reappraise much that had been accepted as unchangeable truth, and the historical accuracy of the Bible was being questioned, about which Oliver had written only a few years before (in *The Symbol of Glory*, lecture 7) that 'It is the most ancient record of facts known in the world . . . On its veracity our holy religion must stand or fall; and therefore our hopes of salvation anchor upon it, as on a rock which can never give way . . . If the slightest doubt could be raised respecting the truth of any single fact or doctrine which it contains, it would cease to be the Book of God, and our Faith and Hope would no longer have a solid base to rest upon':[7] a quite terrifying thought for a Christian today but one which nevertheless reflects the teaching of centuries of English philosophers and theologians. In spite of his amazing ability to keep abreast of scientific development, Oliver was writing for a world that was ceasing to exist and for a masonic audience that thought more of ceremonies, which required action only from a few, than of catechisms, which involved many.

There is nevertheless much in the book of interest to any freemason who wishes to know more about the historical and moral background of the Craft, and many today do find such matters interesting, though probably in smaller doses than Oliver tended to administer. But as an attempt to revitalize the lectures it did not succeed; nor would it succeed today, for though the language of the ritual, which harks back to the 18th century, fits well with ceremony, the pomposity of Victorian writing has neither the bite of today's English nor the grandeur of its ancestral lineage.

The Prefatory Address shows Oliver at his perceptive best in dealing with problems which even in modern times can pose difficulties, as the following extract shows:

'It too often happens that when an intelligent Brother proposes to deliver an original lecture in a Freemasons' Lodge, he forms an incorrect estimate of his hearers' patience; and, by inflicting on them a prosaic homily on some abstruse metaphysical subject of an hour or upwards in length, is surprised to find that, instead of interesting them by a series of appropriate instructions, he has only succeeded in mesmerising their faculties and indisposing them for a repetition of the experiment.

'But all our W[orshipful] Masters are not eloquent, nor do the most fluent speakers always make the best rulers of a Lodge of Masons.'[8]

In the light of what was to come five years later when he undertook to reply to a Papal Allocution against freemasonry, the restatement in the Preface of his view on the relationship between it and the Christian religion should be noted. 'The prosy essayist and the stupid bigot must be disarmed, and Masonry accounted a religious as well as a moral institution. Not a religion, but decidedly impregnated with the purest Christian ethics . . . I have stated my beliefs freely and faithfully, after an experience of more than half a century . . . ; and as an octogenarian, I trust that I am correct in predicating that the removal of opinions thus matured is an occurrence very unlikely to happen.'[9]

Towards the end of the Preface he ruefully remarks 'my prefatory address has already extended to a greater length than I originally designed', reminiscent of his father's words in the sermon preached at the dedication of the Peterborough lodge 60 years before; 'Bear with me, Brethren, I am enraptured by my subject'.[10]

As to the lectures themselves, while there is much of interest in the content, they are now dated. But they contain some gems which again cast light on Oliver's shrewd sense of humour. Thus, 'the strict inviolability of a Landmark is somewhat problematical';[11] 'In many of our Lodges words are substituted for thoughts, and sometimes for knowledge itself';[12] and 'Dr Hemming and his associates in the year 1814, thought it expedient to introduce some peculiar disquisitions from the system of Pythagoras'.[13]

Whilst he had considerable pride in his achievements in masonic research, he had no doubt that others would follow and that their work would overtake his. He would have appreciated Professor Bury's comment on Gibbon made nearly 30 years later when, remarking on 'the danger with which the activities of successors must always threaten the worthies of the past', he wrote 'That Gibbon is behind date in many details, and in some departments of importance, simply signifies that we and our fathers have not lived in an absolutely incompetent world'.[14]

Though he insisted that in reporting traditions he must not be taken as believing them to enshrine truth, he propounded them with such enthusiasm at times as to appear not to doubt their veracity, but in the 45th lecture of *The Freemason's Treasury* he again stresses the point: 'I have distinctly affirmed them to be mere traditions and nothing more, and to be received *quantum valeat* as they are not proveable by any credible authority, and were promulgated long before I became a Mason, and therefore I cannot be responsible for them, or for many other fables and legends which are scattered throughout my voluminous Masonic works, and which were in existence long before I came into the world. That the time is come for their removal there can be no doubt';[15] and in the next lecture he touches on the difficulties that follow from confident assertions in ceremonial so that if something is 'given as a naked and unexplained fact, and recited with all the solemnity of truth, ninety-nine out of every hundred candidates believe it implicitly'.[16] This defensive attack may reflect the impact of the scepticism which was beginning to sweep across his world and which still perists today. The criticism would carry less weight now, largely because many of the myths have vanished into the mist of antiquity. It is interesting that he should have found it necessary at this late stage to repeat in such emphatic terms the disclaimer he had made so many years ago in *The Historical Landmarks*. But it also refutes the charge that has been made against him so often that he had a gullible approach to the work of research and so belonged to the world of the 'romantic' masonic scholars of the 18th century; it would be more realistic to accept him as the first of the so-called 'authentics', or at the least a bridge between the two schools.

The last words of the last lecture sum up the creed that was his constant message: 'It ought to be the chief business of every free and accepted Mason in this life so to prepare himself, by the practice of faith, hope, and charity, that he may inherit an eternity of happiness in another and a better world',[17] though, as he consistently stressed, it was religion, faith, that made it possible to attain that end; freemasonry could only act in a subordinate capacity.

Another honorary membership came to him in 1864, that of the Pelham Pillar Lodge at Great Grimsby, the lodge which had some of the effects of the old Apollo Lodge.[18]

In 1863 he published the text of a lecture he had recently given to the Witham Lodge on 'The Various Rituals of Freemasonry'. Protesting that it was rather late in life for him to appear in the capacity of lecturer, he stated that he did so because he thought he could tell his hearers something not generally known and which he was satisfied from his masonic correspondence that 'many brethren . . . would travel over half the island, and think themselves well paid for their trouble, to acquire'; but these are the words of an old man, and the slightly didactic tone of the whole contrasts with his usual presentation. Shorn of the conceits and presumptions of age it is a remarkable achievement for an octogenarian. The first part is devoted to the history of 18th century ritual, which was supposed to be traceable to King Athelstan; it would seem that Oliver still believed in this legend. He then went on to discuss a ritual attributed, without foundation as we now know, to Sir Christopher Wren, and thence to that of his great mentor William Preston on whose first degree lecture he dilated at length (though in *The Freemasons' Treasury* he comments at one point that 'our worthy Brother Preston appears to have been a believer in the mystical attainments of our ancient brethren'). His presentation is clear and his thoughts flow in orderly and coherent manner, but the impression of an old man speaking is constantly felt, even if the speaker was the best recognized authority in the world on his subject.

On 9 February 1864, he made his will; this was not such a routine precaution as it is today and may have signified a sense of further deterioration in his health. Whatever the reason, the testator survived the experience and in May of the following year was able to enjoy the honour of having a Chapter in Great Grimsby named after him (now no.792). At about the same time the state of his finances was causing concern to his friends and a movement was set on foot to establish a fund to augment his income. An application by the Provincial Grand Secretary for a contribution from the Grand Master drew a frosty refusal from the Grand Secretary:

> 'Lord Zetland believes that Dr Oliver has been a zealous & enthusiastic mason, yet in the opinion of the best and oldest Masons in this Country, Dr Oliver has written a great deal which it would have been better to have left unwritten, and that much both as to the laws of our Order and its ceremonies has been published which is not unlikely to lead Brethren astray. You will please to understand that it is solely on public grounds that Lord Zetland feels compelled to decline allowing his name to be used in any way; for his Lordship is unwilling to do anything that could in any wise lead Brethren to suppose that he either sanctions or agrees in many of Dr Oliver's writings.'[19]

The letter was dated 4 September 1865. As Lord Zetland had allowed the second volume of Landmarks to be dedicated to him in 1846, it would seem that there had been a change of attitude since then. It is unlikely that Oliver's association with the Ancient and Accepted Rite would be responsible; his masonic writings had been concerned with Craft and Royal Arch. It seems probable therefore that it was the publication of The Book of the Lodge, the 3rd edition of which had appeared in 1864, which was the cause of this rebuff.

It was in 1865 also that Pope Pius IX promulgated an Allocution against freemasonry. The policy of the UGL at that time was to take no action against attacks on the Craft but to let them die for want of fuel. Oliver however was so incensed by the papal pronouncement, and so anxious to correct what he saw as its errors, that he wrote a refutation.

To understand the position it is necessary to consider the standing of the Roman Catholic Church in England at the time and the nature of Continental freemasonry.

In 1829 Parliament, responding to pressure from Irish interests, had removed many of the disqualifications which had affected the Roman Catholic Church since the Reformation. By the middle of the century the Catholic population of England had been increased by the large number of Irish immigrants fleeing from the devastation caused by famine, most of whom found work as labourers in the industrial towns and on the railways. The Roman Catholic Church in England grew correspondingly and came to be seen by some as a challenge and by others as an alternative to the Church of England. Further governmental interference in Irish ecclesiastical affairs caused apprehensions in England which found expression in the Oxford Movement ('The Tractarians'); eventually a number of influential supporters of that Movement seceded to the Church of Rome, the most publicized being Newman in 1845.

The effect of these events on the Church of England was to stir it in its lethargy. It was still the Established Church, but it now had a rival which could claim an earlier origin and had a well-established bureaucracy to administer it—and also had an energetic and proselytizing approach that could be seen as a threat, particularly since the Church of England was divided between High and Low Church parties. It was therefore at a very sensitive time in the history of the Established Church that the Papal Allocution appeared.

As to Continental masonry, this had, as already noted, been subject to Napoleonic interference. As a result of this and of the trend to agnosticism or atheism which had grown since the French Revolution at the end of the 18th century, much so-called freemasonry on the Continent no longer required its members to acknowledge the existence of a Supreme Creator; it was also, and sometimes with justice, suspected of desiring the overthrow of established governments. Regular freemasonry as recognized by the Grand Lodges of England, Scotland and Ireland found both these traits unacceptable, first because as a result the Bible no longer lay open in lodge, and second because discussion of politics was, and is, banned in their own lodges. However, to the Catholic hierarchy all freemasonry appeared as tarred with one brush and the stricter code of the authentic Craft as practised here was either not understood or ignored. There had earlier been pronouncements against masonry, but those were on the grounds of secrecy, on the basis that the Catholic Church had no use for a movement where the priest might be banned from meetings.

It was against this background that the Allocution was received in England. So many of the English clergy were staunch supporters of freemasonry that the first reaction would be that the Papal view was another instance of the 'foreignness' of the Roman Church. Probably few English masons realized the extent to which Continental masonry had become both politically oriented and agnostic or atheistic, and certainly the activities of a number of bodies calling themselves freemasons on the Continent had been of a nature that would seem to the religious and political establishments of the day heretical and subversive. To this extent therefore there was clear ground for misunderstanding since freemasonry did not necessarily mean the same thing on the Continent as in England, where it had successfully distanced itself from other societies and was accepted as respectable by the political and, on the whole, by the ecclesiastical hierarchies.

Further, the innate distrust of many native Englishmen for the Papal legions was deep-rooted and sincere. The strength of the Roman Catholic Church here in the early nineteenth century had been among the Irish immigrants; and the defection, as it was seen, of supporters of the English High Church party to Rome in the wake of the Oxford Movement had been condemned with an anger that bordered on panic. After all, it was only little over a hundred years before that the Catholic Stuarts had been finally defeated in their bid for the throne. The last credible claimant of that line had styled himself Henry IX in a manifesto issued in 1788 (less than a hundred years before) and, after becoming a Catholic priest, had been created a cardinal; what was more, he had become Dean of the Sacred College. He had died in 1807 and though by that time a pensioner of the English Crown, his existence had been enough to keep alive memories of the Stuart threat to the Hanoverian dynasty.

As has been seen, it was not at that time the policy of the Grand Lodge to make public pronouncements about freemasonry. It would seem that under Lord Zetland there had been a deliberate attempt to keep the Craft out of the public eye and it was in accordance with this that no statement was made about the Allocution and no open discussion took place. The effect was to leave the Craft without guidance in a matter which, even outside masonic circles, was of considerable interest; to Oliver it may have been reminiscent of those early days when, faced with a skilful opponent, he had found himself unable to argue adequately in support of freemasonry through lack of information on its policies. He decided that whatever the official view he would not be silent. His pamphlet *Papal Teachings in Freemasonry* was printed by Cox and Wyman, Great Queen Street, London, W.C.; the Preface is dated from 32 Eastgate, Lincoln, in January 1866.

He had spent half a century satisfying himself that freemasonry was in every respect compatible with the Christian religion, and the arguments he used now restated those of the Grand Design. The interest of the work for his biographer lies in the preface in which he asserts that 'nothing less than the untenable denunciations against the Divine institution of Freemasonry recently issued by an eminent personage . . . could have induced me, at the age of eighty-four years, to have taken up my pen in its defence' and, claiming that it had not the shadow of a foundation he referred to it as a 'bitter phillipic'. (He was in fact only 83 but had reached the age where additional years are not uncommonly claimed with as much fervour as they are rejected earlier in life).

He seems to have felt satisfied that the completion of the Grand Design had left him with nothing more to say, and the pamphlet is in the nature of a reply to an attack on a theory that has already been proved. His reference to the divine institution shows that he held to the argument about the origin of a universal system of morality as part of God's plan for mankind; clearly he was untouched by the arguments of Darwin and his followers. But he was not blind to the doubts that were beginning to assail theologians in the wake of those arguments and in fact seems to have placed them on a par with the Allocution as the following extract shows:

'. . . one of our Protestant colonial bishops not only repudiates the Pentateuch, and pronounces it to be a forgery of much later age than the time of Moses, but denies the stupendous facts which are recorded in its pages, although abundantly confirmed by the direct and unimpeachable testimony of prophets and apostles. And, finally, his Holiness Pope Pius IX pronounces the beautiful system of freemasonry to be "impious and criminal, inimical to the Church and to God, and dangerous for the security of kingdoms".'[20]

He also quotes from an American source, Grand Master Dalcho who in one of his addresses—which are well worth perusing—said 'There is no institution in which benevolence so pure, and philanthropy so disinterested, are taught, in obedience to the command of God, nor where, but *in the Gospel*, the social and moral duties are enforced with such awful sanctions, as in the Lodges of the Brotherhood'.[21]

It is passages such as these that pose the question to what extent Oliver's arguments on the compatibility of freemasonry with the Christian religion can still be treated as valid. Superficially it would seem they can only do so if his thesis as to the literal truth of the Biblical account of the Creation and other matters in the early books of the Old Testament can be accepted. But this is to ignore the real basis of his argument which is that religion must postulate a moral code; first faith, then works. He believed implicitly in the Redemption of the world by Christ and that the teachings of freemasonry were limited to morality though it required its members to have a religious belief in a Divine Creator. His view was indeed that the morality of freemasonry was more compatible with the Christian religion than with any other, that the ostensible dechristianizing of the ritual under the auspices of the Duke of Sussex had made no difference to this, and that logically it was only the Trinitarian Christian God whom a freemason could acknowledge as his Creator, since he held that the Old Testament stories and prophecies which form the background to much masonic ritual and ceremonial must be considered as leading inevitably to, and culminating in, the mission and gospel of Christ. It is an irony of fate that some Christian attacks on the Order should be directed to the argument that freemasonry postulates the existence of its own peculiar god. The revisions under the Duke of Sussex were intended to make it possible for non-Christians to attend lodges without embarrassment, something which Oliver would have accepted as in keeping with the basic tenets of the Craft; in Lecture 4 of *The Symbol of Glory* he reminds his readers that God has created all mankind as brethren, and saying 'Freemasonry must not however be mistaken for a religious sect', he roundly proclaims 'No matter what may be the birth, language or colour of the skin, every man is a brother if he faithfully performs his duty to God, his neighbour, and himself'.[22] All this, of course, in no way alters the requirement already noted that before he can be admitted to the Craft a candidate must have his own personal religious belief and is expected to practise his religion the more assiduously because he has become a freemason; that is still the rule today and many clergymen might well be surprised to know how many of those who support their churches in practice as well as in theory are in fact members of the Craft: Christians first and freemasons second.

In 1866 a history of Great Grimsby by Oliver was published with the title *Ye Byrde of Gryme*. As he is described on the title page as 'Rector of South Hykeham, Vicar of Scopwick, late Rector of Wolverhampton, and Prebendary in the Collegiate Church there, and Honorary Member of many Literary Societies at home and abroad', it may be assumed that it was written before he formally gave up the two Lincolnshire livings in 1865. The dedication however is dated January 1866 and reads 'At the age of 84 years the following pages are inscribed as a souvenir of friendship and a kindly farewell to the inhabitants of Grimsby and Clee by their former parish minister with sole charge for a period of 17 years and now their obedient servant and wellwisher Geo. Oliver' and is dated from Eastgate, Lincoln. The printer and publisher was A. Gait, 13 Market Place, Grimsby. A reviewer in 'The Athenaeum' wrote of it, 'Our readers will not take the less interest in this little book about Grimsby when they learn that the writer is eighty-four years old, while the style is so light & genial that Sam Weller might claim, "Blest if his heart isn't five and twenty years younger than his body" '.[23] It is extraordinary how Oliver mixed two styles, the open and easy which he used in lighter moments and the heavy depths into which he could stray when propounding the abstruse.

The book itself has something in common with *Revelations of a Square* in that the author selects an unusual character to tell the story for him; this time a raven. The work itself has been heavily criticized for inaccuracy in detail and appears to be somewhat patchily researched and more in the nature of a gossipy collection of legend than a factual account; as such it can be a trap for the unwary. Quite why he wrote it is a mystery but he said it derived from jottings, notes and memoranda contained in his common place book of the time, though only an extract, as the whole 'are sufficiently numerous to fill a thick quarto; which, if I published, I have some apprehension would lack purchasers, and be an unprofitable speculation',[24] a remark which might have caused Claret to stir in his grave. He added that he had extracted a fair proportion of plumbs out of the pudding. Probably, in his retirement he had been going through his records and written the book to pass the time and make a small profit into the bargain to augment his rather straitened circumstances, though he shows he was not particularly hopeful on this latter point by remarking, 'I am not insensible to the fact that the launching of a book of topography on the ocean of public opinion, is like venturing on a stormy sea in a cock boat'.[25]

It seems to have been his custom to maintain a common place book. We have seen that one survives in the possession of the English Supreme Council 33°. It is a small leather-bound pocket book filled with unrelated jottings and seems to have been in use about the time of Oliver's dismissal in 1842. It will also be recalled that in the draft letter to Nicholson which Stevens saw, Oliver referred to his 'memoranda' in a manner which suggests he kept some sort of journal. By the time he retired to Lincoln he must have had a number of such books to browse through and this may in fact account for the origin of this latest work.

An interesting sentence in the first chapter shows his attitude to the more exotic forms of religious expression: 'Is the shock of physical sensibility more to be condemned among our ancestors, than that of religious feeling among ourselves, excited by the disgusting mummeries of mesmerism, phrenology, spirit rapping, or table turning? The former is only repulsive to humanity, while the latter is an outrageous interference with the providence of God'.[26] Later he draws a vivid picture of 'clubism', with its members 'reeling home at the small hours of the morning, in a happy state of ebriety, and counting the stars for want of a better amusement'.[27]

In May 1866, Provincial Grand Lodge was held in Lincoln with the Duke of St Albans in the chair. Oliver delivered an oration on 'The superiority of freemasonry over all other Social Institutions' and then took 'a graceful opportunity of bidding farewell' by a moving speech enlivened by the statement 'I must not refuse, if called on, to edit a new edition of any of my Masonic works, or even to publish a new one if necessary'; and once again affirmed the fact 'that a Clergyman of the establishment, tolerably well versed in antiquarian lore, after a critical examination of the esoteric principles of the Order for more than half a century, has found no reason to change his opinion on its unrivalled purity as a humble handmaiden to religion'.[28]

In spite of his protest that it had not been intended for publication, this speech, the last he would make, was ordered to be printed for the benefit of the Provincial Benevolent Fund.

In 1867 the final version of his history of the Royal Arch appeared, with the title *The Origin of the Royal Arch Order of Masonry historically considered including an Explanatory View of its Primitive Rituals, Doctrines and Symbols. And of their Progressive Improvements to the present time*. On the title page he was described as 'Past Grand Commander of the 33° for England and Wales; past DGM of the Grand Lodge of Massachusetts; past DPGM for Lincolnshire; and Honorary Member of numerous Lodges and Literary Societies'. The book was dedicated to the Duke of St Albans and Oliver wrote that he had 'taken the facts simply as they were brought to my notice; and their existence appears amply sufficient to set this vexed question at rest for ever . . . And it will not be believed that I have deliberately attempted to promulgate a fallacy at my time of life, when I am shortly to be initiated into the greater mysteries, in other words, Death; the arcane secrets of which no mortal man has ever been able to reveal, although perfectly familiar with the exoteric form of the Lesser Mysteries, that is, Sleep, while their esoteric secrets, Dreams, still remain beyond his comprehension'.[29]

In spite of his confidence his explanation has been questioned and is not today found acceptable; but that is a matter for masonic historians rather than a biography. There are however several passages in the book which throw light on his work and character. In the preface he relates that he recalls 'very well, though it were more than sixty years ago, the dead lock which frequently occurred to me when I first entered on the study of masonry, but the absence of books of reference', a deficiency which he states he has in great measure supplied; and with some justice claims that many fallacies, misapprehensions and myths about the nature of freemasonry have been dispelled by the spread of masonic literature. There is also a passage which merits quotation:

'I turn to another subject which I consider of still greater importance, embracing the present opportunity because it is scarcely probable, at my advanced age, that another will occur, of repeating my firm and unshaken conviction that Freemasonry is a Christian institution, established by Christian men, and embracing Christian principles . . . My faith in this respect commenced at my initiation, when I was only eighteen years of age, and has remained unshaken through a long and eventful life, and I rejoice in the opportunity of publicly professing the same faith at the age of eighty-five years.

'I do not deny that its ceremonies bear a reference to the Tabernacle of Moses, and the Temples erected by Solomon and Zerubbabel; but those edifices, and the rites and observances performed within their courts, were intended merely as signs and symbols to prefigure a better and more perfect dispensation, and afford no valid argument to prove Freemasonry to be a Jewish or even latitudinarian institution.'[30]

But as he also remarks, 'I am not ignorant that when a prejudice has taken possession of the mind, however fallacious it may be, the difficulty of removing it is unsurmountable'.[31]

His conviction as to the essential Christianity of freemasonry has often been referred to in this biography. Now, at the end of his life, he stated it again in vigorous and uncompromising terms:

' . . . it is a well-known fact that the numerous prayers of masonry are uniformly sealed by an invocation to TGAOTU, or in other words, to Jesus Christ the Maker of the World and the Redeemer of mankind.

'Now, should any doubt whether the Redeemer of mankind is rightly identified in Freemasonry with TGAOTU I would tell him that St John the Evangelist, one of our traditional patrons, plainly asserts that the second person in the Trinity was the builder of the world, in these words: "All things were made by Him, and without Him was nothing made that was made". . .

' . . . a few dissentients in the masonic body . . . contend that "all was altered at the Union; and the above title transferred from the Second to the First Person in the Trinity". I should like to see the authority for the presumed change; because it was provided in the third Article of the Union, that "no alteration whatever should be permitted". . .

'But is it really true that freemasonry fails to contribute such collateral aid to our holy religion as may humbly be afforded by a society purely human? I have already said that it was founded by Christian men for a Christian purpose; I now add that it embodies a series of Christian types, which are explained in its rituals on Christian principles; its doctrines and duties are framed on Christian models; it is acknowledged and protected by Christian laws; and therefore I am at a loss to understand how it can truly be pronounced an anti-Christian institution.'[32]

Chapter Twenty-One

EPILOGUE

(Lincoln)

George Oliver died on 3 March 1867 at his Lincoln home after a short illness, almost his last act being to pay his subscription to the new Provincial Benevolent Fund.[1] *The Origin of the Royal Arch* was in the printer's hands, and the publisher, Spencer, included a note 'In Memoriam' after the preface; much of it had appeared in the *Stamford Mercury* for 8 March 1867 so whether or not Spencer was the original author cannot be stated. From it the following quotations are extracted:

'The close of the life of a good old man is always suggestive, in the minds of the survivors, of mixed feelings of regret and melancholy pleasure . . . [He] has incontrovertibly shown that there is no antagonism between Christianity and Freemasonry; that on the contrary, the latter is the handmaid of the former, its truest and staunchest friend and helper, and that a good mason must necessarily be a good man . . . Having led an active life in the discharge of his professional duties and in literary pursuits, his voice began to fail at the age of seventy-two, and being obliged to confide the charge of his parishes to curates, he passed the remainder of his life in dignified retirement, honoured and beloved . . . [In] May last . . . he took his farewell of the Grand Lodge of Lincolnshire by delivering . . . a warmly uttered address, which was listened to by those present with evident emotion, as the words fell from the lips of a kind old man who had then outlived the limit of human existence. . . He was of a kind and genial disposition, charitable in the highest sense of the word, "thinking no evil", courteous, affable, self-denying and beneficent, humble, unassuming and unaffected; ever ready to oblige, easy of approach, amiable, yet firm in the right'.

And even the author of a more critical letter in the Library at Grimsby confirmed his popularity: 'Poor Dr Oliver—just dead at 90 or 91. Perhaps you did not know him. A great masonic gun, O. is to be buried with the honours. Wrote immensely on behalf of the Order. Had the living of Scopwick latterly—when I was a youth was the Grimsby schoolmaster. A great antiquary & yet a small one. Immense in facts yet quite unable to do justice to them. Grimsby & Beverley he made books on. But there was a thorough kindly simplicity what made everyone like him'. Dixon's description of his character has been repeated in the Preface.

Oliver's will was proved at Lincoln on 6 April 1867 by the two named executors, John William Danby, his solicitor, and Henry Goddard, Architect; it will be recalled that Goddard, as Provincial Grand Secretary, had adopted a friendly and helpful attitude to him in the fracas that followed the dismissal. The estate was sworn at under £2000.

There were few legacies; his printed masonic books were left to Charles, who seems in the event to have received most of his father's papers; any claim by his executors in respect of the security for £300 given in regard to Charles was released. Of his daughters, Mary (now Mrs Rainforth) was left £10 for mourning 'she being otherwise provided for' and Caroline (now Mrs Pears) received the residue, her reward for acting as his secretary as well as keeping house for him after his wife's death. According to an unattributed note in Grimsby Public Library she proceeded to sell everything she did not require herself and invest the proceeds in an annuity, to the indignation of the rest of the family. Apparently the silver of the Oliver Testimonial was included so that it never reached its intended destinations. The estrangement lasted for many years until, according to the same source, Mrs Pears became blind and joined some of the family in Louth towards the end of her life.

Oliver's funeral took place at St Swithin's Church, Lincoln and he was buried in the cemetery in Rosemary Avenue nearby, beside his wife; the funeral was accompanied with masonic ceremonial, a practice disapproved of today. On the slab covering the grave is a low ridged memorial stone inscribed 'In memory of the Reverend George Oliver, D.D., who died the 3rd of March 1867 in the 85th year of his age'. On the other side is a similar inscription 'In memory of Mary Ann, wife of the Reverend George Oliver, D.D., who died the 13th of October 1856 in the 80th year of her age'. There is no reference to his achievements other than his status as a priest and his doctorate. In spite of a statement by S. Race,[2] the tombstone still protects and identifies the grave.

The freemasons of Lincolnshire later subscribed for a memorial window to Oliver's memory in the Church at South Hykeham. The Crucefixion forms its main theme, with underneath a view of the interior of King Solomon's Temple showing the altar of sacrifice, the veils (blue, crimson and purple) drawn aside; below that again are a number of masonic symbols and at the bottom an inscription in fraternal remembrance.

Provincial Grand Lodge was held at Great Grimsby (appropriately, in the Mechanics' Institute) on 2 May 1867. The Duke of St Albans paid this moving tribute to Oliver from the chair:

'Few indeed are spared to be united to masonry for so long a period . . . and still fewer who can leave behind them so magnificent a proof how truly and constantly during a period of 65 years our revered Brother's heart beat in accordance with the highest principles of the Craft, and how hard he laboured to advance the prosperity of the Order.'

We live in a very different world to any that Oliver knew, though there is the similarity that scientific knowledge is again growing almost too fast for our absorption. It is however a much more secular age and Christianity is on the defensive. Moral standards have changed too, so much that there are those who would question their existence. There is a need and a place for movements which seek to uphold what is good and discountenance what is evil. Freemasonry as practised under the UGL stands now on the same basis as that on which it stood in Oliver's day; brotherly love, relief and truth are its objectives; the individual's duty to his God, his neighbour and himself provide its standards; the ancient craft of the freemason supplies its symbolism; and the allegorical legends of the building of the first and second Temples at Jerusalem form the basis of its teaching in Craft and Royal Arch. It stipulates that its members should have acknowledged that the world was created but it does not postulate the name of the Creator, though in the Royal Arch the Ineffable Name revealed in the Old Testament is honoured. It postulates that the individual freemason should practise the religion he professes. It requires that the Bible should lie open in lodge, but insists that Obligations shall be taken by the individual on whatever Book he regards as Holy and as binding to his oath. It cannot exist therefore except in the shadow of religion, using that term generically. That the religion acknowledged by the majority of English freemasons should doubt its credentials is not necessarily a comment only on the Craft.

Oliver wrote sincerely and thoughtfully. His sermons were rooted in the Gospel of Christ and the teaching of the Bible. He was first, foremost and for ever a priest and his beliefs were more strictly confined to the teachings of the Bible than seems to be acceptable today. Yet in spite of this strict interpretation he found freemasonry wholly compatible with his religion. Had he not been able to assure himself fully of this he would without hesitation have resigned from the Craft. He made this clear at the Testimonial dinner in Lincoln in 1844 where he referred at length to the anxious researches which had led him to this conclusion:

'I instituted a strict search into Masonic facts; I penetrated into the dark and abstruse regions of Masonic antiquities; and the further I advanced in my enquiries, the more I became convinced of the absolute necessity of some systematic attempt to identify Freemasonry with the religious institutions of ancient nations, as typical of the universal religion of Christ. While I was engaged in these investigations, I found an opinion promulgated in several learned writings, that Freemasonry was nothing more than a scion from the Eleusynian mysteries. It was contended that their internal construction, their external ceremonies, and their legend of initiation, resembled each other in so many important particulars, that it was impossible for any candid mind to doubt their identity. This opinion, I regret to say, was hastily taken up, not only by some uninitiated persons, who were very glad of a pretext to throw discredit on the Order, but also—owing to the undoubted resemblance of the legend and ceremonies—by some well-meaning members of our own fraternity. A conclusion, so disastrous to Freemasonry, was forbidding; and I determined, as a Christian divine, to abandon it altogether, if the charge should prove to be true. To satisfy myself on this point, I determined to investigate the evidence of both these institutions. With care and circumspection I waded through all the ancient and modern writers who had treated on the subject; and, after mature deliberation on every point and bearing of the case, which occupied my attention, at intervals, for several years of my life, I came to a conclusion which proved the origin of much anxiety and much labour, and ended in the production of those publications to which my worshipful friend has so pointedly referred [the chairman had displayed on the table a specially-bound set of Oliver's masonic works in proposing his health] . . . Still the series is not complete . . . A great principle remains to be established, on which I have bestowed much care and attention. This principle is intended to show, not only that the legends, symbols and lectures of Freemasonry bear an undoubted reference to the Messiah promised at the fall of man; but also that the Order itself, in the earliest days, was a legitimate branch of true religion. To establish these points, I have commenced a periodical work, the first numbers of which are in your hands'.[3] [This last remark was a reference to *Landmarks*, then appearing in monthly parts.]

There could not be clearer evidence of his sincere determination to have nothing to do with anything that was not in every way compatible with his calling as a Christian minister than his decision to abandon the Craft in which he was so happy and whose tenets he so much admired should these allegations not be disproved.

Many sincere Christians are freemasons, practising their religion in both faith and works and finding it easier to do so because of the masonic lessons they have learnt and the support and fellowship they have found both in Church and Craft. Nor should it be overlooked that the presence of Christians, particularly of priests and ministers, in lodge makes for a bond which can help in those times when faith is dimmed; for a man will talk of such things to (and be guided by) one whom he regularly meets and respects as a brother; while he will often be desperate indeed before he seeks out a stranger. Christian freemasons can hardly be blamed if they find the present attitude of some of their fellow Christians towards them puzzling and may perhaps be forgiven if they wonder whether the Churches would not be better employed than in turning upon their friends; but sincerity of belief, even belief in the same God, has never been a protection where theological differences are thought to arise. Charges of heresy and blasphemy are hurled against the imagined enemy with all the passion of proselytizing zeal. In this respect regrettably the world has not changed. Those who, for whatever reason, challenge freemasonry's compatibility with a specific religion are forced to claim that it is a religion; yet it has no religious dogma, though it does insist that the universe must have been super-naturally created. The prayers in its rituals are not specifically Christian; but do Christians consider prayers in inter-faith services, where the mediation of a Redeemer is not invoked, to be a sham? When Grace is said before and after meals, as is the case on masonic occasions, must it be specifically Christian even when adherents of other faiths are present? Oliver believed that freemasonry was essentially Christian; not all Christian freemasons would agree but all would accept that freemasonry and the companionship of freemasons encourage and strengthen them in living Christian lives. The dictum that freemasonry is the humble handmaiden of religion is a simple profundity about which all parties to the argument might well think.

Today few can accept Oliver's fundamentalist beliefs. But that does not destroy the validity of his arguments. He saw more clearly than many of us. Freemasons will appreciate that his views about explaining the Craft to the public are accepted policy today and many of them will feel he was right to lament the failure to revise the lectures. He revived freemasonry in Lincolnshire and taught the masons of the Province and a far wider audience in both hemispheres to appreciate its moral teachings and its subservient relationship to religion. He was an affectionate husband and father and a loyal son. He rescued the villagers of Scopwick from squalor and neglect and gave them new heart. He was no respecter of persons in the discharge of his sacred duties as a Christian pastor and was ever the friend of the poor and distressed. Well aware of the fame he had achieved, he was unspoilt by his reputation and remained at all times the humble but determined servant of his God. In describing the Oliver testimonial dinner in a pamphlet almost certainly written by Crucefix, the contrast between 'the sage and historian of masonry' at the dinner and the Vicar of Scopwick on the following Sunday was noted with the instinct of a reporter. Oliver had enjoyed the great occasion to the full, but in the 'little rustic church' with its small congregation of villagers and visitors he was engaged in the real business of life.[4]

His interests outside the church and freemasonry were in history and the social problems of the age. His abilities as a researcher were restricted by the fundamentalist tenets of his time and the limited facilities for travel and analysis; and in research, to quote Bury again, 'Accuracy is relevant to opportunity'.[5] He used his ability as a writer to spread knowledge and propound arguments. Freemasonry appealed to him because it welcomed all ranks of society to 'meet on the level and part on the square'; because it welcomed to its ranks only those who confessed a belief in a Divine Creator; because it required its members to practise the religion they professed and to maintain high moral standards; and because it was founded on tenets of brotherly love, relief and truth. It has not altered and this is all as true today as in Oliver's time. He found it compatible with his religion as a Christian priest and published his findings in books anyone can obtain. If it be alleged that freemasonry is not exclusively Christian, that is so; but neither are other societies which require their members to have a religious belief without requiring them to be Christians; the Scout and Guide movements are cases in point. But George Oliver, and not any controversy of the present time, is the subject of this biography. Nevertheless there could be lessons for today in this. It has been shown that many priests of his day shared his view that Christianity and freemasonry are not incompatible; many do today in spite of recent pronouncements by Christian Churches. If the Craft had not adopted the secretive policy towards the public which became its rule in the mid-nineteenth century, but had retained the more open attitude of earlier years of which Oliver was so strong an advocate, it might be better understood now.

Though of towering stature as a freemason revered around the world in the teeth of powerful disapproval, Oliver was, above all else, a priest—an Anglican priest; Nicholson less formally but with more meaning described him as a Christian

Pastor.[6] He had a deeply-held and fervently proclaimed faith in the Gospel of Christ and served the Church of England well for over half a century, restoring the churches and caring for the communities in Great Grimsby and Scopwick, whether Anglican or not. He was at all times the shepherd of his flock, fully acknowledging that he was responsible for them to his Master; he was not only a pastor but a friend to them and would not be diverted from his duty even by the enmity and abuse to which he was subjected in Wolverhampton. He had his foibles, his conceits, his fears and, in Wolverhampton, his failures. But he laboured faithfully in the vineyard. Among his contemporaries he inspired love and affection on a scale that it is given to few to achieve; and that perhaps should be his epitaph.

Requiescat in Pace.

NOTES

- For full names of abbreviated titles, refer to List of Abbreviations at front of book.
- Page numbers in Oliver's works sometimes vary with different printings so that it may be necessary to search adjoining pages to trace a reference.
- Unless otherwise noted, letters referred to are to be found in the Library of the United Grand Lodge of England. Words italicized in letters are underlined for emphasis in the originals.

Preface

1. *The Pythagorean Triangle*, 119. cf. *The Existing Remains of the Ancient Britons . . .* (1846), 44: ' . . . brevity is the soul of wit; although I am free to acknowledge that the shortest dissertations are sometimes extremely dull.'
2. Dixon, 302–3.

Chapter 1: Background

1. *Antiquities*, 32, note (1843 edn).
2. *Mirror*, Dedication.
3. *Papal Teachings*, Preface iii.
4. FQR 1847, 303.
5. ibid. 301.
6. Dixon, 263.
7. *Golden Remains*, IV, 33 (note).
8. See article by S. Race in *Transactions of Lodge of Research, 2429* (Leicester), 1954–5, p. 23 sqq.
9. *Golden Remains*, V. 111.

Chapter 2: Early Days (1802–1809)

1. Dixon, 268.
2. S. Race in article referred to at note 8 to Chapter 1.
3. For the arguments, see AQC 1985, 28–9.
4. FQR, 1843, p. 305. *Symbol*, 200.
5. According to an article in *Lincolnshire Life*, March 1981 p. 24, he applied for a post as master at this school in 1803 'while clerk to an attorney in Holbeach'.

Chapter 3: The Start of a Career

1. Letter to C. Tennyson, 10 May 1819, in Public Library, Great Grimsby.
2. Address to Pelham Pillar Lodge, 792, 2 March 1967.
3. *The History of Initiation* (1829).
4. Anderson Bates, *The History of Freemasonry in Grimsby from its introduction to 1892*, (1892).
5. *Mirror*, 13.
6. *Offering*, 14.
7. See note 1 above.
8. *The History and Antiquities of St James' Church, Great Grimsby*, (1829), p. 44.
9. *Farewell Address to the Inhabitants of Great Grimsby, comprising a brief account of the results of his ministry during a period of sixteen years by the Revd Geo. Oliver, M.A.S.E.: late Curate. Grimsby*. Printed and sold by H. Palmer.
10. Preface to *Landmarks*, Vol. 2, xiv.
11. Letter to Sir Edward Ffrench Bromhead, Bart., quoted in preface to *Landmarks*, Vol. 2, vii.

Chapter 4: Priest, Mason, Writer

1. *Antiquities*, 20.
2. e.g. *Landmarks*, Vol. 2, 668; *Farewell to Provincial Grand Lodge* (1866); *Star* (1841 edn.), p. 7 (note); *Mirror*, 13; *Signs and Symbols*, 103. He may have taken up the phrase from a sermon preached by the Revd Jethro Inwood, then Provincial Grand Chaplain for Kent, at Woolwich in 1798: see *Golden Remains*, Vol. IV, Sermon X, p. 282, 'the beautiful handmaid of Christianity'.
3. AQC, vol. 98, (1985), 39.
4. *Landmarks* I, Lecture 4, 128.
5. ibid. Lecture 15, 386–7.
6. *Valedictory*, xi.
7. *Star* (1841 edn.), 10–11.
8. ibid. p.7, note.
9. *The Pythagorean Triangle*, ch.X., 221–3.
10. *Valedictory*, xviii.
11. ibid. xx.
12. See e.g. *Offering*, 7, 24, *Offering to Dr Crucefix*, p. 27.
13. *Valedictory*, xx.
14. *Signs and Symbols*, Preface, vii.
15. Letter in UGL Library.
16. *The Book of the Lodge*, 3rd. edn, Aquarian Press—reprint (1985), 206–7.
17. *Valedictory*, xxi.
18. Reprint (1841). Published in London by Richard Spencer, 314 High Holborn.
19. Grimsby Corporation Court Book, 25 September 1821.
20. In Public Library, Great Grimsby.
21. Lincoln Diocesan Archives show the quarrel became so bitter that on 7 October 1831 Attwood 'most solemnly conjured' the Bishop 'for the sake of the spiritual welfare of this place, not to collate or institute Mr Oliver' to

Scopwick: an exhortation rather diminished by the condition 'until he withdraws his opposition to me'.

Chapter 5: 'A Secluded Village'
1. *Farewell Address, Great Grimsby.* (See Chapter 3, note 9).
2. *Scopwickiana, or Sketches and Illustrations of a secluded village in Lincolnshire. By the Vicar thereof. Lincoln, E. B. Drury. Gazette office. MDCCCVIII.* Unless otherwise noted, quotations in this and the next Chapter are from that work.
3. Dixon, 301.
4. A letter (29 November 1831) in the Diocesan Archives refers to '3 lower rooms with Mudd Floors . . . 3 chambers 2′6″ open to thatch'.
5. Diocesan records suggest the Church authorities defrayed the expense.
6. *Jacob's Ladder.* See Chapter 15.

Chapter 6: Success
1. *The Existing Remains of the Ancient Britons . . .* (1846), 21.
2. Anderson Bates. See Chapter 3, note 4.
3. *Offering*, 15.
4. ibid, 15.
5. Quoted *Centenary of the Witham lodge* (1842), 7.
6. FQR. 1840, 417. *Offering to Dr Crucefix*, 10 sqq.

Chapter 7: Problems
1. I have found the history of Wolverhampton by Mr Mander, completed by Mr Norman W. Tildesley, very helpful in unravelling this tangled story, and am particularly grateful to Mr Tildesley for his help, and for permission to quote from the work.
2. General William Dyott, Diary, Vol. 2, 90, 29 October 1830.
3. Oliver wrote to the Bishop on 30 March 1835: 'I consented to quit Lincolnshire only because the alteration in the corn average of Scopwick had reduced the income so considerably, as to leave absolutely nothing to subsist on'. Other correspondence in 1839 shows strained relations between Hobart and Oliver, who was finding the Wolverhampton living 'a fruitful source of trouble, annoyance, and Loss of both health and property'—the last-named being a reference to the loss of anticipated fees as a result of the claims of Mr Clare.
4. Details of proceedings at the various meetings of the Provincial Grand Lodge of Lincolnshire are taken from FQR reports in the absence of the relevant minutes.
5. For an account of the building of this neo-gothic monstrosity by D'Eyncourt's father, and their aspirations to revive the extinct D'Eyncourt barony, see *Alfred Tennyson* by Charles Tennyson, pub. Macmillan, 1949.

Chapter 8: Industrial Revolution
1. *Scopwickiana*, 37.

2. See *A History of Freemasonry in the Province of Staffordshire* by F. W. Wilmore (1905).
3. Quoted FQR 1840, advertisements, p.7; see also p. 346.
4. Reported FQR 1840, 236–7, with comment 'Dr Oliver is a truly liberal divine'.

Chapter 9: Family Life
1. Registers in Lincolnshire Archives, The Castle, Lincoln.
2. FQR 1844, 146.
3. Reported FQR 1842, 63.

Chapter 10: Disasters
1. For an account of the Tennyson family at this time, see *Alfred Tennyson* by Charles Tennyson, Macmillan, 1949.
2. op. cit., 137.
3. Letter from G. Oliver, junior, to his father, 21 July 1842.
4. *Masonic Offering to Dr Crucefix* in UGL Library, based on FQR report.
5. Quoted Dixon, 272.

Chapter 11: Reactions
1. Proceedings reported FQR, 1842, 211–215.
2. A report appeared in FQR, 1842, 193–206 with a note that 'The provincial press has very generally denounced the authors of the ungracious treatment of Dr Oliver' and quoted some of 'the mildest opinions offered on the subject'.
3. Stevens had attempted in 1840 to persuade Grand Lodge to enact that a PGM who did not hold a Pr. Grand Lodge for 2 successive years should be deemed to have vacated his appointment, a move clearly aimed at D'Eyncourt: FQR, 1840, p. 463.

Chapter 12: Theories
1. op. cit., 295.
2. AQC (1985), 50.
3. AQC (1961), 54.
4. For early history of the Rose Croix in England, See *Rose Croix, A History of the Ancient and Accepted Rite for England and Wales* by A. C. F. Jackson, London 1980 (revised 1987).

Chapter 13: Testimonial
1. This account is based on reports in FQR, 1842, 377–382, Dixon, 296 et seq, and letters in UGL Library.
2. Cutting with Keene-Oliver papers in UGL Library.
3. At which D'Eyncourt said he 'trembled when he looked back on the last few hours'. FQR, 1842, p.380.
4. op. cit., 297.

Chapter 14: 'The Sage of Masonry'

1. *Valedictory*, xxiv.
2. *Theocratic*, 1.
3. ibid, 295.
4. ibid, 292.
5. *Discrepancies*, 4–5.
6. ibid, 9.
7. ibid, 10, 11.
8. ibid, 21–23.
9. ibid, 14–17.
10. H. Mendoza, Prestonian Lecture 1984; AQC 98 (1985), 14–25.
11. *Discrepancies*, 52.
12. ibid, 168.
13. *Offering*, 14.
14. *Signs and Symbols*, 1; G. Claret, *Masonic Gleanings* (1844), No. III.
15. *Preface to present Edition* (1842), xiii.
16. *Valedictory*, xxxi.
17. *Landmarks* Vol. 1, preface, 2 & 30.
18. *Deuteronomy*, xxvii, 17.
19. *Landmarks*, Vol. 1, Lecture X, 266 (note).
20. *Treasury*, 16–17.
21. *Landmarks*, Vol. 2, v–vi.
22. ibid, Vol. 2, 186 (note).
23. ibid, Vol. 2, 657–666.

Chapter 15: The Christian Freemason

1. *Landmarks*, Vol. 1, 11–13
2. Review of *The Existing Remains of the Ancient Britons* . . . FQR (1846), 262.
3. A letter from Grand Secretary General, NMJ, to Crucefix dated 1 June 1846 refers to 'the indisposition of Bro. Oliver'. An arch erected in the vicarage garden at Scopwick commemorates his recovery from serious illness in 1849.
4. *Ladder*, iv–v.
5. ibid, 49.
6. ibid, 63–4.
7. ibid, 80 (Isaiah, xi. 9).
8. ibid, 128–131.
9. ibid, 26–27.
10. ibid, 194–5.

Chapter 16: Challenges

1. FQR, 1846, 202.
2. ibid, 201.
3. Unattributed cutting in UGL Library, Keene-Oliver bequest.
4. Draft letter in UGL Library (Keene-Oliver bequest).
5. *Valedictory*, xxxii–xxxiii.

6. *Apology*, 8.
7. ibid, 15.

Chapter 17: An Interim Period

1. *Golden Remains*, I, 2.
2. *Mirror*, 17.
3. ibid, Dedicatory Letter, iii.
4. ibid, 34, 40.
5. ibid, Letter 6, end.
6. ibid, 147–8.
7. ibid, 172–3.
8. Letter, Spencer to Oliver, 4 May 1846.
9. *Golden Remains*, I.iii.
10. ibid, I.30. Text of pamphlet at III, 78 sqq.
11. ibid, III, 107.
12. ibid, III, 167.
13. ibid, III, 311.
14. *Charge after Initiation*, Emulation ritual.
15. op. cit., III, 320. It is not clear whether Oliver himself wrote these words but he clearly approved them.
16. ibid, IV, 2–9.
17. See Chapter 15, note 2 ante.
18. *Golden Remains*, V, 44.
19. ibid, IV, 218.
20. ibid, IV, 219.
21. ibid, II, 237 sqq.
22. Aquarian Press reprint (1985), 111–140.
23. *Valedictory*, xv.

Chapter 18: The Grand Design

1. FQR, 1847, 301–303.
2. See Chapter 4, note 2.
3. *Symbol*, 338.
4. ibid, 333.
5. *Valedictory*, viii.
6. *Valedictory*, vi.
7. ibid, vii & viii.
8. *The Book of the Lodge* (Aquarian Press reprint, 1985), 33.
9. *Valedictory*, xliii.
10. ibid, xxviii.
11. *Symbol*, 2.
12. ibid, 81–82.
13. ibid, 112.
14. ibid, 141, 142.
15. ibid, 199–201.
16. FQR, 1840, 7; also letter, Crucefix to Oliver, 22 September 1842.

17. *Symbol*, 330–331.
18. ibid, 331.
19. See Chapter 4, Note 12.
20. *Symbol*, 208.
21. ibid, 337.
22. ibid, 7.
23. ibid, 7.
24. ibid, 71–2.

Chapter 19: Later Works

1. *Ante*, chapter 18, note 9, and chapter 15, note 3.
2. For details of early days of this Council, refer to Chapter 12, note 4, *ante*.
3. Letter, Grand Secretary General, Supreme Council 33rd Degree, NMJ, to Crucefix, Jackson, op.cit., 176.
4. Dixon, 301.
5. ibid, 301, and unattributed paper in UGL file.
6. *Revelations of a Square* (1855), Preface, v.
7. *The Life of Samuel Johnson, LL.D.*: 14 September 1777.
8. *A new and complete Directory of Great Grimsby and Cleethorpes* (by John Shepherd) ' . . . with a sketch of the town and port of Great Grimsby by the Revd George Oliver, D.D.'

Chapter 20: The Last Years

1. UGL, ref. BE 10 (Mas).
2. The list is corrupt in one respect: no. 348 was St John's Lodge, Leicester (now no. 279) and no. 349 was Worcester Lodge, Worcester (now no. 280); Oliver presumably intended to refer to both. Neither no. 191, New York, nor no. 342, Rising Star, Bombay (presumably the same as 'Rising Star of Western India Lodge' to whom lecture XI of *The Symbol of Glory* had been dedicated) are mentioned in Lane's List of Lodges and appear therefore to be outside the English Constitution. The remainder are:

48	Royal Cumberland, Bath	Now 41
176	Albany, Isle of Wight	Now 151
319	Phoenix, Portsmouth	Now 257
326	Social Friendship, Madras	Erased 1862
329	Bank of England, London	Now 263
356	Shakespere, Warwick	Now 284
374	Witham, Lincoln	Now 297
523	Hope & Charity, Kidderminster	Now 377
607	St Peter's, Wolverhampton	Now 419
643	St George's, Montreal	Now 440, Quebec
646	St Peter's Peterborough	Now 442
689	First Lodge of Light,	Now 468
690	Hundred of Elloe, Spalding	Now 469
773	Lodge of Australasia	Now under G. Lodge of Victoria

3. *Treasury*, preface, v.
4. AQC, Vol. 98 (1985), 54–5.
5. *Treasury*, xv–xvi.
6. *Offering*, 13.
7. *Symbol*, 172–4.
8. *Treasury*, preface, vi.
9. ibid, xv.
10. *A Masonic Sermon preached in St John's Church*, Peterborough, 24 July 1802 . . . by Brother The Revd S. Oliver, R.A.M., chaplain . . . ' p. 30.
11. *Treasury*, 17.
12. ibid, 89.
13. ibid, 273.
14. Preface to Gibbon's *Decline and Fall of the Roman Empire*, Macmillan edition (1896–1900), xvii.
15. *Treasury*, 291.
16. ibid, 292.
17. ibid, 335.
18. He also accepted honorary membership of a lodge in Hong Kong about this time. His letter of acceptance contains some details about his early masonic career but is unreliable so far as dates are concerned. The lodge commissioned a portrait of him by (presumably) a Chinese artist working from a well-known print; this portrait, after vicissitudes, is now in the UGL Museum and gives the doctor a distinctly Oriental look.
19. Quoted Dixon, 304.
20. *Papal Teachings*, 14.
21. Quoted ibid, 15.
22. *Symbol*, Lecture IV, 85, 86. See too ibid. 10–11.
23. Review in *The Athenaeum*.
24. *Ye Byrde of Gryme* 7–8.
25. ibid, 9.
26. ibid, 10.
27. ibid, 15.
28. *Farewell Address to Provincial Grand Lodge, 10 May 1866.*
29. *The Origin of the Royal Arch*, Dedication.
30. ibid, Preface xxiii–xix.
31. ibid, xx.
32. ibid, xxii–xxvi.

Chapter 21: Epilogue

1. Dixon, 302.
2. *Transactions of The Lodge of Research*, Leicester, no. 2429, 1954–5, 31.
3. *Offering*, 14–15.
4. *Offering*, 24; *ante* p. 79.
5. Preface to Gibbon: see Chapter 20, note 12 *ante*.
6. *Ante*, p. 77.

BIBLIOGRAPHICAL INDEX

Part One: Works by Dr George Oliver
Titles from The Grand Design are listed in *italics*.

1821   A Vindication of the Fundamental Doctrines of Christianity
1823   *The Antiquities of Freemasonry*
1825   The Monumental Antiquities of Great Grimsby
        The Star in the East
        (?) Essay on Education
1826   *Signs and Symbols*
1829   Preston's Illustrations of Masonry (14th edition: edited with notes by Oliver.
            Editions 15–17 were also edited by him)
        The History of Initiation
        The History and Antiquities of St James' Church, Great Grimsby
        History and Antiquities of Beverley and its Collegiate Church
        [Notes on] Clee
        [Notes on] Ratcliffe
        [Notes on] Castor [Caistor]
1831   The Apostolic Institution of the Church of England Examined
        Farewell Address to the Inhabitants of Great Grimsby
1833   (?) Letter to the Archbishop of Canterbury
1834   An Introductory Address to the Inhabitants of Wolverhampton
1835   A Candid Statement of the Question relating to St George's Church
        Second Pastoral Address to the Inhabitants of Wolverhampton
1836   Hints for Improving the Societies and Institutions Connected with Education and
            Science in the Town of Wolverhampton
        The History and Antiquities of the Collegiate Church, Wolverhampton
1837   History of the Holy Trinity Guild at Sleaford
1838   Scopwickiana
        Letters to his Curate
1840   *The Theocratic Philosophy of Freemasonry*
        An Address . . . in reply to Misrepresentations in a Circular . . .
1841   *The History of Freemasonry, 1829–1840*
        A Brief History of the Witham Lodge No.374
        Oration (at Crucefix testimonial dinner)
1842   On Popular Superstition
        An Account of the Centenary of the Witham Lodge No. 374. including 'a Narra-
            tive of the circumstances attending the author's removal from the Deputy
            Provincial Grand Masip of the Province'

Part Two: Other Works

Ars Quatuor Coronatorum, *Transactions of Quatuor Coronati Lodge 2076*, published
    annually
Ashe, Jonathan, *The Masonic Manual*, London 1814
Bates, Anderson, *History of Freemasonry in Great Grimsby ...*, Grimsby 1892
Clare, Revd G.B., *Reply (to 'A Candid Statement')*, 1835
Claret, George, *Masonic Gleanings ...*, London 1894
Darwin, Charles, *On the Origin of Species ...*, 1859
Dixon, W., *History of Freemasonry in Lincolnshire*, 1894
Freemason's Quarterly Review, 1834–42: new series 1843–4, 2nd series, 1845–9
Gentleman's Magazine
Gordon, W., *Young Man's Companion*, 1765 (earliest edition with article on
    Freemasonry)
Hutchinson, William, *The Spirit of Masonry*, 1775

Jackson, A.C.F., *Rose Croix, A History of the Ancient and Accepted Rite for England and Wales*, London 1980, 1987

James, P.R., *The Crucefix–Oliver affair*, paper to Quatuor Coronati Lodge, 5 May 1961

Kant, Immanuel, *Critique of Pure Reason*, 1781

Lane, John, Masonic Records 1717–1894, 2nd edn, London 1895

Mander and Tildesley, *History of Wolverhampton*

Masonic Offerings (*see* 'Testimonial' infra)

Preston, William, *Illustrations of Freemasonry*, 1772

Race, S., 'Samuel and George Oliver', *Transactions*, The Lodge of Research, 2429, Leicester, 1954–5

Scott, Sir Walter, various works

'Testimonial to Dr Crucefix' (Account of *Proceedings*, London 1841)

'Testimonial to Dr Oliver' (Account of *Proceedings*, reprinted from FQR, new series, no. 6)

Transactions of Quatuor Coronati Lodge, *see* 'Ars Quatuor Coronatorum'

Wilmore, F.W., *A History of Freemasonry in the Province of Staffordshire, Wolverhampton & London*, 1905

Wilson, E.H.E., *Address to Pelham Pillar Lodge, 792*, 2 March 1967

GENERAL INDEX

Note: A date (in brackets) in the Index means that the publication is listed in the Bibliographical Index, Part One, under that year;

'*(BI)*' means that the references will be found in the Bibliographical Index, Part Two, which is alphabetical. The full form of abbreviated titles appears in the list of abbreviations at the beginning of the book.

'n' means that the reference will be found in the notes to the given page.